Practical Data Science Cookbook

Second Edition

Practical recipes on data pre-processing, analysis and visualization using R and Python

Prabhanjan Tattar
Tony Ojeda
Sean Patrick Murphy
Benjamin Bengfort
Abhijit Dasgupta

BIRMINGHAM - MUMBAI

MW00844170

Practical Data Science Cookbook

Second Edition

Copyright © 2017 Packt Publishing

All rights reserved. No part of this book may be reproduced, stored in a retrieval system, or transmitted in any form or by any means, without the prior written permission of the publisher, except in the case of brief quotations embedded in critical articles or reviews.

Every effort has been made in the preparation of this book to ensure the accuracy of the information presented. However, the information contained in this book is sold without warranty, either express or implied. Neither the authors, nor Packt Publishing, and its dealers and distributors will be held liable for any damages caused or alleged to be caused directly or indirectly by this book.

Packt Publishing has endeavored to provide trademark information about all of the companies and products mentioned in this book by the appropriate use of capitals. However, Packt Publishing cannot guarantee the accuracy of this information.

First published: September 2014

Second Edition: June 2017

Production reference: 1270617

Published by Packt Publishing Ltd.
Livery Place
35 Livery Street
Birmingham
B3 2PB, UK.

ISBN 978-1-78712-962-7

www.packtpub.com

Credits

Authors
Prabhanjan Tattar
Tony Ojeda
Sean Patrick Murphy
Benjamin Bengfort
Abhijit Dasgupta

Reviewers
Alberto Boschetti
Abhinav Rai

Commissioning Editor
Amey Varangaonkar

Acquisition Editor
Tushar Gupta

Content Development Editor
Cheryl Dsa

Technical Editor
Karan Thakkar

Copy Editors
Vikrant Phadkay
Safis Editing

Project Coordinator
Nidhi Joshi

Proofreader
Safis Editing

Indexer
Pratik Shirodkar

Production Coordinator
Shantanu Zagade

About the Authors

Prabhanjan Tattar has 9 years of experience as a statistical analyst. His main thurst has been to explain statistical and machine learning techniques through elegant programming which will clear the nuances of the underlying mathematics. Survival analysis and statistical inference are his main areas of research/interest, and he has published several research papers in peer-reviewed journals and also has authored two books on R: *R Statistical Application Development by Example, Packt Publishing*, and *A Course in Statistics with R, Wiley*. He also maintains the R packages gpk, RSADBE, and ACSWR.

I would like to thank the readers for their encouragement and feedback that lead to the improvements in this edition and hope that they find the current edition useful. Thanks are due to Tushar Gupta for introducing me to this project, Cheryl Dsa for bearing with the delays, Karan Thakkar for the eagle-eyed editing, and the entire Packt team for every little support. The authors of the first edition need to be thanked by me as their platform is largely carried forward. On the personal front, I continue to thank my family: Pranathi the kiddo, Chandrika the wifey, Lakshmi the goddess mother, and Narayanachar the beloved father.

Tony Ojeda is an accomplished data scientist and entrepreneur, with expertise in business process optimization and over a decade of experience creating and implementing innovative data products and solutions. He has a master's degree in finance from Florida International University and an MBA with a focus on strategy and entrepreneurship from DePaul University. He is the founder of District Data Labs, is a cofounder of Data Community DC, and is actively involved in promoting data science education through both organizations.

Sean Patrick Murphy spent 15 years as a senior scientist at *The Johns Hopkins University*, Applied Physics Laboratory, where he focused on machine learning, modeling and simulation, signal processing, and high performance computing in the Cloud. Now, he acts as an advisor and data consultant for companies in San Francisco, New York, and Washington DC. He completed graduation from The Johns Hopkins University and got his MBA from the University of Oxford. He currently co-organizes the Data Innovation DC meetup and co-founded the Data Science MD meetup. He is also a board member and co-founder of Data Community DC.

Benjamin Bengfort is an experienced data scientist and Python developer who has worked in the military, industry, and academia for the past 8 years. He is currently pursuing his PhD in Computer Science at the University of Maryland, College Park, doing research in Metacognition and Natural Language Processing. He holds a Master's degree in Computer Science from North Dakota State University, where he taught undergraduate Computer Science courses. He is also an adjunct faculty member at Georgetown University, where he teaches Data Science and Analytics. Benjamin has been involved in two data science start-ups in the DC region: leveraging large-scale machine learning and Big Data techniques across a variety of applications. He has a deep appreciation for the combination of models and data for entrepreneurial effect, and he is currently building one of these start-ups into a more mature organization.

Abhijit Dasgupta is a data consultant working in the greater DC-Maryland-Virginia area, with several years of experience in biomedical consulting, business analytics, bioinformatics, and bioengineering consulting. He has a PhD in biostatistics from the University of Washington and over 40 collaborative peer-reviewed manuscripts, with strong interests in bridging the statistics/machine-learning divide. He is always on the lookout for interesting and challenging projects, and is an enthusiastic speaker and discussant on new and better ways to look at and analyze data. He is a member of Data Community DC and a founding member and co-organizer of Statistical Programming DC (formerly R Users DC).

About the Reviewer

Alberto Boschetti is a data scientist, with strong expertise in signal processing and statistics. He holds a PhD in telecommunication engineering and currently lives and works in London. In his work projects he daily faces challenges spanning among natural language processing (NLP), machine learning, and distributed processing. He is very passionate about his job and he always tries to be updated on the latest development of data science technologies, attending meetups, conferences and other events. He is the author of *Python Data Science Essentials, Regression Analysis with Python*, and *Large Scale Machine Learning with Python*, all published by Packt.

> *I would like to thank my family, friends, and colleagues. Also, a big thanks to the open source community.*

Abhinav Rai has been working as a Data Scientist for nearly a decade, currently working at Microsoft. He has experience working in telecom, retail marketing, and online advertisement. His areas of interest include the evolving techniques of Machine Learning and the associated technologies. He is especially more interested in analyzing large and humongous datasets and likes to generate deep insights in such scenarios. Academically holding a double master's degree in Mathematics from Deendayal Upadhyay Gorakhpur University with an NBHM scholarship and in Computer Science from Indian Statistical Institute, rigor and sophistication is a surety with his analytical deliveries.

www.PacktPub.com

For support files and downloads related to your book, please visit www.PacktPub.com. Did you know that Packt offers eBook versions of every book published, with PDF and ePub files available? You can upgrade to the eBook version at www.PacktPub.comand as a print book customer, you are entitled to a discount on the eBook copy. Get in touch with us at service@packtpub.com for more details. At www.PacktPub.com, you can also read a collection of free technical articles, sign up for a range of free newsletters and receive exclusive discounts and offers on Packt books and eBooks.

https://www.packtpub.com/mapt

Get the most in-demand software skills with Mapt. Mapt gives you full access to all Packt books and video courses, as well as industry-leading tools to help you plan your personal development and advance your career.

Why subscribe?

- Fully searchable across every book published by Packt
- Copy and paste, print, and bookmark content
- On demand and accessible via a web browser

Customer Feedback

Thanks for purchasing this Packt book. At Packt, quality is at the heart of our editorial process. To help us improve, please leave us an honest review on this book's Amazon page at https://www.amazon.com/dp/1787129624.

If you'd like to join our team of regular reviewers, you can e-mail us at customerreviews@packtpub.com. We award our regular reviewers with free eBooks and videos in exchange for their valuable feedback. Help us be relentless in improving our products!

Table of Contents

Preface

Welcome to the second edition of *Practical Data Science Cookbook*. It was the positive feedback and usefulness that the book has found for its readers that made a second edition possible. When Packt asked me to co-author the second edition, I had a preview of some of its reviews across the web and immediately found the reasons for the popularity of the book and its little weakness. Thus, the current version retains the positives of the acceptance and removes the pain points as much as possible. The two new chapters: Chapter 10, *German Credit Data Analysis* and Chapter 11, *Forecasting New Zealand Overseas Visitors* are included to enhance the usefulness of the book.

We live in the age of data. As increasing amounts are generated each year, the need to analyze and create value from this asset is more important than ever. Companies that know what to do with their data and how to do it well will have a competitive advantage over companies that don't. Due to this, there will be an increasing demand for people who possess both the analytical and technical abilities to extract valuable insights from data and the business acumen to create valuable and pragmatic solutions that put these insights to use. This book provides multiple opportunities to learn how to create value from data through a variety of projects that run the spectrum of types of contemporary data science projects. Each chapter stands on its own, with step-by-step instructions that include screenshots, code snippets, and more detailed explanations where necessary and with a focus on process and practical application. The goal of this book is to introduce the data science pipeline, show you how it applies to a variety of different data science projects, and get you comfortable enough to apply it in future to projects of your own. Along the way, you'll learn different analytical and programming lessons, and the fact that you are working through an actual project while learning will help cement these concepts and facilitate your understanding of them.

What this book covers

Chapter 1, *Preparing Your Data Science Environment*, introduces the data science pipeline and helps you get your data science environment properly set up with instructions for the Mac, Windows, and Linux operating systems. This chapter is a guideline for setting up the environment for R and Python on the preceding platforms.

Chapter 2, *Driving Visual Analysis with Automobile Data with R*, takes you through the process of analyzing and visualizing automobile data to identify trends and patterns in fuel efficiency over time. The chapter will give you a taste of acquisition, exploration, munging, analysis, and communication. The concepts will be implemented in R.

Chapter 3, *Creating Application-Oriented Analyses Using Tax Data and Python*, shows you how to use Python to transition your analyses from one-off, custom efforts to reproducible and production-ready code using income distribution data as the base for the project.

Chapter 4, *Modeling Stock Market Data*, shows you how to build your own stock screener and use moving averages to analyze historical stock prices. You will learn how to acquire, summarize, clean, and generate relative evaluations of data.

Chapter 5, *Visually Exploring Employment Data*, shows you how to obtain employment and earnings data from the Bureau of Labor Statistics and conduct geospatial analysis at different levels with R. The same will be implemented using Python. The focus of this chapter is on the transformation, manipulation, and visualization of data.

Chapter 6, *Driving Visual Analyses with Automobile Data*, mirrors the automobile data analyses and visualizations in Chapter 2, *Driving Visual Analysis with Automobile Data with R*, but does so using the powerful programming language, Python. It focuses on the implementation of the analysis model using Python.

Chapter 7, *Working with Social Graphs*, shows you how to build, visualize, and analyze a social network that consists of comic book character relationships. You will also see the R and Python implementation.

Chapter 8, *Recommending Movies at Scale (Python)*, walks you through building a movie recommender system with Python. You will also learn the R and Python code to implement a predictive model and the use of collaborative filtering to implement a predictive model.

Chapter 9, *Harvesting and Geolocating Twitter Data (Python)*, shows you how to connect to the Twitter API and plot the geographic information contained in profiles. You will also learn the use of RESTful APIs in TextMining

Chapter 10, *Forecasting New Zealand Overseas Visitors*, explains how to create time series objects and describes various methods to visualize time series data. You will also learn how to build an appropriate model for the data and identify if the data has any trends and seasonal components.

Chapter 11, *German Credit Data Analysis*, demonstrates Exploratory Data Analysis (EDA), with a few basic tree methods and random forest. You will learn the method to apply EDA, tree-based methods and random forest on some particular data.

What you need for this book

For this book, you will need a computer with access to the Internet and the ability to install the open source software needed for the projects. The primary software we will be using consists of the R and Python programming languages, with a myriad of freely available packages and libraries. Installation instructions are in the first chapter.

Who this book is for

This book is intended for aspiring data scientists who want to learn data science and numerical programming concepts through hands-on, real-world projects. Whether you are brand new to data science or you are a seasoned expert, you will benefit from learning about the structure of real-world data science projects and the programming examples in R and Python.

Sections

In this book, you will find several headings that appear frequently (Getting ready, How to do it, How it works, There's more, and See also). To give clear instructions on how to complete a recipe, we use these sections as follows.

Getting ready

This section tells you what to expect in the recipe, and describes how to set up any software or any preliminary settings required for the recipe.

How to do it...

This section contains the steps required to follow the recipe.

How it works...

This section usually consists of a detailed explanation of what happened in the previous section.

There's more...

This section consists of additional information about the recipe in order to make the reader more knowledgeable about the recipe.

See also

This section provides helpful links to other useful information for the recipe.

Conventions

In this book, you will find a number of text styles that distinguish between different kinds of information. Here are some examples of these styles and an explanation of their meaning. Code words in text, database table names, folder names, filenames, file extensions, pathnames, dummy URLs, user input, and Twitter handles are shown as follows: "Create a new user for JIRA in the database and grant the user access to the jiradb database we just created using the following command:"

A block of code is set as follows:

```
<Contextpath="/jira"docBase="${catalina.home}
/atlassian- jira" reloadable="false" useHttpOnly="true">
```

Any command-line input or output is written as follows:

```
mysql -u root -p
```

New terms and **important words** are shown in bold. Words that you see on the screen, for example, in menus or dialog boxes, appear in the text like this: "Select **System info** from the **Administration** panel."

Warnings or important notes appear in a box like this.

 Tips and tricks appear like this.

Reader feedback

Feedback from our readers is always welcome. Let us know what you think about this book-what you liked or disliked. Reader feedback is important for us as it helps us develop titles that you will really get the most out of. To send us general feedback, simply e-mail feedback@packtpub.com, and mention the book's title in the subject of your message. If there is a topic that you have expertise in and you are interested in either writing or contributing to a book, see our author guide at www.packtpub.com/authors.

Customer support

Now that you are the proud owner of a Packt book, we have a number of things to help you to get the most from your purchase.

Downloading the example code

You can download the example code files for this book from your account at http://www.packtpub.com. If you purchased this book elsewhere, you can visit http://www.packtpub.com/support and register to have the files e-mailed directly to you. You can download the code files by following these steps:

1. Log in or register to our website using your e-mail address and password.
2. Hover the mouse pointer on the **SUPPORT** tab at the top.
3. Click on **Code Downloads & Errata**.
4. Enter the name of the book in the **Search** box.
5. Select the book for which you're looking to download the code files.
6. Choose from the drop-down menu where you purchased this book from.
7. Click on **Code Download**.

You can also download the code files by clicking on the **Code Files** button on the book's webpage at the Packt Publishing website. This page can be accessed by entering the book's name in the **Search** box. Please note that you need to be logged in to your Packt account. Once the file is downloaded, please make sure that you unzip or extract the folder using the latest version of:

- WinRAR / 7-Zip for Windows
- Zipeg / iZip / UnRarX for Mac
- 7-Zip / PeaZip for Linux

The code bundle for the book is also hosted on GitHub at `https://github.com/PacktPublishing/Practical-Data-Science-Cookbook-Second-Edition`. We also have other code bundles from our rich catalog of books and videos available at `https://github.com/PacktPublishing/`. Check them out!

Downloading the color images of this book

We also provide you with a PDF file that has color images of the screenshots/diagrams used in this book. The color images will help you better understand the changes in the output. You can download this file from `https://www.packtpub.com/sites/default/files/downloads/PracticalDataScienceCookbookSecondEditon_ColorImages.pdf`.

Errata

Although we have taken every care to ensure the accuracy of our content, mistakes do happen. If you find a mistake in one of our books-maybe a mistake in the text or the code-we would be grateful if you could report this to us. By doing so, you can save other readers from frustration and help us improve subsequent versions of this book. If you find any errata, please report them by visiting `http://www.packtpub.com/submit-errata`, selecting your book, clicking on the **Errata Submission Form** link, and entering the details of your errata. Once your errata are verified, your submission will be accepted and the errata will be uploaded to our website or added to any list of existing errata under the Errata section of that title. To view the previously submitted errata, go to `https://www.packtpub.com/books/content/support` and enter the name of the book in the search field. The required information will appear under the **Errata** section.

Piracy

Piracy of copyrighted material on the Internet is an ongoing problem across all media. At Packt, we take the protection of our copyright and licenses very seriously. If you come across any illegal copies of our works in any form on the Internet, please provide us with the location address or website name immediately so that we can pursue a remedy. Please contact us at copyright@packtpub.com with a link to the suspected pirated material. We appreciate your help in protecting our authors and our ability to bring you valuable content.

Questions

If you have a problem with any aspect of this book, you can contact us at questions@packtpub.com, and we will do our best to address the problem.

1
Preparing Your Data Science Environment

A traditional cookbook contains culinary recipes of interest to the authors, and helps readers expand their repertoire of foods to prepare. Many might believe that the end product of a recipe is the dish itself and one can read this book, in much the same way. Every chapter guides the reader through the application of the stages of the data science pipeline to different datasets with various goals. Also, just as in cooking, the final product can simply be the analysis applied to a particular set.

We hope that you will take a broader view, however. Data scientists learn by doing, ensuring that every iteration and hypothesis improves the practioner's knowledge base. By taking multiple datasets through the data science pipeline using two different programming languages (R and Python), we hope that you will start to abstract out the analysis patterns, see the bigger picture, and achieve a deeper understanding of this rather ambiguous field of data science.

We also want you to know that, unlike culinary recipes, data science recipes are ambiguous. When chefs begin a particular dish, they have a very clear picture in mind of what the finished product will look like. For data scientists, the situation is often different. One does not always know what the dataset in question will look like, and what might or might not be possible, given the amount of time and resources. Recipes are essentially a way to dig into the data and get started on the path towards asking the right questions to complete the best dish possible.

If you are from a statistical or mathematical background, the modeling techniques on display might not excite you per se. Pay attention to how many of the recipes overcome practical issues in the data science pipeline, such as loading large datasets and working with scalable tools to adapting known techniques to create data applications, interactive graphics, and web pages rather than reports and papers. We hope that these aspects will enhance your appreciation and understanding of data science and apply good data science to your domain.

Practicing data scientists require a great number and diversity of tools to get the job done. Data practitioners scrape, clean, visualize, model, and perform a million different tasks with a wide array of tools. If you ask most people working with data, you will learn that the foremost component in this toolset is the language used to perform the analysis and modeling of the data. Identifying the best programming language for a particular task is akin to asking which world religion is correct, just with slightly less bloodshed.

In this book, we split our attention between two highly regarded, yet very different, languages used for data analysis - R and Python and leave it up to you to make your own decision as to which language you prefer. We will help you by dropping hints along the way as to the suitability of each language for various tasks, and we'll compare and contrast similar analyses done on the same dataset with each language.

When you learn new concepts and techniques, there is always the question of depth versus breadth. Given a fixed amount of time and effort, should you work towards achieving moderate proficiency in both R and Python, or should you go all in on a single language? From our professional experiences, we strongly recommend that you aim to master one language and have awareness of the other. Does that mean skipping chapters on a particular language? Absolutely not! However, as you go through this book, pick one language and dig deeper, looking not only to develop conversational ability, but also fluency.

To prepare for this chapter, ensure that you have sufficient bandwidth to download up to several gigabytes of software in a reasonable amount of time.

Understanding the data science pipeline

Before we start installing any software, we need to understand the repeatable set of steps that we will use for data analysis throughout the book.

How to do it...

The following are the five key steps for data analysis:

1. **Acquisition**: The first step in the pipeline is to acquire the data from a variety of sources, including relational databases, NoSQL and document stores, web scraping, and distributed databases such as HDFS on a Hadoop platform, RESTful APIs, flat files, and hopefully this is not the case, PDFs.

2. **Exploration and understanding**: The second step is to come to an understanding of the data that you will use and how it was collected; this often requires significant exploration.

3. **Munging, wrangling, and manipulation**: This step is often the single most time-consuming and important step in the pipeline. Data is almost never in the needed form for the desired analysis.

4. **Analysis and modeling**: This is the fun part where the data scientist gets to explore the statistical relationships between the variables in the data and pulls out his or her bag of machine learning tricks to cluster, categorize, or classify the data and create predictive models to see into the future.

5. **Communicating and operationalizing**: At the end of the pipeline, we need to give the data back in a compelling form and structure, sometimes to ourselves to inform the next iteration, and sometimes to a completely different audience. The data products produced can be a simple one-off report or a scalable web product that will be used interactively by millions.

How it works...

Although the preceding list is a numbered list, don't assume that every project will strictly adhere to this exact linear sequence. In fact, agile data scientists know that this process is highly iterative. Often, data exploration informs how the data must be cleaned, which then enables more exploration and deeper understanding. Which of these steps comes first often depends on your initial familiarity with the data. If you work with the systems producing and capturing the data every day, the initial data exploration and understanding stage might be quite short, unless something is wrong with the production system. Conversely, if you are handed a dataset with no background details, the data exploration and understanding stage might require quite some time (and numerous non-programming steps, such as talking with the system developers).

The following diagram shows the data science pipeline:

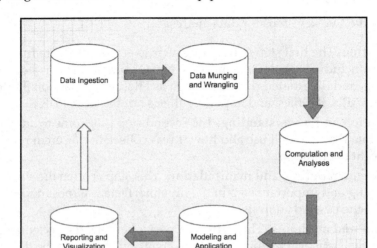

As you have probably heard or read by now, data munging or wrangling can often consume 80 percent or more of project time and resources. In a perfect world, we would always be given perfect data. Unfortunately, this is never the case, and the number of data problems that you will see is virtually infinite. Sometimes, a data dictionary might change or might be missing, so understanding the field values is simply not possible. Some data fields may contain garbage or values that have been switched with another field. An update to the web app that passed testing might cause a little bug that prevents data from being collected, causing a few hundred thousand rows to go missing. If it can go wrong, it probably did at some point; the data you analyze is the sum total of all of these mistakes.

The last step, communication and operationalization, is absolutely critical, but with intricacies that are not often fully appreciated. Note that the last step in the pipeline is not entitled data visualization and does not revolve around simply creating something pretty and/or compelling, which is a complex topic in itself. Instead, data visualizations will become a piece of a larger story that we will weave together from and with data. Some go even further and say that the end result is always an argument as there is no point in undertaking all of this effort unless you are trying to persuade someone or some group of a particular point.

Installing R on Windows, Mac OS X, and Linux

Straight from the R project, *R is a language and environment for statistical computing and graphics,* and it has emerged as one of the de-facto languages for statistical and data analysis. For us, it will be the default tool that we use in the first half of the book.

Getting ready Make sure you have a good broadband connection to the Internet as you may have to download up to 200 MB of software.

How to do it...

Installing R is easy; use the following steps:

1. Go to **Comprehensive R Archive Network (CRAN)** and download the latest release of R for your particular operating system:
    - For Windows, go to http://cran.r-project.org/bin/windows/base/
    - For Linux, go to http://cran.us.r-project.org/bin/linux/
    - For Mac OS X, go to http://cran.us.r-project.org/bin/macosx/

    As of June 2017, the latest release of R is Version 3.4.0 from April 2017.

2. Once downloaded, follow the excellent instructions provided by CRAN to install the software on your respective platform. For both Windows and Mac, just double-click on the downloaded install packages.

3. With R installed, go ahead and launch it. You should see a window similar to that shown in the following screenshot:

4. An important modification of CRAN is available at `https://mran.microsoft.com/` and it is a Microsoft contribution to R software. In fact, the authors are a fan of this variant and strongly recommend the Microsoft version as it has been demonstrated on multiple occasions that **MRAN** version is much faster than the CRAN version and all codes run the same on both the variants. So, there is a bonus reason to use MRAN R versions.

5. You can stop at just downloading R, but you will miss out on the excellent **Integrated Development Environment (IDE)** built for R, called RStudio. Visit `http://www.rstudio.com/ide/download/` to download RStudio, and follow the online installation instructions.

6. Once installed, go ahead and run RStudio. The following screenshot shows one of our author's customized RStudio configurations with the **Console** panel in the upper-left corner, the editor in the upper-right corner, the current variable list in the lower-left corner, and the current directory in the lower-right corner:

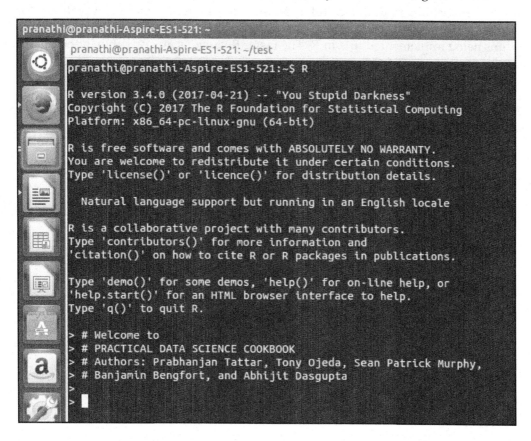

How it works...

R is an interpreted language that appeared in 1993 and is an implementation of the S statistical programming language that emerged from Bell Labs in the '70s (S-PLUS is a commercial implementation of S). R, sometimes referred to as GNU S due to its open source license, is a **domain-specific language (DSL)** focused on statistical analysis and visualization. While you can do many things with R, not seemingly related directly to statistical analysis (including web scraping), it is still a domain-specific language and not intended for general-purpose usage.

R is also supported by CRAN, the Comprehensive R Archive Network (http://cran.r-project.org/). CRAN contains an accessible archive of previous versions of R, allowing for analyses depending on older versions of the software to be reproduced. Further, CRAN contains hundreds of freely downloaded software packages, greatly extending the capability of R. In fact, R has become the default development platform for multiple academic fields, including statistics, resulting in the latest and greatest statistical algorithms being implemented first in R. The faster R versions are available in the Microsoft variants at https://mran.microsoft.com/.

RStudio (http://www.rstudio.com/) is available under the *GNU Affero General Public License v3* and is open source and free to use. RStudio, Inc., the company, offers additional tools and services for R as well as commercial support.

See also

You can also refer to the following:

- Refer to the *Getting Started with R* article at https://support.rstudio.com/hc/en-us/articles/201141096-Getting-Started-with-R
- Visit the home page for RStudio at http://www.rstudio.com/
- Refer to the *Stages in the Evolution of S* article at http://cm.bell-labs.com/cm/ms/departments/sia/S/history.html
- Refer to the *A Brief History of S PS* file at http://cm.bell-labs.com/stat/doc/94.11.ps

Installing libraries in R and RStudio

R has an incredible number of libraries that add to its capabilities. In fact, R has become the default language for many college and university statistics departments across the country. Thus, R is often the language that will get the first implementation of newly developed statistical algorithms and techniques. Luckily, installing additional libraries is easy, as you will see in the following sections.

Getting ready

As long as you have R or RStudio installed, you should be ready to go.

How to do it...

R makes installing additional packages simple:

1. Launch the R interactive environment or, preferably, RStudio.
2. Let's install ggplot2. Type the following command, and then press the *Enter* key:

```
install.packages("ggplot2")
```

 Note that for the remainder of the book, it is assumed that, when we specify entering a line of text, it is implicitly followed by hitting the Return or *Enter* key on the keyboard

3. You should now see text similar to the following as you scroll down the screen:

```
trying URL 'http://cran.rstudio.com/bin/macosx/contrib/3.0/
 ggplot2_0.9.3.1.tgz'Content type 'application/x-gzip' length
2650041 bytes (2.5
 Mb)
opened URL
==================================================
downloaded 2.5 Mb

The downloaded binary packages are in
/var/folders/db/z54jmrxn4y9bjtv8zn_1z1b00000gn/T//Rtmpw0N1dA/
 downloaded_packages
```

4. You might have noticed that you need to know the exact name, in this case, `ggplot2`, of the package you wish to install. Visit `http://cran.us.r-project.org/web/packages/available_packages_by_name.html` to make sure you have the correct name.

5. RStudio provides a simpler mechanism to install packages. Open up RStudio if you haven't already done so.

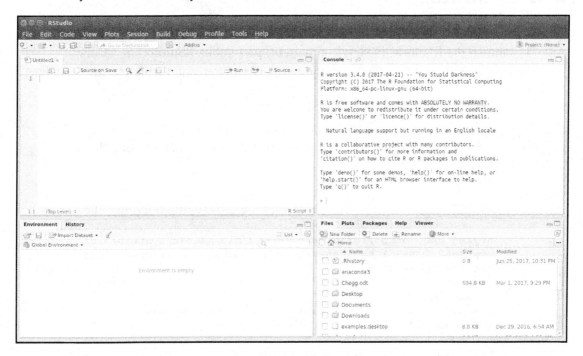

6. Go to **Tools** in the menu bar and select **Install Packages ...**. A new window will pop up, as shown in the following screenshot:

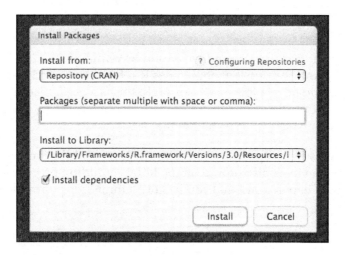

7. As soon as you start typing in the **Packages** field, RStudio will show you a list of possible packages. The autocomplete feature of this field simplifies the installation of libraries. Better yet, if there is a similarly named library that is related, or an earlier or newer version of the library with the same first few letters of the name, you will see it.

8. Let's install a few more packages that we highly recommend. At the R prompt, type the following commands:

```
install.packages("lubridate")
install.packages("plyr")
install.packages("reshape2")
```

You can download the example code files for all Packt books you have purchased from your account at http://www.packtpub.com. If you purchased this book elsewhere, you can visit http://www.packtpub.com/support and register to have the files E-mailed directly to you.

How it works...

Whether you use RStudio's graphical interface or the install.packages command, you do the same thing. You tell R to search for the appropriate library built for your particular version of R. When you issue the command, R reports back the URL of the location where it has found a match for the library in CRAN and the location of the binary packages after download.

There's more...

R's community is one of its strengths, and we would be remiss if we didn't briefly mention two things. R-bloggers is a website that aggregates R-related news and tutorials from over 750 different blogs. If you have a few questions on R, this is a great place to look for more information. The Stack Overflow site (`http://www.stackoverflow.com`) is a great place to ask questions and find answers on R using the tag `rstats`.

Finally, as your prowess with R grows, you might consider building an R package that others can use. Giving an in-depth tutorial on the library building process is beyond the scope of this book, but keep in mind that community submissions form the heart of the R movement.

See also

You can also refer to the following:

- Refer to the *10 R packages I wish I knew about earlier* article at `http://blog.yhathq.com/posts/10-R-packages-I-wish-I-knew-about-earlier.html`
- Visit the R-bloggers website at `http://www.r-bloggers.com/`
- Refer to the *Creating R Packages: A Tutorial* at `http://cran.r-project.org/doc/contrib/Leisch-CreatingPackages.pdf`
- Refer to the *Top 100 R packages for 2013 (Jan-May)!* article at `http://www.r-bloggers.com/top-100-r-packages-for-2013-jan-may/`
- Visit the Learning R blog website at `http://learnr.wordpress.com`

Installing Python on Linux and Mac OS X

Luckily for us, Python comes pre-installed on most versions of Mac OS X and many flavors of Linux (both the latest versions of Ubuntu and Fedora come with Python 2.7 or later versions out of the box). Thus, we really don't have a lot to do for this recipe, except check whether everything is installed.

For this book, we will work with Python 3.4.0.

Getting ready

Just make sure you have a good Internet connection in case we need to install anything.

How to do it...

Perform the following steps in the command prompt:

1. Open a new Terminal window and type the following command:

   ```
   which python
   ```

2. If you have Python installed, you should see something like this:

   ```
   /usr/bin/python
   ```

3. Next, check which version you are running with the following command:

   ```
   python --version
   ```

How it works...

If you are planning on using OS X, you might want to set up a separate Python distribution on your machine for a few reasons. First, each time Apple upgrades your OS, it can and will obliterate your installed Python packages, forcing a reinstall of all previously installed packages. Secondly, new versions of Python will be released more frequently than Apple will update the Python distribution included with OS X. Thus, if you want to stay on the bleeding edge of Python releases, it is best to install your own distribution. Finally, Apple's Python release is slightly different from the official Python release and is located in a nonstandard location on the hard drive.

There are a number of tutorials available online to help walk you through the installation and setup of a separate Python distribution on your Mac. We recommend an excellent guide, available at `http://docs.python-guide.org/en/latest/starting/install/osx/`, to install a separate Python distribution on your Mac.

See also

You can also refer to the following:

- Refer to the *Python For Beginners* guide at
  `http://www.python.org/about/gettingstarted/`
- Refer to *The Hitchhiker's Guide to Python* at
  `http://docs.python-guide.org/en/latest/`
- Refer to the *Python Development Environment on Mac OS X Mavericks 10.9* article at
  `http://hackercodex.com/guide/python-development-environment-on-mac-osx/`

Installing Python on Windows

Installing Python on Windows systems is complicated, leaving you with three different options. First, you can choose to use the standard Windows release with executable installer from Python.org available at `http://www.python.org/download/releases/`. The potential problem with this route is that the directory structure, and therefore, the paths for configuration and settings will be different from the standard Python installation. As a result, each Python package that was installed (and there will be many) might have path problems. Further, most tutorials and answers online won't apply to a Windows environment, and you will be left to your own devices to figure out problems. We have witnessed countless tutorial-ending problems for students who install Python on Windows in this way. Unless you are an expert, we recommend that you do not choose this option.

The second option is to install a prebundled Python distribution that contains all scientific, numeric, and data-related packages in a single install. There are two suitable bundles, one from **Enthought** and another from **Continuum Analytics**. Enthought offers the Canopy distribution of Python 3.5 in both 32- and 64-bit versions for Windows. The free version of the software, Canopy Express, comes with more than 50 Python packages pre-configured so that they work straight out of the box, including pandas, NumPy, SciPy, IPython, and matplotlib, which should be sufficient for the purposes of this book. Canopy Express also comes with its own IDE reminiscent of MATLAB or RStudio.

Continuum Analytics offers Anaconda, a completely free (even for commercial work) distribution of Python 2.7, and 3.6, which contains over 100 Python packages for science, math, engineering, and data analysis. Anaconda contains NumPy, SciPy, pandas, IPython, matplotlib, and much more, and it should be more than sufficient for the work that we will do in this book.

The third, and best option for purists, is to run a virtual Linux machine within Windows using the free VirtualBox (`https://www.virtualbox.org/wiki/Downloads`) from Oracle software. This will allow you to run Python in whatever version of Linux you prefer. The downside to this approach to that virtual machines tend to run a bit slower than native software, and you will have to get used to navigating via the Linux command line, a skill that any practicing data scientist should have.

How to do it...

Perform the following steps to install Python using VirtualBox:

1. If you choose to run Python in a virtual Linux machine, visit `https://www.virtualbox.org/wiki/Downloads` to download VirtualBox from Oracle Software for free.
2. Follow the detailed install instructions for Windows at `https://www.virtualbox.org/manual/ch01.html#intro-installing`.
3. Continue with the instructions and walk through the sections entitled 1.6. Starting VirtualBox, 1.7 Creating your first virtual machine, and 1.8 Running your virtual machine.
4. Once your virtual machine is running, head over to the Installing Python on Linux and Mac OS X recipe.

If you want to install Continuum Analytics' Anaconda distribution locally instead, follow these steps:

1. If you choose to install Continuum Analytics' Anaconda distribution, go to `http://continuum.io/downloads` and select either the 64- or 32-bit version of the software (the 64-bit version is preferable) under Windows installers.
2. Follow the detailed installation instructions for Windows at `http://docs.continuum.io/anaconda/install.html`.

How it works...

For many readers, choosing between a prepackaged Python distribution and running a virtual machine might be easy based on their experience. If you are wrestling with this decision, keep reading. If you come from a windows-only background and/or don't have much experience with a `*nix` command line, the virtual machine-based route will be challenging and will force you to expand your skill set greatly. This takes effort and a significant amount of tenacity, both useful for data science in general (trust us on this one). If you have the time and/or knowledge, running everything in a virtual machine will move you further down the path to becoming a data scientist and, most likely, make your code easier to deploy in production environments. If not, you can choose the backup plan and use the Anaconda distribution, as many people choose to do.

For the remainder of this book, we will always include Linux/Mac OS X-oriented Python package install instructions first and supplementary Anaconda install instructions second. Thus, for Windows users we will assume you have either gone the route of the Linux virtual machine or used the Anaconda distribution. If you choose to go down another path, we applaud your sense of adventure and wish you the best of luck! Let Google be with you.

See also

You can also refer to the following:

- Refer to the Anaconda web page at
  `https://store.continuum.io/cshop/anaconda/`
- Visit the Enthought Canopy Express web page at
  `https://www.enthought.com/canopy-express/`
- Visit the VirtualBox website at `https://www.virtualbox.org/`
- Various installers of Python packages for Windows at `http://www.lfd.uci.edu/~gohlke/pythonlibs`

Installing the Python data stack on Mac OS X and Linux

While Python is often said to have *batteries included*, there are a few key libraries that really take Python's ability to work with data to another level. In this recipe, we will install what is sometimes called the SciPy stack, which includes NumPy, SciPy, pandas, matplotlib, and Jupyter.

Getting ready

This recipe assumes that you have a standard Python installed.

 If, in the previous section, you decided to install the Anaconda distribution (or another distribution of Python with the needed libraries included), you can skip this recipe.

To check whether you have a particular Python package installed, start up your Python interpreter and try to import the package. If successful, the package is available on your machine. Also, you will probably need root access to your machine via the sudo command.

How to do it...

The following steps will allow you to install the Python data stack on Linux:

1. When installing this stack on Linux, you must know which distribution of Linux you are using. The flavor of Linux usually determines the package management system that you will be using, and the options include apt-get, yum, and rpm.
2. Open your browser and navigate to http://www.scipy.org/install.html, which contains detailed instructions for most platforms.
3. These instructions may change and should supersede the instructions offered here, if different:
   1. Open up a shell.
   2. If you are using Ubuntu or Debian, type the following:

      ```
      sudo apt-get install build-essential python-dev python-
        setuptools python-numpy python-scipy python-matplotlib
      ipython
        ipython-notebook python-pandas python-sympy python-nose
      ```

   3. If you are using Fedora, type the following:

      ```
      sudo yum install numpy scipy python-matplotlib ipython
      python-pandas sympy python-nose
      ```

4. You have several options to install the Python data stack on your Macintosh running OS X. These are:
   1. The first option is to download pre-built installers (`.dmg`) for each tool, and install them as you would any other Mac application (this is recommended).
   2. The second option is if you have MacPorts, a command line-based system to install software, available on your system. You will also probably need XCode with the command-line tools already installed. If so, you can enter:

      ```
      sudo port install py27-numpy py27-scipy py27-matplotlib
      py27- ipython +notebook py27-pandas py27-sympy py27-nose
      ```

   3. As the third option, *Chris Fonnesbeck* provides a bundled way to install the stack on the Mac that is tested and covers all the packages we will use here. Refer to `http://fonnesbeck.github.io/ScipySuperpack`.

All the preceding options will take time as a large number of files will be installed on your system.

How it works...

Installing the SciPy stack has been challenging historically due to compilation dependencies, including the need for Fortran. Thus, we don't recommend that you compile and install from source code, unless you feel comfortable doing such things.

Now, the better question is, what did you just install? We installed the latest versions of NumPy, SciPy, matplotlib, IPython, IPython Notebook, pandas, SymPy, and nose. The following are their descriptions:

- **SciPy**: This is a Python-based ecosystem of open source software for mathematics, science, and engineering and includes a number of useful libraries for machine learning, scientific computing, and modeling.
- **NumPy**: This is the foundational Python package providing numerical computation in Python, which is C-like and incredibly fast, particularly when using multidimensional arrays and linear algebra operations. NumPy is the reason that Python can do efficient, large-scale numerical computation that other interpreted or scripting languages cannot do.

- **matplotlib**: This is a well-established and extensive 2D plotting library for Python that will be familiar to MATLAB users.
- **IPython**: This offers a rich and powerful interactive shell for Python. It is a replacement for the standard Python **Read-Eval-Print Loop** (**REPL**), among many other tools.
- **Jupyter Notebook**: This offers a browser-based tool to perform and record work done in Python with support for code, formatted text, markdown, graphs, images, sounds, movies, and mathematical expressions.
- **pandas**: This provides a robust data frame object and many additional tools to make traditional data and statistical analysis fast and easy.
- **nose**: This is a test harness that extends the unit testing framework in the Python standard library.

There's more...

We will discuss the various packages in greater detail in the chapter in which they are introduced. However, we would be remiss if we did not at least mention the Python IDEs. In general, we recommend using your favorite programming text editor in place of a full-blown Python IDE. This can include the open source Atom from GitHub, the excellent Sublime Text editor, or TextMate, a favorite of the Ruby crowd. Vim and Emacs are both excellent choices not only because of their incredible power but also because they can easily be used to edit files on a remote server, a common task for the data scientist. Each of these editors is highly configurable with plugins that can handle code completion, highlighting, linting, and more. If you must have an IDE, take a look at **PyCharm** (the community edition is free) from the IDE wizards at JetBrains, Spyder, and Ninja-IDE. You will find that most Python IDEs are better suited for web development as opposed to data work.

See also

You can also take a look at the following for reference:

- For more information on pandas, refer to the *Python Data Analysis Library* article at http://pandas.pydata.org/
- Visit the NumPy website at http://www.numpy.org/
- Visit the SciPy website at http://www.scipy.org/
- Visit the matplotlib website at http://matplotlib.org/
- Visit the IPython website at http://ipython.org/

- Refer the *History of SciPy* article at http://wiki.scipy.org/History_of_SciPy
- Visit the MacPorts home page at http://www.macports.org/
- Visit the XCode web page at https://developer.apple.com/xcode/features/
- Visit the XCode download page at https://developer.apple.com/xcode/downloads/

Installing extra Python packages

There are a few additional Python libraries that you will need throughout this book. Just as R provides a central repository for community-built packages, so does Python in the form of the **Python Package Index (PyPI)**. As of August 28, 2014, there were 48,054 packages in **PyPI**.

Getting ready

A reasonable Internet connection is all that is needed for this recipe. Unless otherwise specified, these directions assume that you are using the default Python distribution that came with your system, and not Anaconda.

How to do it...

The following steps will show you how to download a Python package and install it from the command line:

1. Download the source code for the package in the place you like to keep your downloads.
2. Unzip the package.
3. Open a terminal window.
4. Navigate to the base directory of the source code.
5. Type in the following command:

   ```
   python setup.py install
   ```

6. If you need root access, type in the following command:

   ```
   sudo python setup.py install
   ```

To use pip, the contemporary and easiest way to install Python packages, follow these steps:

1. First, let's check whether you have pip already installed by opening a terminal and launching the Python interpreter. At the interpreter, type:

   ```
   >>>import pip
   ```

2. If you don't get an error, you have pip installed and can move on to step 5. If you see an error, let's quickly install pip.

3. Download the `get-pip.py` file from `https://raw.github.com/pypa/pip/master/contrib/get-pip.py` onto your machine.

4. Open a terminal window, navigate to the downloaded file, and type:

   ```
   python get-pip.py
   ```

   Alternatively, you can type in the following command:

   ```
   sudo python get-pip.py
   ```

5. Once pip is installed, make sure you are at the system command prompt.

6. If you are using the default system distribution of Python, type in the following:

   ```
   pip install networkx
   ```

   Alternatively, you can type in the following command:

   ```
   sudo pip install networkx
   ```

7. If you are using the Anaconda distribution, type in the following command:

   ```
   conda install networkx
   ```

8. Now, let's try to install another package, `ggplot`. Regardless of your distribution, type in the following command:

   ```
   pip install ggplot
   ```

   Alternatively, you can type in the following command:

   ```
   sudo pip install ggplot
   ```

How it works...

You have at least two options to install Python packages. In the preceding *old fashioned* way, you download the source code and unpack it on your local computer. Next, you run the included `setup.py` script with the `install` flag. If you want, you can open the `setup.py` script in a text editor and take a more detailed look at exactly what the script is doing. You might need the `sudo` command, depending on the current user's system privileges.

As the second option, we leverage the pip installer, which automatically grabs the package from the remote repository and installs it to your local machine for use by the system-level Python installation. This is the preferred method, when available.

There's more...

The `pip` is capable, so we suggest taking a look at the user guide online. Pay special attention to the very useful `pip freeze > requirements.txt` functionality so that you can communicate about external dependencies with your colleagues.

Finally, `conda` is the package manager and pip replacement for the Anaconda Python distribution or, in the words of its home page, *a cross-platform, Python-agnostic binary package manager*. Conda has some very lofty aspirations that transcend the Python language. If you are using Anaconda, we encourage you to read further on what `conda` can do and use it, and not pip, as your default package manager.

See also

You can also refer to the following:

- Refer to the pip *User Guide* at
  `http://www.pip-installer.org/en/latest/user_guide.html`
- Visit the Conda home page at `http://conda.pydata.org`
- Refer to the Conda blog posts from *Continuum Blog* at
  `http://www.continuum.io/blog/conda`

Installing and using virtualenv

virtualenv is a transformative Python tool. Once you start using it, you will never look back. virtualenv creates a local environment with its own Python distribution installed. Once this environment is activated from the shell, you can easily install packages using `pip install` into the new local Python.

At first, this might sound strange. Why would anyone want to do this? Not only does this help you handle the issue of package dependencies and versions in Python but also allows you to experiment rapidly without breaking anything important. Imagine that you build a web application that requires Version 0.8 of the `awesome_template` library, but then your new data product needs the `awesome_template` library Version 1.2. What do you do? With virtualenv, you can have both.

As another use case, what happens if you don't have admin privileges on a particular machine? You can't install the packages using `sudo pip install` required for your analysis so what do you do? If you use virtualenv, it doesn't matter.

Virtual environments are development tools that software developers use to collaborate effectively. Environments ensure that the software runs on different computers (for example, from production to development servers) with varying dependencies. The environment also alerts other developers to the needs of the software under development. Python's virtualenv ensures that the software created is in its own holistic environment, can be tested independently, and built collaboratively.

Getting ready

Assuming you have completed the previous recipe, you are ready to go for this one.

How to do it...

Install and test the virtual environment using the following steps:

1. Open a command-line shell and type in the following command:

   ```
   pip install virtualenv
   ```

   Alternatively, you can type in the following command:

   ```
   sudo pip install virtualenv
   ```

2. Once installed, type `virtualenv` in the command window, and you should be greeted with the information shown in the following screenshot:

3. Create a temporary directory and change location to this directory using the following commands:

```
mkdir temp
cd temp
```

4. From within the directory, create the first virtual environment named venv:

```
virtualenv venv
```

5. You should see text similar to the following:

```
New python executable in venv/bin/python
Installing setuptools, pip...done.
```

6. The new local Python distribution is now available. To use it, we need to activate venv using the following command:

```
source ./venv/bin/activate
```

7. The activated script is not executable and must be activated using the source command. Also, note that your shell's command prompt has probably changed and is prefixed with venv to indicate that you are now working in your new virtual environment.

8. To check this fact, use which to see the location of Python, as follows:

```
which python
```

   You should see the following output:

```
/path/to/your/temp/venv/bin/python
```

   So, when you type python once your virtual environment is activated, you will run the local Python.

9. Next, install something by typing the following:

```
pip install flask
```

   Flask is a micro-web framework written in Python; the preceding command will install a number of packages that Flask uses.

10. Finally, we demonstrate the versioning power that virtual environment and pip offer, as follows:

```
pip freeze > requirements.txt
cat requirements.txt
```

This should produce the following output:

```
Flask==0.10.1
Jinja2==2.7.2
MarkupSafe==0.19
Werkzeug==0.9.4
itsdangerous==0.23
wsgiref==0.1.2
```

11. Note that not only the name of each package is captured, but also the exact version number. The beauty of this `requirements.txt` file is that, if we have a new virtual environment, we can simply issue the following command to install each of the specified versions of the listed Python packages:

```
pip install -r requirements.txt
```

12. To deactivate your virtual environment, simply type the following at the shell prompt:

```
deactivate
```

How it works...

virtualenv creates its own virtual environment with its own installation directories that operate independently from the default system environment. This allows you to try out new libraries without polluting your system-level Python distribution. Further, if you have an application that just works and want to leave it alone, you can do so by making sure the application has its own `virtualenv`.

There's more...

`virtualenv` is a fantastic tool, one that will prove invaluable to any Python programmer. However, we wish to offer a note of caution. Python provides many tools that connect to C-shared objects in order to improve performance. Therefore, installing certain Python `packages`, such as NumPy and SciPy, into your virtual environment may require external dependencies to be compiled and installed, which are system specific. Even when successful, these compilations can be tedious, which is one of the reasons for maintaining a virtual environment. Worse, missing dependencies will cause compilations to fail, producing errors that require you to troubleshoot alien error messages, dated make files, and complex dependency chains. This can be daunting even to the most veteran data scientist.

A quick solution is to use a package manager to install complex libraries into the system environment (aptitude or Yum for Linux, Homebrew or MacPorts for OS X, and Windows will generally already have compiled installers). These tools use precompiled forms of the third-party packages. Once you have these Python packages installed in your system environment, you can use the `--system-site-packages` flag when initializing a `virtualenv`. This flag tells the `virtualenv` tool to use the system site packages already installed and circumvents the need for an additional installation that will require compilation. In order to nominate packages particular to your environment that might already be in the system (for example, when you wish to use a newer version of a package), use `pip install -I` to install dependencies into `virtualenv` and ignore the global packages. This technique works best when you only install large-scale packages on your system, but use `virtualenv` for other types of development.

For the rest of the book, we will assume that you are using a `virtualenv` and have the tools mentioned in this chapter ready to go. Therefore, we won't enforce or discuss the use of virtual environments in much detail. Just consider the virtual environment as a safety net that will allow you to perform the recipes listed in this book in isolation.

See also

You can also refer to the following:

- Read an introduction to virtualenv at
  `http://www.virtualenv.org/en/latest/virtualenv.html`
- Explore virtualenvwrapper at
  `http://virtualenvwrapper.readthedocs.org/en/latest/`
- Explore virtualenv at `https://pypi.python.org/pypi/virtualenv`

2
Driving Visual Analysis with Automobile Data with R

In this chapter, we will cover the following:

- Acquiring automobile fuel efficiency data
- Preparing R for your first project
- Importing automobile fuel efficiency data into R
- Exploring and describing fuel efficiency data
- Analyzing automobile fuel efficiency over time
- Investigating the makes and models of automobiles

Introduction

The first project we will introduce in this book is an analysis of automobile fuel economy data. The primary tool that we will use to analyze this dataset is the R statistical programming language. R is often referred to as the *lingua franca* of data science since it is currently the most popular language for statistics and data analysis. As you'll see from the examples in this book, R is an excellent tool for data manipulation, analysis, modeling, visualization, and creating useful scripts to get analytical tasks done.

The recipes in this chapter will roughly follow these five steps in the data science pipeline:

- Acquisition
- Exploration and understanding
- Munging, wrangling, and manipulation
- Analysis and modeling
- Communication and operationalization

Process-wise, the backbone of data science is the data science pipeline, and in order to get good at data science, you need to gain experience going through this process while swapping various tools and methods along the way so that you always use the ones that are appropriate for the dataset you are analyzing.

The goal of this chapter is to guide you through an analysis project on automobile fuel efficiency via step-by-step examples that you can learn from and then apply to other datasets and analysis projects in the future. Think of this chapter as a warm-up for the longer and more challenging chapters to come.

Acquiring automobile fuel efficiency data

Every data science project starts with data and this chapter begins in the same manner. For this recipe, we will dive into a dataset that contains fuel efficiency performance metrics, measured in **Miles Per Gallon (MPG)** over time, for most makes and models of automobiles available in the US since 1984. This data is courtesy of the U.S. Department of Energy and the US Environmental Protection Agency. In addition to fuel efficiency data, the dataset also contains several features and attributes of the automobiles listed, thereby providing the opportunity to summarize and group data to determine which groups tend to have better fuel efficiency historically and how this has changed over the years. The latest version of the dataset is available at `http://www.fueleconomy.gov/feg/epadata/vehicles.csv.zip`, and information about the variables in the dataset can be found at `http://www.fueleconomy.gov/feg/ws/index.shtml#vehicle`. The data was last updated on December 4, 2013 and was downloaded on December 8, 2013.

 We recommend that you use the copy of the dataset provided with the code for this book to ensure that the results described in this chapter match what your efforts produce.

Getting ready

To complete this recipe, you will need a computer with access to the Internet and a text editor of your choice.

How to do it...

Perform the following simple steps to acquire the data needed for the rest of this chapter:

1. Download the dataset from:
   `http://www.fueleconomy.gov/feg/epadata/vehicles.csv.zip`

2. Unzip `vehicles.csv` with the decompression tool of your choice and move it to your working code directory.

3. Take a moment and open the unzipped `vehicles.csv` file with Microsoft Excel, Google Spreadsheet, or a simple text editor. **Comma-separated value** (**CSV**) files are very convenient to work with as they can be edited and viewed with very basic and freely available tools. With the file open, scroll through some of the data and get a sense of what you will be working with.

4. Navigate to `http://www.fueleconomy.gov/feg/ws/index.shtml#vehicle`.

5. Select and copy all the text below the vehicle heading under **Data Description**, and paste it into a text file. Do not include the emissions heading. Save this file in your working directory as `varlabels.txt`. The first five lines of the file are as follows:

```
atvtype - type of alternative fuel or advanced technology
vehicle
barrels08 - annual petroleum consumption in barrels for
fuelType1 (1)
barrelsA08 - annual petroleum consumption in barrels for
fuelType2 (1)
charge120 - time to charge an electric vehicle in hours at 120
V
charge240 - time to charge an electric vehicle in hours at 240
V
```

Note that this file is provided for your convenience in the repository containing this chapter's code.

How it works...

There isn't much to explain in this first simple recipe, but note that we are starting off relatively easily here. In many data science projects, you will not be able to access and view the data so easily.

Preparing R for your first project

For the following recipes, you will need the R statistical programming language installed on your computer (either the base R or RStudio, but the authors strongly recommend using the excellent and free RStudio) and the automobile fuel efficiency dataset. This quick recipe will help you ensure that you have everything that you will need to complete this analysis project.

Getting ready

You will need an internet connection to complete this recipe, and we assume that you have installed RStudio for your particular platform, based on the instructions in the previous chapter.

How to do it...

If you are using RStudio, the following three steps will get you ready to roll:

1. Launch RStudio on your computer.
2. At the R console prompt, install the three R packages needed for this project:

```
install.packages("plyr")
install.packages("ggplot2")
install.packages("reshape2")
```

3. Load the R packages as follows:

```
library(plyr)
library(ggplot2)
library(reshape2)
```

There's more...

R's strength comes from the community that has developed around the language and the packages that have been created and made available by the ones in the community. There are currently over 4,000 packages and libraries that you can import and utilize to make your data analysis tasks much easier.

Dr. Hadley Wickham is a notable member of the R community and he has produced a large number of highly regarded and often-used R packages. In this chapter you will primarily use two of his biggest hits, `plyr` and `ggplot2` and a third package called `reshape2`. The package `plyr` will be used to apply the split-apply-combine data analysis pattern, explained later in this chapter, to our dataset and `ggplot2` will make complex data visualizations significantly easier.

See also

- *The R Project for Statistical Computing* web page at http://www.r-project.org/
- Visit the RStudio home page at http://www.rstudio.com/
- Refer to the *R Tutorial* at http://www.cyclismo.org/tutorial/R/
- A comprehensive guide to R at http://www.statmethods.net/about/sitemap.html
- Refer to the `plyr` reference manual at http://cran.r-project.org/web/packages/plyr/plyr.pdf
- Refer to the `ggplot2` reference manual at http://cran.r-project.org/web/packages/ggplot2/ggplot2.pdf
- Visit Dr. Wickham's home page http://had.co.nz/

Importing automobile fuel efficiency data into R

Once you have downloaded and installed everything in the previous recipe, *Preparing R for your first project*, you can import the dataset into R to start doing some preliminary analysis and get a sense of what the data looks like.

Getting ready

Much of the analysis in this chapter is cumulative, and the efforts of the previous recipes will be used for subsequent recipes. Thus, if you completed the previous recipe, you should have everything you need to continue.

How to do it...

The following steps will walk you through the initial import of the data into the R environment:

1. First, set the working directory to the location where we saved the `vehicles.csv.zip` file:

   ```
   setwd("path")
   ```

   Substitute the path for the actual directory.

2. We can load the data directly from compressed (ZIP) files, as long as you know the filename of the file inside the ZIP archive that you want to load:

   ```
   vehicles <- read.csv(unz("vehicles.csv.zip", "vehicles.csv"),
       stringsAsFactors = F)
   ```

3. To see whether this worked, let's display the first few rows of data using the **head** command:

   ```
   head(vehicles)
   ```

   You should see the first few rows of the dataset printed on your screen.

    Note that we could have used the tail command, which would have displayed the last few rows of the data frame instead of the first few rows.

4. The `labels` command gives the variable labels for the `vehicles.csv` file. Note that we use `labels`, since `labels` is a function in R. A quick look at the file shows that the variable names and their explanations are separated by –. So we will try to read the file using – as the separator:

   ```
   labels <- read.table("varlabels.txt", sep = "-", header = FALSE)
   ## Error: line 11 did not have 2 elements
   ```

5. This doesn't work! A closer look at the error shows that in line 11 of the data file, there are two – symbols, and it thus gets broken into three parts rather than two, unlike the other rows. We need to change our file-reading approach to ignore hyphenated words:

```
labels <- do.call(rbind, strsplit(readLines("varlabels.txt"), " -
"))
```

6. To check whether it works, we use the head function again:

```
head(labels)
```

```
            [,1]            [,2]
[1,] "atvtype"    "type of alternative fuel or advanced
     technology vehicle"
[2,] "barrels08"  "annual petroleum consumption in barrels for
     fuelType1 (1)"
[3,] "barrelsA08" "annual petroleum consumption in barrels for
     fuelType2 (1)"
[4,] "charge120"  "time to charge an electric vehicle in hours
     at 120 V"
[5,] "charge240"  "time to charge an electric vehicle in hours
     at 240 V"
```

How it works...

Let's break down the last complex statement in *step 5*, piece-by-piece, starting from the innermost portion and working outwards. First, let's read the file line by line:

```
x <- readLines("varlabels.txt")
```

Each line needs to be split at the string –. The spaces are important, so we don't split hyphenated words (such as in *line 11*). This results in each line split into two parts as a vector of strings, and the vectors stored in a single list:

```
y <- strsplit(x, " - ")
```

Now, we stack these vectors together to make a matrix of strings, where the first column is the variable name and the second column is the description of the variable:

```
labels <- do.call(rbind, y)
```

There's more...

Astute readers might have noticed that the `read.csv` function call included
`stringsAsFactors = F` as its final parameter. By default, R converts strings to a datatype,
known as factors in many cases. Factors are the names for R's categorical datatype, which
can be thought of as a label or tag applied to the data. Internally, R stores factors as integers
with a mapping to the appropriate label. This technique allows older versions of R to store
factors in much less memory than the corresponding character.

Categorical variables do not have a sense of order (where one value is considered greater
than another). In the following snippet, we create a quick toy example converting four
values of the `character` class to factor and do a comparison:

```
colors <- c('green', 'red', 'yellow', 'blue')
colors_factors <- factor(colors)
colors_factors
[1] green   red     yellow blue
Levels: blue green red yellow
colors_factors[1] > colors_factors[2]
[1] NA
Warning message:
In Ops.factor(colors_factors[1], colors_factors[2]) :
>not meaningful for factors
```

However, there is an ordered categorical variable, also known in the statistical world as
ordinal data. Ordinal data is just like categorical data, with one exception. There is a sense
of scale or value to the data. It can be said that one value is larger than another, but the
magnitude of the difference cannot be measured.

Furthermore, when importing data into R, we often run into the situation where a column
of numeric data might contain an entry that is non-numeric. In this case, R might import the
column of data as factors, which is often not what was intended by the data scientist.
Converting from factor to character is relatively routine, but converting from factor to
numeric can be a bit tricky.

R is capable of importing data from a wide range of formats. In this recipe, we handled a
CSV file, but we could have used a Microsoft Excel file as well. CSV files are preferred as
they are universally supported across operating systems and are far more portable.
Additionally, R can import data from numerous popular statistical programs, including
SPSS, **Stata**, and **SAS**.

See also

- Refer to the *R Data Import/Export* guide at
  `http://cran.r-project.org/doc/manuals/r-release/R-data.html`
- Explore the datatypes in R at
  `http://www.statmethods.net/input/datatypes.html`

Exploring and describing fuel efficiency data

Now that we have imported the automobile fuel efficiency data into R and learned a little about the nuances of importing, the next step is to do some preliminary analysis of the dataset. The purpose of this analysis is to explore what the data looks like and get your feet wet with some of R's most basic commands.

Getting ready

If you have completed the previous recipe, you should have everything that you need to continue.

How to do it...

The following steps will lead you through the initial exploration of our dataset, where we compute some of its basic parameters:

1. First, let's find out how many observations (rows) are in our data:

   ```
   nrow(vehicles)
   ## 34287
   ```

2. Next, let's find out how many variables (columns) are in our data:

   ```
   ncol(vehicles)
   ## 74
   ```

3. Now, let's get a sense of which columns of data are present in the data frame using the **names** function:

   ```
   > names(vehicles)
   ```

The preceding command will give you the following output:

```
> names(vehicles)
 [1] "barrels08"       "barrelsA08"       "charge120"        "charge240"       "city08"          "city08U"
 [7] "cityA08"         "cityA08U"         "cityCD"           "cityE"           "cityUF"          "co2"
[13] "co2A"            "co2TailpipeAGpm"  "co2TailpipeGpm"   "comb08"          "comb08U"         "combA08"
[19] "combA08U"        "combE"            "combinedCD"       "combinedUF"      "cylinders"       "displ"
[25] "drive"           "engId"            "eng_dscr"         "feScore"         "fuelCost08"      "fuelCostA08"
[31] "fuelType"        "fuelType1"        "ghgScore"         "ghgScoreA"       "highway08"       "highway08U"
[37] "highwayA08"      "highwayA08U"      "highwayCD"        "highwayE"        "highwayUF"       "hlv"
[43] "hpv"             "id"               "lv2"              "lv4"             "make"            "model"
[49] "mpgData"         "phevBlended"      "pv2"              "pv4"             "range"           "rangeCity"
[55] "rangeCityA"      "rangeHwy"         "rangeHwyA"        "trany"           "UCity"           "UCityA"
[61] "UHighway"        "UHighwayA"        "VClass"           "year"            "youSaveSpend"    "guzzler"
[67] "trans_dscr"      "tCharger"         "sCharger"         "atvType"         "fuelType2"       "rangeA"
[73] "evMotor"         "mfrCode"          "trany2"
>
```

Luckily, a lot of these column or variable names are pretty descriptive and give us an idea of what they might contain. Remember, a more detailed description of the variables is available at http://www.fueleconomy.gov/feg/ws/index.shtml#vehicle.

4. Let's find out how many unique years of data are included in this dataset by computing a vector of the unique values in the year column, and then computing the length of that vector:

```
length(unique(vehicles[, "year"]))
```

```
## 31
```

5. Now we determine the first and last years present in the dataset using the min and max functions:

```
first_year <- min(vehicles[, "year"])
## 1984
last_year <- max(vehicles[, "year"])
## 2014
```

 Note that we could have used the tail command, which would have displayed the last few rows of the data frame instead of the first few rows.

6. Also, since we might use the `year` variable a lot, let's make sure that we have each year covered. The list of years from 1984 to 2014 should contain 31 unique values. To test this, use the following command:

```
> length(unique(vehicles$year))

[1] 31
```

7. Next, let's find out what types of fuel are used as the automobiles' primary fuel types:

```
table(vehicles$fuelType1)

##              Diesel       Electricity Midgrade Gasoline
Natural Gas
##                1025                56                  41
57
##   Premium Gasoline   Regular Gasoline
##               8521              24587
```

From this, we can see that most cars in the dataset use regular gasoline, and the second most common fuel type is premium gasoline.

8. Let's explore the types of transmissions used by these automobiles. We first need to take care of all missing data by setting it to `NA`:

```
vehicles$trany[vehicles$trany == ""] <- NA
```

9. Now, the `trany` column is **text**, and we only care about whether the car's transmission is automatic or manual. Thus, we use the `substr` function to extract the first four characters of each `trany` column value and determine whether it is equal to `Auto`. If so, we set a new variable, `trany2`, equal to `Auto`; otherwise, the value is set to `Manual`:

```
vehicles$trany2 <- ifelse(substr(vehicles$trany, 1, 4) == "Auto",
                                                        "Auto",
"Manual")
```

10. Finally, we convert the new variable to a factor and then use the table function to see the distribution of values:

```
vehicles$trany <- as.factor(vehicles$trany)
table(vehicles$trany2)
##    Auto Manual
## 22451  11825
```

We can see that there are roughly twice as many automobile models with automatic transmission as there are models with manual transmission.

How it works...

The data frame is an incredibly powerful datatype used by R, and we will leverage it heavily throughout this recipe. The data frame allows us to group variables of different datatypes (numeric, strings, logical, factors, and so on) into rows of related information. One example will be a data frame of customer information. Each row in the data frame can contain the name of the person (a string), along with an age (numeric), a gender (a factor), and a flag to indicate whether they are a current customer (Boolean). If you are familiar with relational databases, this is much like a table in a database.

Furthermore, in this recipe, we looked at several ways of getting a quick read on a dataset imported into R. Most notably, we used the powerful `table` function to create a count of the occurrence of values for the `fuelType1` variable. This function is capable of much more, including cross tabulations, as follows:

```
with(vehicles, table(sCharger, year))
```

The preceding command will give you the following output:

```
> with(vehicles, table(sCharger, year))
        year
sCharger 1984 1985 1986 1987 1988 1989 1990 1991 1992 1993 1994 1995 1996 1997 1998 1999 2000 2001 2002 2003 2004 2005
         1964 1701 1210 1247 1130 1149 1074 1130 1116 1088  979  962  767  757  800  840  826  891  949 1015 1089 1136
       S    0    0    0    0    0    4    4    2    5    5    3    5    6    5   12   12   14   20   26   29   33   30
        year
sCharger 2006 2007 2008 2009 2010 2011 2012 2013 2014
         1067 1098 1152 1166 1091 1077 1125 1141 1051
       S   37   28   35   19   18   20   28   42   57
> |
```

Here, we looked at the number of automobile models by year, with and without a super charger (and we saw that super chargers have seemingly become more popular more recently than they were in the past).

Also, note that we use the `with` command. This command tells R to use vehicles as the default data when performing the subsequent command, in this case, table. Thus, we can omit prefacing the `sCharger` and `year` column names with the name of the data frame and vehicles, followed by the dollar sign.

There's more...

To provide a cautionary tale about data import, let's look at the sCharger and tCharger columns more closely. Note that these columns indicate whether the car contains a super charger or a turbo charger, respectively.

Starting with sCharger, we look at the class of the variable and the unique values present in the data frame:

```
> class(vehicles$sCharger)
[1] "character"
> unique(vehicles$sCharger)
[1] ""   "S"
```

We next look at tCharger, expecting things to be the same:

```
> class(vehicles$tCharger)
[1] "logical"
> unique(vehicles$tCharger)
[1]    NA TRUE
```

However, what we find is that these two seemingly similar variables are different datatypes completely. While the tCharger variable is a logical variable, also known as a Boolean variable in other languages, and it is used to represent the binary values of TRUE and FALSE, the sCharger variable appears to be the more general character datatype. Something seems wrong. In this case, because we can, let's check the original data. Luckily, the data is in a .csv file, and we can use a simple text editor to open and read the file (Notepad on Windows and vi on Unix systems are recommended for the task, but feel free to use your favorite, basic text editor). When we open the file, we can see that sCharger and tCharger data columns either are blank or contain an **S** or **T**, respectively.

Thus, R has read in the **T** character in the tCharger column as a Boolean TRUE variable, as opposed to the character T. This isn't a fatal flaw and might not impact an analysis. However, undetected bugs such as this can cause problems far down the analytical pipeline and necessitate significant repeated work.

Analyzing automobile fuel efficiency over time

We have now successfully imported the data and looked at some important high-level statistics that provided us with a basic understanding of what values are in the dataset and how frequently some features appear. With this recipe, we continue the exploration by looking at some of the fuel efficiency metrics over time and in relation to other data points.

Getting ready

If you completed the previous recipe, you should have everything you need to continue.

How to do it...

The following steps will use both `plyr` and the graphics library, `ggplot2`, to explore the dataset:

1. Let's start by looking at whether there is an overall trend of how MPG changes over time on average. To do this, we use the `ddply` function from the `plyr` package to take the `vehicles` data frame, aggregate rows by year, and then, for each group, we compute the mean highway, city, and combine fuel efficiency. The result is then assigned to a new data frame, `mpgByYr`. Note that this is our first example of split-apply-combine. We split the data frame into groups by year, we apply the mean function to specific variables, and then we combine the results into a new data frame:

   ```
   mpgByYr <- ddply(vehicles, ~year, summarise, avgMPG =
   mean(comb08), avgHghy = mean(highway08), avgCity =
   mean(city08))
   ```

2. To gain a better understanding of this new data frame, we pass it to the `ggplot` function, telling it to plot the `avgMPG` variable against the `year` variable, using points. In addition, we specify that we want axis labels, a title, and even a smoothed conditional `mean` (`geom_smooth()`) represented as a shaded region of the plot:

```
ggplot(mpgByYr, aes(year, avgMPG)) + geom_point() +
  geom_smooth() + xlab("Year") + ylab("Average MPG") +
  ggtitle("All cars")
## geom_smooth: method="auto" and size of largest group is <1000,
so using
## loess. Use 'method = x' to change the smoothing method.
```

The preceding commands will give you the following plot:

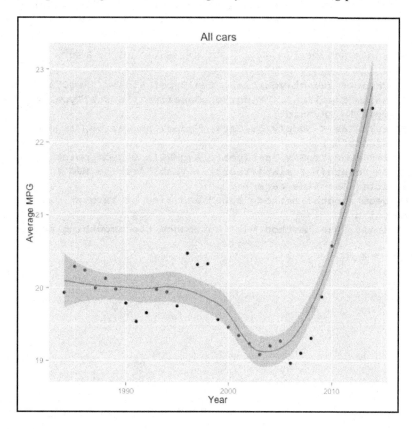

3. Based on this visualization, one might conclude that there has been a tremendous increase in the fuel economy of cars sold in the last few years. However, this can be a little misleading as there have been more hybrid and non-gasoline vehicles in later years, which is shown as follows:

```
table(vehicles$fuelType1)
```

```
##              Diesel      Electricity Midgrade Gasoline
Natural Gas
##                1025              56                 41
57
##   Premium Gasoline  Regular Gasoline
##               8521             24587
```

4. Let's look at just gasoline cars, even though there are not many non-gasoline powered cars, and redraw the preceding plot. To do this, we use the subset function to create a new data frame, gasCars, which only contains the rows of vehicles in which the fuelType1 variable is one among a subset of values:

```
gasCars <- subset(vehicles, fuelType1 %in% c("Regular Gasoline",
"Premium Gasoline", "Midgrade Gasoline") & fuelType2 == "" &
atvType != "Hybrid")
mpgByYr_Gas <- ddply(gasCars, ~year, summarise, avgMPG =
mean(comb08))
ggplot(mpgByYr_Gas, aes(year, avgMPG)) + geom_point() +
 geom_smooth() + xlab("Year") + ylab("Average MPG") +
ggtitle("Gasoline cars")
## geom_smooth: method="auto" and size of largest group is <1000,
so using
## loess. Use 'method = x' to change the smoothing method.
```

The preceding commands will give you the following plot:

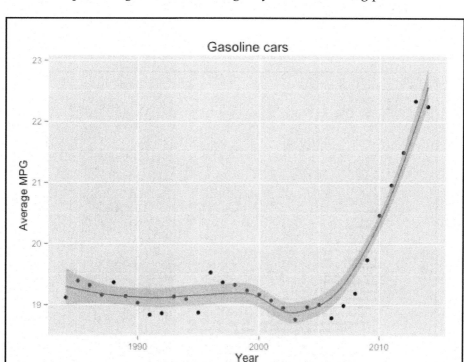

5. Have fewer large engine cars been made recently? If so, this can explain the increase. First, let's verify whether cars with larger engines have worse fuel efficiency. We note that the `displ` variable, which represents the displacement of the engine in liters, is currently a string variable that we need to convert to a numeric variable:

```
typeof(gasCars$displ)

##   "character"
gasCars$displ <- as.numeric(gasCars$displ)
ggplot(gasCars, aes(displ, comb08)) + geom_point() +
  geom_smooth()

## geom_smooth: method="auto" and size of largest group is >=1000,
so using
## gam with formula: y ~ s(x, bs = "cs"). Use 'method = x' to
change the
## smoothing method.
## Warning: Removed 2 rows containing missing values
```

```
(stat_smooth).
## Warning: Removed 2 rows containing missing values
(geom_point).
```

The preceding commands will give you the following plot:

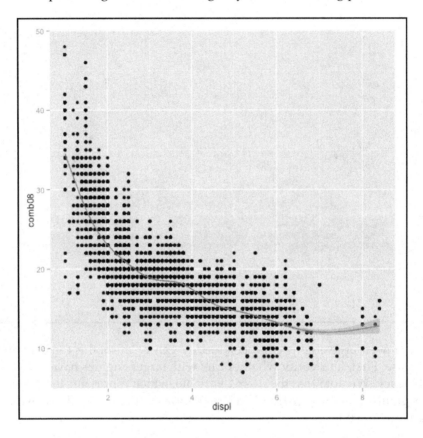

This scatter plot of the data offers the convincing evidence that there is a negative, or even inverse correlation, between engine displacement and fuel efficiency; thus, smaller cars tend to be more fuel-efficient.

6. Now, let's see whether more small cars were made in later years, which can explain the drastic increase in fuel efficiency:

```
avgCarSize <- ddply(gasCars, ~year, summarise, avgDispl =
mean(displ))

ggplot(avgCarSize, aes(year, avgDispl)) + geom_point() +
  geom_smooth() + xlab("Year") + ylab("Average engine displacement
```

```
(1)")
```

```
## geom_smooth: method="auto" and size of largest group is <1000,
so using
## loess. Use 'method = x' to change the smoothing method.
## Warning: Removed 1 rows containing missing values (stat_smooth).
## Warning: Removed 1 rows containing missing values (geom_point).
```

The preceding commands will give you the following plot:

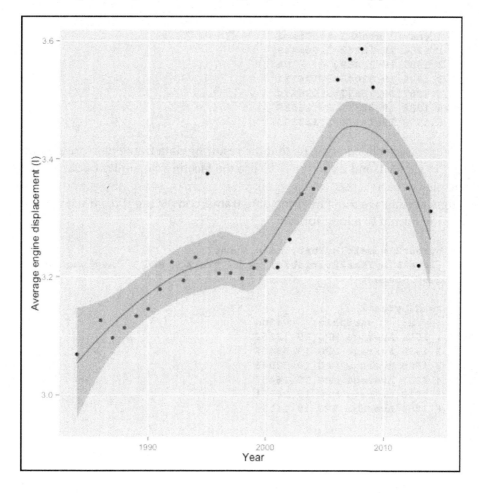

7. From the preceding figure, the average engine displacement has decreased substantially since 2008. To get a better sense of the impact this might have had on fuel efficiency, we can put both MPG and displacement by year on the same graph. Using `ddply`, we create a new data frame, `byYear`, which contains both the average fuel efficiency and the average engine displacement by year:

```
byYear <- ddply(gasCars, ~year, summarise, avgMPG = mean(comb08),
  avgDispl = mean(displ))

> head(byYear)
  year   avgMPG avgDispl
1 1984 19.12162 3.068449
2 1985 19.39469       NA
3 1986 19.32046 3.126514
4 1987 19.16457 3.096474
5 1988 19.36761 3.113558
6 1989 19.14196 3.133393
```

8. The `head` function shows us that the resulting data frame has three columns: `year`, `avgMPG`, and `avgDispl`. To use the faceting capability of `ggplot2` to display `Average MPG` and `Avg engine displacement` by year on separate but aligned plots, we must melt the data frame, converting it from what is known as a wide format to a long format:

```
byYear2 = melt(byYear, id = "year")
 levels(byYear2$variable) <- c("Average MPG", "Avg engine
displacement")

head(byYear2)
  year    variable    value
1 1984 Average MPG 19.12162
2 1985 Average MPG 19.39469
3 1986 Average MPG 19.32046
4 1987 Average MPG 19.16457
5 1988 Average MPG 19.36761
6 1989 Average MPG 19.14196
```

9. If we use the `nrow` function, we can see that the `byYear2` data frame has 62 rows and the `byYear` data frame has only 31. The two separate columns from `byYear` (`avgMPG` and `avgDispl`) have now been melted into one new column (`value`) in the `byYear2` data frame. Note that the variable column in the `byYear2` data frame serves to identify the column that the value represents:

```
ggplot(byYear2, aes(year, value)) + geom_point() +
 geom_smooth() + facet_wrap(~variable, ncol = 1, scales =
 "free_y") + xlab("Year") + ylab("")
## geom_smooth: method="auto" and size of largest group is <1000,
so using
## loess. Use 'method = x' to change the smoothing method.
 ## geom_smooth: method="auto" and size of largest group is <1000,
so using
## loess. Use 'method = x' to change the smoothing method.
## Warning: Removed 1 rows containing missing values (stat_smooth).
## Warning: Removed 1 rows containing missing values (geom_point).
```

The preceding commands will give you the following plot:

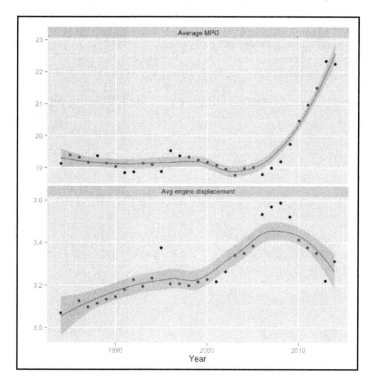

From this plot, we can see the following:

- Engine sizes have generally increased until 2008, with a sudden increase in large cars between 2006 and 2008.
- Since 2009, there has been a decrease in the average car size, which partially explains the increase in fuel efficiency.
- Until 2005, there was an increase in the average car size, but the fuel efficiency remained roughly constant. This seems to indicate that engine efficiency has increased over the years.
- The years 2006-2008 are interesting. Though the average engine size increased quite suddenly, the MPG remained roughly the same as in previous years. This seeming discrepancy might require more investigation.

10. Given the trend towards smaller displacement engines, let's see whether automatic or manual transmissions are more efficient for four cylinder engines, and how the efficiencies have changed over time:

```
gasCars4 <- subset(gasCars, cylinders == "4")
```

```
ggplot(gasCars4, aes(factor(year), comb08)) + geom_boxplot() +
facet_wrap(~trany2, ncol = 1) + theme(axis.text.x =
element_text(angle = 45)) + labs(x = "Year", y = "MPG")
```

The preceding command will give you the following plot:

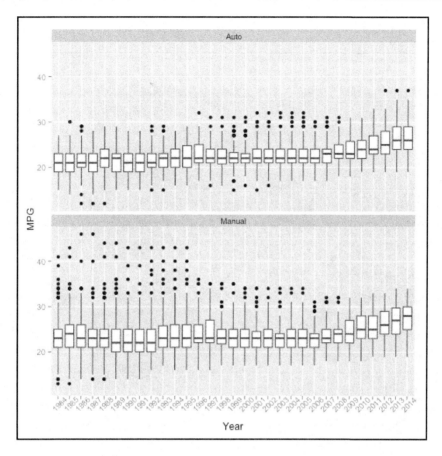

11. This time, `ggplot2` was used to create box plots that help visualize the distribution of values (and not just a single value, such as a mean) for each year.

12. Next, let's look at the change in proportion of manual cars available each year:

```
ggplot(gasCars4, aes(factor(year), fill = factor(trany2))) +
geom_bar(position = "fill") + labs(x = "Year", y = "Proportion
of cars", fill = "Transmission") + theme(axis.text.x =
element_text(angle = 45)) + geom_hline(yintercept = 0.5,
linetype = 2)
```

The preceding command will give you the following plot:

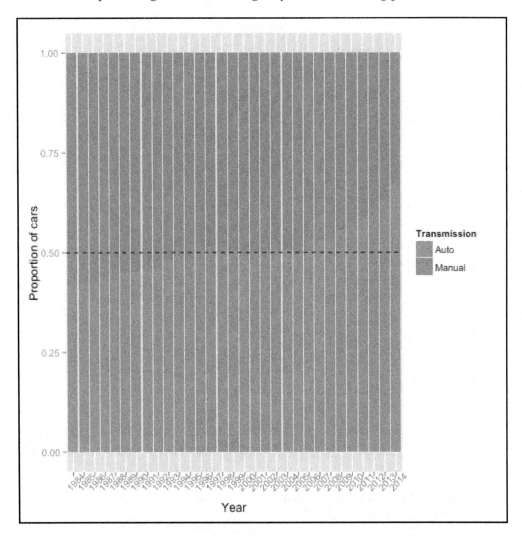

How it works...

The ggplot2 library is an open source implementation of the foundational grammar of graphics by Wilkinson, Anand, and Grossman for R. **The Grammar of Graphics** attempts to decompose statistical data visualizations into component parts to better understand how such graphics are created. With ggplot2, Hadley Wickham takes these ideas and implements a layered approach, allowing the user to assemble complex visualizations from individual pieces very quickly. Take, for example, the first graph for this recipe, which shows the average fuel efficiency of all models of cars in a particular year over time:

```
ggplot(mpgByYr, aes(year, avgMPG)) + geom_point() + geom_smooth() +
    xlab("Year") + ylab("Average MPG") + ggtitle("All cars")
```

To construct this plot, we first tell ggplot the data frame that will serve as the data for the plot (mpgByYr), and then the aesthetic mappings that will tell ggplot2 which variables will be mapped into visual characteristics of the plot. In this case, aes(year, avgMPG) implicitly specifies that the year will be mapped to the x axis and avgMPG will be mapped to the y axis. geom_point() tells the library to plot the specified data as points and a second geom, geom_smooth(), adds a shaded region showing the smoothed mean (with a confidence interval set to 0.95, by default) for the same data. Finally, the xlab(), ylab(), and ggtitle() functions are used to add labels to the plot. Thus, we can generate a complex, publication quality graph in a single line of code; ggplot2 is capable of doing far more complex plots.

Also, it is important to note that ggplot2, and the grammar of graphics in general, does not tell you how best to visualize your data, but gives you the tools to do so rapidly. If you want more advice on this topic, we strongly recommend looking into the works of *Edward Tufte*, who has numerous books on the matter, including the classic *The Visual Display of Quantitative Information, Graphics Press USA*. Furthermore, ggplot2 does not allow for dynamic data visualizations.

There's more...

In *step 9*, it appears that manual transmissions are more efficient than automatic transmissions, and they both exhibit the same increase, on an average, since 2008. However, there is something odd here. There appears to be many very efficient cars (less than 40 MPG) with automatic transmissions in later years, and almost no manual transmission cars with similar efficiencies in the same time frame. The pattern is reversed in earlier years. Is there a change in the proportion of manual cars available each year? Yes.

With this recipe, we threw you into the deep end of data analysis with R, using two very important R packages, `plyr` and `ggplot2`. Just as traditional software development has design patterns for common constructs, a few such patterns are emerging in the field of data science. One of the most notable is the split-apply-combine pattern highlighted by *Dr. Hadley Wickham*. In this strategy, one breaks up the problem into smaller, more manageable pieces by some variable. Once aggregated, you perform an operation on the new grouped data, and then combine the results into a new data structure. As you can see in this recipe, we used this strategy of split-apply-combine repeatedly, examining the data from many different perspectives, as a result.

Beyond `plyr`, this recipe heavily leveraged the `ggplot2` library, which deserves additional exposition. We will refrain from providing an extensive `ggplot2` tutorial as there are a number of excellent tutorials available online. What is important is that you understand the important idea of how `ggplot2` allows you to construct such complex statistical visualizations in such a terse fashion.

See also

- Refer to *The Split-Apply-Combine Strategy for Data Analysis* paper at `http://www.jstatsoft.org/v40/i01/paper`
- Refer to *The Grammar of Graphics, Leland Wilkinson, Springer Science & Business Media*
- Refer to the *Package 'ggplot2'* article from CRAN at `http://cran.r-project.org/web/packages/ggplot2/ggplot2.pdf`
- Refer to the *A Layered Grammar of Graphics* article at `http://vita.had.co.nz/papers/layered-grammar.pdf`

Investigating the makes and models of automobiles

With the first set of questions asked and answered about this dataset, let's move on to additional analyses.

Getting ready

If you completed the previous recipe, you should have everything you need to continue.

How to do it...

This recipe will investigate the makes and models of automobiles and how they have changed over time:

1. Let's look at how the makes and models of cars inform fuel efficiency over time. First, let's look at the frequency of the makes and models of cars available in the US over this time and concentrate on four-cylinder cars:

```
carsMake <- ddply(gasCars4, ~year, summarise, numberOfMakes =
length(unique(make)))

ggplot(carsMake, aes(year, numberOfMakes)) + geom_point() + labs(x
= "Year", y = "Number of available makes") + ggtitle("Four cylinder
cars")
```

We see in the following graph that there has been a decline in the number of makes available over this period, though there has been a small uptick in recent times.

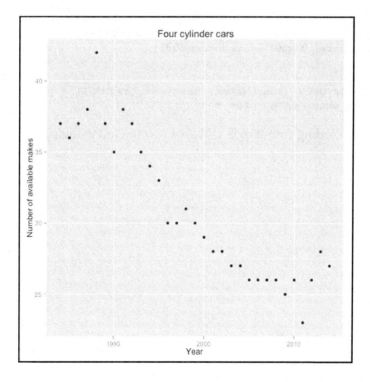

2. Can we look at the makes that have been available for every year of this study? We find that there are only 12 manufactures that made four-cylinder cars every year during this period:

```
uniqMakes <- dlply(gasCars4, ~year, function(x)
  unique(x$make))

commonMakes <- Reduce(intersect, uniqMakes)
commonMakes
##  [1] "Ford"       "Honda"       "Toyota"      "Volkswagen"
 "Chevrolet"
##  [6] "Chrysler"   "Nissan"      "Dodge"       "Mazda"
 "Mitsubishi"
## [11] "Subaru"     "Jeep"
```

3. How have these manufacturers done over time with respect to fuel efficiency? We find that most manufacturers have shown improvement over this time, though several manufacturers have demonstrated quite sharp fuel efficiency increases in the last five years:

```
carsCommonMakes4 <- subset(gasCars4, make %in% commonMakes)
avgMPG_commonMakes <- ddply(carsCommonMakes4, ~year + make,
  summarise, avgMPG = mean(comb08))


ggplot(avgMPG_commonMakes, aes(year, avgMPG)) + geom_line() +
  facet_wrap(~make, nrow = 3)
```

The preceding commands will give you the following plot:

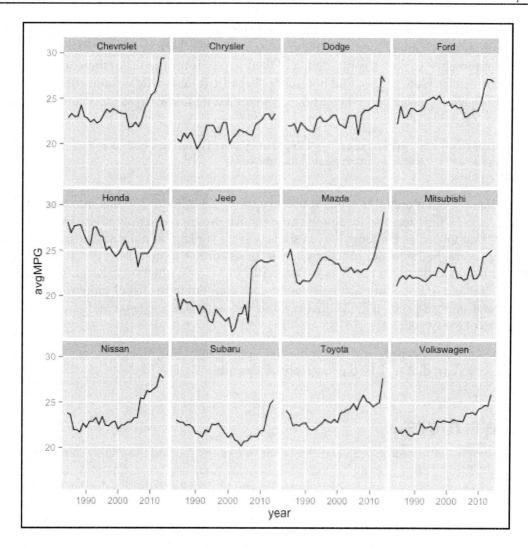

How it works...

In *step 2*, there is definitely some interesting magic at work, with a lot being done in only a few lines of code. This is both a beautiful and a problematic aspect of R. It is beautiful because it allows the concise expression of programmatically complex ideas, but it is problematic because R code can be quite inscrutable if you are not familiar with the particular library.

In the first line, we use `dlply` (not `ddply`) to take the `gasCars4` data frame, split it by year, and then apply the unique function to the `make` variable. For each year, a list of the unique available automobile makes is computed, and then `dlply` returns a list of these lists (one element each year). Note `dlply`, and not `ddply`, because it takes a data frame (d) as input and returns a list (l) as output, whereas `ddply` takes a data frame (d) as input and outputs a data frame (d):

```
uniqMakes <- dlply(gasCars4, ~year, function(x) unique(x$make))
commonMakes <- Reduce(intersect, uniqMakes)
commonMakes
```

The next line is even more interesting. It uses the `Reduce` higher order function, and this is the same `Reduce` function and idea in the map reduce programming paradigm introduced by Google that underlies Hadoop. R is, in some ways, a functional programming language and offers several higher order functions as part of its core. A higher order function accepts another function as input. In this line, we pass the `intersect` function to `Reduce`, which will apply the `intersect` function pairwise to each element in the list of unique makes per year that was created previously. Ultimately, this results in a single list of automobile makes that is present every year.

The two lines of code express a very simple concept (determining all automobile makes present every year) that took two paragraphs to describe.

There's more...

The final graph in this recipe is an excellent example of the faceted graphics capabilities of `ggplot2`. Adding `+facet_wrap(~make, nrow = 3)` tells `ggplot2` that we want a separate set of axes for each make of automobile and to distribute these subplots between three different rows. This is an incredibly powerful data visualization technique as it allows us to clearly see patterns that might only manifest for a particular value of a variable.

We kept things simple in this first data science project. The dataset itself was small--only 12 megabytes uncompressed, easily stored, and handled on a basic laptop. We used R to import the dataset, check the integrity of some (but not all) of the data fields, and summarize the data. We then moved on to exploring the data by asking a number of questions and using two key libraries, `plyr` and `ggplot2`, to manipulate the data and visualize the results. In this data science pipeline, our final stage was simply the text that we wrote to summarize our conclusions and the visualizations produced by `ggplot2`.

See also

- Read a great post titled *Higher Order Functions in R, John Myles White* at `http://www.johnmyleswhite.com/notebook/2010/09/23/higher-order-functions-in-r/`

3

Creating Application-Oriented Analyses Using Tax Data and Python

In this chapter, we will cover:

- Preparing for the analysis of top incomes
- Importing and exploring the world's top incomes dataset
- Analyzing and visualizing the top income data of the US
- Furthering the analysis of the top income groups of the US
- Reporting with Jinja2
- Repeating the analysis in R

Introduction

In this book, we take a practical approach to data analysis with R and Python. With relative ease, we can answer questions about particular datasets, produce models, and export visualizations. For this reason, R is an excellent choice for rapid prototyping and analytics since it is a domain-specific language designed for statistical data analysis, and it does its job well.

In this book, we will take a look at a different approach to analytics that is more geared towards production environments and applications. The data science pipeline of hypothesis, acquisition, cleaning and munging, analysis, modeling, visualization, and application is not a clean and linear process by any means. Moreover, when the analysis is meant to be reproducible at scale in an automated fashion, many new considerations and requirements enter into the picture. Thus, many data applications require a broader toolkit. This toolkit should still provide rapid prototyping, be generally available on all systems, and provide full support for a range of computing operations, including network operations, data operations, and scientific operations. Given these requirements, Python becomes a clear contender as the tool of choice for application-oriented analyses.

Python is an interpreted language (sometimes referred to as a scripting language), much like R. It requires no special IDE or software compilation tools and is therefore as fast as R to develop with and prototype. Like R, it also makes use of C shared objects to improve computational performance. Additionally, Python is a default system tool on Linux, Unix, and macOS X machines and is available for Windows too. Python is loaded with batteries which means that the standard library is widely inclusive of many modules from multiprocessing to compression toolsets. Python is a flexible computing powerhouse that can tackle any domain problem. If you find yourself in need of libraries that are outside of the standard library, Python also comes with a package manager (like R) that allows the download and installation of other code bases.

Python's computational flexibility means that some analytical tasks take more lines of code than their counterpart in R. However, Python does have the tools that allow it to perform the same statistical computing. This leads to an obvious question: *When do we use R over Python and vice versa?* This chapter attempts to answer this question by taking an application-oriented approach to statistical analyses.

An introduction to application-oriented approaches

Data applications and data products are interminably becoming part of our everyday lives. These products have much farther reach than simple data-driven web applications which include all manner of frontend web and mobile applications that are backed by a database and include middleware to handle transactions. By this definition, a simple blog is not fundamentally different from a large-scale e-commerce site. Instead, data products and appliances acquire their value from the data itself and create more data as a result.

These types of applications can be utilized to enrich traditional applications such as semantic tagging for the blog or recommendation engines for an e-commerce site. On the other hand, they can be standalone data products in their own right, including everything from quantified self devices to self-driving vehicles.

The treatment and analyses of data in a live or streaming context seem to be the defining characteristic of application-oriented analyses, unlike more traditional data mining or statistical evaluations of a static dataset. In order to deal with such data, a fair amount of programmatic nimbleness or dynamic approaches are required and flexibility is precisely where Python shines in the data science context.

Consider a specific example for a reporting task. Taking a snapshot of a data window and manually compiling a report from gathered analytics with charting graphics and visualizations is good practice to understand changing data and get a feel for larger patterns. When this report needs to be run daily on lower data volumes, schedulers could merely dump the report out to a file every day. However, when the reporting task becomes hourly, or on demand, it means the visualization application has become a static web application and will probably require a central location. As this task and the data size grow, adding constraints or queries on the report becomes important. This is a typical life cycle for data applications and Python development is well suited to handle these changing requirements.

We will describe, model, and visualize a dataset that contains the world's top incomes and discuss the statistical toolkit in Python. However, as we go through this chapter, we will also include notes on how the analyses and methodologies we are utilizing can be framed in an application-oriented context.

Preparing for the analysis of top incomes

For the following recipes, you will need Python installed on your computer and you will need the world's top incomes dataset. This recipe will help ensure you have set up everything you need to complete this analysis project.

Getting ready

To step through this recipe, you will need a computer with access to the internet. Make sure you have downloaded and installed Python and the necessary Python libraries to complete this project.

Refer to Chapter 1, *Preparing Your Data Science Environment*, to set up a Python development environment using virtualenv and install the required libraries for matplotlib and NumPy.

How to do it...

The following steps will guide you to download the world's top incomes dataset and install the necessary Python libraries to complete this project:

The original dataset for the world's top incomes can be downloaded from http://topincomes.g-mond.parisschoolofeconomics.eu/. However, the site has been updated several times, which has changed the output format of the data (from .csv to .xlsx). This recipe assumes a .csv file format.

This chapter's repository contains the properly formatted version of the input data file.

1. Save the world's top incomes dataset to a location on your computer where you will be able to find it.
2. Open up a terminal window and start a Python interpreter.
3. Check to make sure that the following three libraries, NumPy, matplotlib, and Jinja2, are installed; try to import each:

```
In [2]: import numpy as np
   ...: import jinja2
   ...: import matplotlib as plt
```

Each of the preceding libraries should import without a comment or remark from Python. If they do, you are good to go. If not, refer to `Chapter 1`, *Preparing Your Data Science Environment*, to set up your system.

How it works...

NumPy is the fundamental scientific computing library for Python; it is therefore essential to any data science toolkit, and we will leverage it in many places throughout the Python chapters. However, since NumPy is an external library that must be compiled for your system, we will discuss alternative native-Python approaches alongside the NumPy approach.

Importing and exploring the world's top incomes dataset

Once you have downloaded and installed everything in the previous recipe, you can read the dataset with Python and then start doing some preliminary analysis to get a sense of what the data you have looks like.

The dataset that we'll explore in this chapter was created by *Alvaredo, Facundo, Anthony B. Atkinson, Thomas Piketty*, and *Emmanuel Saez*, The World Top Incomes Database, `http://top incomes.g-mond.parisschoolofeconomics.eu/`, *10/12/2013*. It contains global information about the highest incomes per country for approximately the past 100 years, gleaned from tax records.

Getting ready

If you've completed the previous recipe, *Preparing for the analysis of top incomes*, you should have everything you need to continue.

How to do it...

Let's use the following sequence of steps to import the data and start our exploration of this dataset in Python:

1. With the following snippet, we will create a Python list in memory that contains dictionaries of each row, where the keys are the column names (the first row of the CSV contains the header information) and the values are the values for that particular row:

```
In [3]: import csv
   ...: data_file = "../data/income_dist.csv"
   ...: with open(data_file, 'r') as csvfile:
   ...: reader = csv.DictReader(csvfile)
   ...: data = list(reader)
```

 Note that the input file, `income_dist.csv`, might be in a different directory in your system depending on where you place it.

2. We perform a quick check with `len` to reveal the number of records:

```
In [4]: len(data)
   ...:
Out[4]: 2180
```

3. When utilizing CSV data with headers, we check the field names on the CSV reader itself, as well as getting the number of variables:

```
In [5]: len(reader.fieldnames)
   ...:
Out[5]: 354
```

4. While this data is not too large, let's start using best practices when accessing it. Rather than holding all of the data in memory, we use a generator to access the data one row at a time.

> Generators are Python expressions that allow you to create functions that act as iterables; rather than returning all of the data, they yield data one part at a time in a memory-efficient iteration context. As our datasets get larger, it's useful to use generators to perform filtering on demand and clean data as you read it:

```
In [6]: def dataset(path):
   ...: with open(path, 'r') as csvfile:
   ...: reader = csv.DictReader(csvfile)
   ...: for row in reader:
   ...: yield row
```

> Also, take note of the with `open(path, 'r') as csvfile` statement. This statement ensures that the CSV file is closed when the with block is exited, even (or especially) if there is an exception. Python with blocks replace the try, except, and finally statements, and are syntactically brief while semantically more correct programming constructs.

5. Using our new function, we can take a look to determine which countries are involved in our dataset:

```
In [7]: print(set([row["Country"] for row in dataset(data_file)]))

   ...: set(['Canada', 'Italy', 'France', 'Netherlands',
'Ireland',...])
```

6. We can also inspect the range of years that this dataset covers, as follows:

```
In [8]: print(min(set([int(row["Year"]) for row in
dataset(data_file)])))
   ...:
1875

In [9]: print(max(set([int(row["Year"]) for row in
dataset(data_file)])))
   ...:
2010
```

7. In both of these previous examples, we used a Python list comprehension to generate a set. A comprehension is a concise statement that generates an iterable, much like the earlier memory-safe generators. The output variable (or variables) is specified, along with the for keyword, and the iterable to express the variable, along with an optional if condition. In Python 3.6, set and dictionary comprehensions also exist. The previous country set could also be expressed as follows:

```
In [10]: {row["Country"] for row in dataset(data_file)}
    ...: set(['Canada', 'Italy', 'France', 'Netherlands',
'Ireland',...])
Out[10]: {'Netherlands', Ellipsis, 'Ireland', 'Canada', 'Italy',
'France'}
```

8. Finally, let's filter just the data for the United States so we can analyze it exclusively:

```
In [11]: filter(lambda row: row["Country"] == "United States",
    ...: dataset(data_file))

Out[11]: <filter at 0xb1aeac8>
```

The Python filter function creates a list from all of the values of a sequence or iterable (the second parameter) that make the function specified by the first parameter true. In this case, we use an anonymous function (a Lambda function) to check whether the value in the specified row's Country column is equal to United States.

9. With this initial discovery and exploration of the dataset, we can now take a look at some of the data using matplotlib, one of the main scientific plotting packages available for Python and very similar to the plotting capabilities of MATLAB:

```
In [12]: import csv
    ...: import numpy as np
    ...: import matplotlib.pyplot as plt

In [13]: def dataset(path, filter_field=None, filter_value=None):
    ...: with open(path, 'r') as csvfile:
    ...: reader = csv.DictReader(csvfile)
    ...: if filter_field:
    ...: for row in filter(lambda row:
    ...: row[filter_field]==filter_value, reader):
    ...: yield row
    ...: else:
```

```
     ...: for row in reader:
     ...: yield row

In [14]: def main(path):
     ...: data = [(row["Year"], float(row["Average income per tax
unit"]))
     ...: for row in dataset(path, "Country", "United States")]
     ...: width = 0.35
     ...: ind = np.arange(len(data))
     ...: fig = plt.figure()
     ...: ax = plt.subplot(111)
     ...: ax.bar(ind, list(d[1] for d in data))
     ...: ax.set_xticks(np.arange(0, len(data), 4))
     ...: ax.set_xticklabels(list(d[0] for d in
data)[0::4],rotation=45)
     ...: ax.set_ylabel("Income in USD")
     ...: plt.title("U.S. Average Income 1913-2008")
     ...: plt.show()

In [15]: if __name__ == "__main__":
         ...: main("income_dist.csv")
```

The preceding snippet will give us the following output:

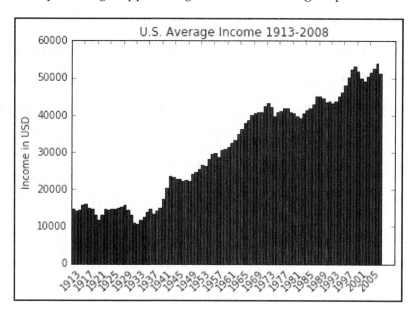

The preceding example of data exploration with Python should seem familiar from many of the R chapters. Loading the dataset, filtering, and computing ranges required a few more lines of code and specific typecasting, but we quickly created analyses in a memory-safe fashion.

10. When we moved on to creating charts, we started using NumPy and matplotlib a bit more. NumPy can be used in a very similar fashion to R, to load data from a CSV file to an array in memory and dynamically determine the type of each column. To do this, the following two module functions can be used:

- genfromtext: This function creates an array from tabular data stored in a text file with two main loops. The first converts each line of the file to string sequences, and the second converts each string to an appropriate datatype. It is a bit slower and not as memory efficient, but the result is a convenient data table stored in memory. This function also handles missing data, which other faster and simpler functions cannot.
- recfromcsv: This function is a helper function based on genfromtext that has default arguments set to provide access to a CSV file.

Have a look at the following snippet:

```
In [16]: import numpy as np

    ...: dataset = np.recfromcsv(data_file, skip_header=1)

    ...: dataset

array([[            nan,   1.93200000e+03,             nan, ...,
           nan,   1.65900000e+00,   2.51700000e+00],
       [            nan,   1.93300000e+03,             nan, ...,
           nan,   1.67400000e+00,   2.48400000e+00],
       [            nan,   1.93400000e+03,             nan, ...,
           nan,   1.65200000e+00,   2.53400000e+00],
       ...,
       [            nan,   2.00600000e+03,   4.52600000e+01, ...,
        1.11936337e+07,   1.54600000e+00,   2.83000000e+00],
       [            nan,   2.00700000e+03,   4.55100000e+01, ...,
        1.19172976e+07,   1.53000000e+00,   2.88500000e+00],
       [            nan,   2.00800000e+03,   4.56000000e+01, ...,
        9.14119000e+06,   1.55500000e+00,   2.80300000e+00]])
```

The first argument to the function should be the data source. It should be either a string that points to a local or remote file or a file-like object with a read method. URLs will be downloaded to the current working directory before they are loaded. Additionally, the input can be either text or a compressed file. The function recognizes `gzip` and `bzip2`. These files need to have the `.gz` or `.bz2` extensions to be readable. Notable optional arguments to `genfromtext` include the delimiter, `,` (comma) by default in `recfromcsv`; `skip_header` and `skip_footer`, which take an optional number of lines to skip from the top or bottom respectively; and `dtype`, which specifies the datatype of the cells. By default, the `dtype` is None, and NumPy will attempt to detect the correct format.

11. We can now get an overall sense of the scope of our data table:

```
In [17]: dataset.size

   ...:
Out[17]: 2179

In [18]: (len(dataset)+1)*len(dataset.T[1]) # works on 3.6
   ...:
Out[18]: 771720
In [19]: dataset.shape
   ...:
Out[19]: (2179,)
```

Depending on your version of NumPy, you might see slightly different output. The dataset.size statement might report back the number of rows of data (2179), and the shape might output as (2179,).

The size property on `ndarray` returns the number of elements in the matrix. The shape property returns a tuple of the dimensions in our array. CSVs are naturally two-dimensional, therefore the `(m, n)` tuple indicates the number of rows and columns, respectively.

However, there are a couple of gotchas with using this method. First, note that we had to skip our header line; genfromtxt does allow named columns by setting the keyword argument names to True (and in this case, you won't set skip_headers=1). Unfortunately, in this particular dataset, the column names might contain commas. The CSV reader deals with this correctly since the strings that contain commas are quoted, but genfromtxt is not a CSV reader in general. To fix this, either the headers have to be fixed, or some other names need to be added. Secondly, the Country column has been reduced to NaN, and the Year column has been turned into a floating point integer, which is not ideal.

12. A manual fix on the dataset is necessary, and this is not uncommon. Since we know that there are 354 columns and the first two columns are Country and Year, we can precompute our column names and datatypes:

```
In [20]: names = ["country", "year"]

   ...: names.extend(["col%i" % (idx+1) for idx in range(352)])
   ...: dtype = "S64,i4," + ",".join(["f18" for idx in
range(352)])
   ...:
In [21]: dataset = np.genfromcsv(data_file, dtype=np.dtype,
names=names,
   ...: delimiter=",", skip_header=1, autostrip=2)
   ...:
```

We name the first two columns country and year, respectively, and assign them datatypes of S64 or string-64, and then assign the year column as i4 or integer-4. For the rest of the columns, we assign them the name coln, where n is an integer from 1 to 352, and the datatype is f18 or float-18. These character lengths allow us to capture as much data as possible, including exponential floating point representations.

Unfortunately, as we look through the data, we can see a lot of nan values that represent **Not a Number**, a fixture in floating point arithmetic used to represent values that are not numbers nor are equivalent to infinity. Missing data is a very common issue in the data wrangling and cleaning stage of the pipeline. It appears that the dataset contains many missing or invalid entries, which makes sense given the historical data, and countries that may not have had effective data collection for given columns.

13. In order to clean the data, we use a NumPy masked array, which is actually a combination of a standard NumPy array and a mask, a set of Boolean values that indicate whether the data in that position should be used in computations or not. This can be done as follows:

```
import numpy.ma as ma
ma.masked_invalid(dataset['col1'])
masked_array(data = [-- -- -- ...,  45.2599983215332
  45.5099983215332 45.599998474121094],
  mask = [ True   True   True ..., False False False],fill_value =
  1e+20)
```

How it works...

Our dataset function has been modified to filter on a single field and value if desired. If no filter has been specified, it generates the entire CSV. The main piece of interest is what happens in the main function. Here, we generate a bar chart of average incomes in the United States per year using matplotlib. Let's walk through the code.

We collect our data as (`year`, `avg_income`) tuples in a list comprehension that utilizes our special dataset method to filter data only for the United States.

We have to cast the average income per tax unit to a float in order to compute on it. In this case, we leave the year as a string since it simply acts as a label; however, in order to perform `datetime` computations, we might want to convert that year to a date using `datetime.strptime (row['Year'], '%Y').date()`.

After we have performed our data collection, filtering, and conversions, we set up the chart. The width is the maximum width of a bar. An `ind` iterable (`ndarray`) refers to the *x* axis locations for each bar; in this case, we want one location for every data point in our set. A NumPy `np.arange` function is similar to the built-in `xrange` functions; it returns an iterable (`ndarray`) of evenly spaced values in the given interval. In this case, we provide a stop value that is the length of the list and use the default start value of 0 and step size of 1, but these can also be specified. The use of `arange` allows floating point arguments, and it is typically much faster than simply instantiating the full array of values.

The `figure` and `subplot` module functions utilize the `matplotlab.pyplot` module to create the base figure and axes, respectively. The `figure` function creates a new figure, or returns a reference to a previously created figure. The `subplot` function returns a subplot axis positioned by the grid definition with the following arguments: the number of rows, number of columns, and plot number. This function has a convenience when all three arguments are less than 10. Simply supplying a three-digit number with the respective values, for example, `plot.subplot (111)`, creates *1 x 1* axes in subplot 1.

We then use the subplot to create a bar chart from our data. Note the use of another comprehension that passes the values of the incomes from our dataset along with the indices we created with `np.arange`. On setting the *x* axis labels, however, we notice that if we add all years as individual labels, the *x* axis is unreadable. Instead, we add ticks for every 4 years, starting with the first year. In this case, you can see that we use a step size of 4 in `np.arange` to set our ticks, and similarly, in our labels, we use slices on the Python list to step through every four labels. For example, for a given list, we will use:

```
mylist[s:e:t]
```

The slice of the list starts at `s`, ends at `e`, and has the step size `t`. Negative numbers are also supported in slices to be iterated from the end of the list; for example, `mylist[-1]` will return the last item of the list.

There's more...

NumPy is an incredibly useful and powerful library, but we should note some very important differences. The list datatype in Python is wildly different from the `numpy` array. The Python list can contain any number of different datatypes, including lists. Thus, the following example list is perfectly valid:

```
python_list = ['bob' , 5.1, True, 1, [5, 3, 'sam'] ]
```

Underneath the hood, the Python list contains pointers to the memory locations of the elements of the list. To access the first element of the list, Python goes to the memory location for the list and grabs the first value stored there. This value is a memory address for the first element. Python then jumps to this new memory location to grab the value for the actual first element. Thus, grabbing the first element of the list requires two memory lookups.

NumPy arrays are very much like C. They must contain a single datatype, and this allows the array to be stored in a contiguous block of memory, which makes reading the array significantly faster. When reading the first element of the array, Python goes to the appropriate memory address that contains the actual value to be retrieved. When the next element in the array is needed, it is right next to the location of the first element in memory, which makes reading much faster.

See also

- The NumPy documentation at `http://docs.scipy.org/doc/numpy/reference/`
- A strong tutorial on NumPy and SciPy at `http://www.engr.ucsb.edu/~shell/che210d/numpy.pdf`

Analyzing and visualizing the top income data of the US

Now that we've imported and explored the top incomes dataset a bit, let's drill down on a specific country and conduct some analyses on their income distribution data. In particular, the United States has excellent data relating to the top incomes by percentile, so we'll use the data of the United States in the following exercises. If you choose other countries to leverage their datasets, beware that you may need to use different fields to get the same analyses.

Getting ready

In order to conduct our analyses, we're going to create a few helper methods that we will use continually throughout this chapter. Application-oriented analyses typically produce reusable code that performs singular tasks in order to adapt quickly to changing data or analysis requirements. In particular, let's create two helper functions: one that extracts data by a particular country and one that creates a time series from a set of particular rows:

```
In [22]: def dataset(path, country="United States"):
    ...:     """
    ...:     Extract the data for the country provided. Default is United
States.
    ...:     """
    ...:     with open(path, 'r') as csvfile:
    ...:         reader = csv.DictReader(csvfile)
```

```
...: for row in filter(lambda row: row["Country"]==country, reader):
...: yield row
...:

In [23]: def timeseries(data, column):
...: """
...: Creates a year based time series for the given column.
...: """
...: for row in filter(lambda row: row[column], data):
...: yield (int(row["Year"]), row[column])
...:
```

The first function iterates through the dataset using the `csv.DictReader` filter on a particular country using Python's built-in filter function. The second function leverages the fact that there is a `Year` column to create a time series for the data, a generator that yields (year, value) tuples for a particular column in the dataset. Note that this function should be passed in a generator created by the dataset function. We can now utilize these two functions for a series of analyses across any column for a single country.

How to do it...

Generally speaking, the data for the United States is broken up into six groups:

- Top 10 percent income share
- Top 5 percent income share
- Top 1 percent income share
- Top 0.5 percent income share
- Top 0.1 percent income share
- Average income share

These groups reflect aggregations for data points collected in those specific bins. An easy and quick first analysis is to simply plot these percentages of income shares over time for each of the top income groups. Since plotting several time series is going to be a common task, let's once again create a `helper` function that wraps matplotlib and generates a line chart for each time series that is passed to it:

```
In [24]: def linechart(series, **kwargs):
...: fig = plt.figure()
...: ax = plt.subplot(111)
...: for line in series:
...: line = list(line)
...: xvals = [v[0] for v in line]
...: yvals = [v[1] for v in line]
```

```
...: ax.plot(xvals, yvals)
...: if 'ylabel' in kwargs:
...: ax.set_ylabel(kwargs['ylabel'])
...: if 'title' in kwargs:
...: plt.title(kwargs['title'])
...: if 'labels' in kwargs:
...: ax.legend(kwargs.get('labels'))
...: return fig
...:
```

This function is very simple. It creates a `matplotlib.pyplot` figure as well as the axis subplot. For each line in the series, it gets the *x* axis values (remember that the first item in our time series time tuple is `Year`) as the first item of the tuple and the *y* axis, which is the second value. It splits these into separate generators and then plots them on the figure. Finally, any options we want for our chart, such as labels or legends, we can simply pass as keyword arguments, and our function will handle them for us! The following steps will walk you through this recipe of application-oriented analysis.

In order to generate our chart, we simply need to use our time series function on the columns we would like and pass them to the `linechart` function. This simple task is now repeatable, and we'll use it a few times for the next few charts:

```
In [25]: def percent_income_share(source):
    ...: """
    ...: Create Income Share chart
    ...: """
    ...: columns = (
    ...: "Top 10% income share",
    ...: "Top 5% income share",
    ...: "Top 1% income share",
    ...: "Top 0.5% income share",
    ...: "Top 0.1% income share",
    ...: )
    ...: source = list(dataset(source))
    ...: return linechart([timeseries(source, col) for col in columns],
    ...: labels=columns,
    ...: ,
    ...: ylabel="Percentage")
    ...:
    ...:
```

Note that I wrapped the generation of this chart in a function as well; this way, we modify the chart as needed, and the function wraps the configuration and generation of the chart itself. The function identifies the columns for the line series and then fetches the dataset. For each column, it creates a time series and then passes these time series to our `linechart` function with our configuration options:

1. To generate the plot, we define the input parameter to the `percent_income_source function`:

   ```
   In [26]: percent_income_share(data_file)

        ...:
   Out[26]:
   ```

   The following screenshot shows the result, and you will use a similar pattern in the rest of this chapter to use the functions to create the needed plots:

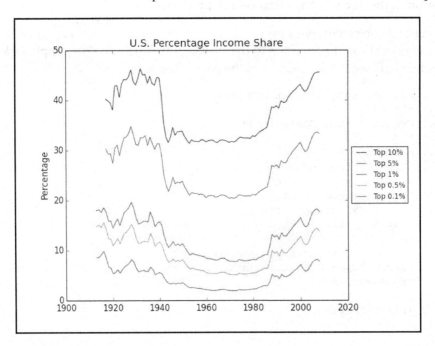

This graph tells us that the raw percentages for the income groups tend to move in the same direction. When one group's income increases, the other groups' incomes also increase. This seems like a good sanity check as folks who are in the top 0.1 percent income bracket are also in the top 10 percent income bracket, and they contribute a lot to the overall mean for each bin. There is also a clear, persistent difference between each of the lines.

2. Looking at the raw percentages is useful, but we may also want to consider how the percentages have changed over time, relative to what the average percentage has been for that income group. In order to do this, we can calculate the means of each group's percentages and then divide all of the group's values by the mean we just calculated.

   Since mean normalization is another common function that we might want to perform on a range of datasets, we will once again create a function that will accept a time series as input and return a new time series whose values are divided by the mean:

```
In [27]: def normalize(data):

    ...: """

    ...: Normalizes the data set. Expects a timeseries input
    ...: """
    ...: data = list(data)
    ...: norm = np.array(list(d[1] for d in data), dtype="f8")
    ...: mean = norm.mean()
    ...: norm /= mean
    ...: return zip((d[0] for d in data), norm)
    ...:
```

3. We can now easily write another function that takes these columns and computes the mean normalized time series:

```
In [28]: def mean_normalized_percent_income_share(source):
    ...: columns = (
    ...: "Top 10% income share",
    ...: "Top 5% income share",
    ...: "Top 1% income share",
    ...: "Top 0.5% income share",
    ...: "Top 0.1% income share",
    ...: )
    ...: source = list(dataset(source))
    ...: return linechart([normalize(timeseries(source, col)) for
col in columns],
    ...: labels=columns,
```

```
...: ,
...: ylabel="Percentage")
...: mean_normalized_percent_income_share(data_file)
...: plt.show()
...:
```

Note how the following command snippet is very similar to the previous function, except when it performs the normalization:

```
>>> fig = mean_normalized_percent_income_share(DATA)
>>> fig.show()
```

The preceding commands give us the following graph:

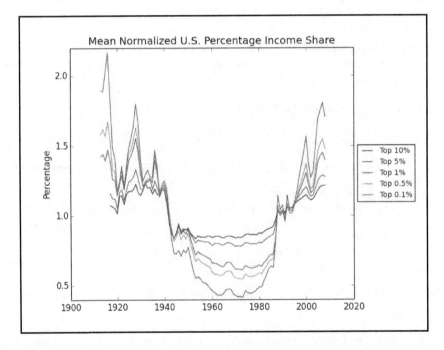

This graph shows us that the wealthier the group, the larger the percentage-wise swings we tend to see in their incomes.

4. The dataset also breaks the group's income into categories, such as income that includes capital gains versus income without capital gains. Let's take a look at how each group's capital gains income fluctuates over time.

Another common functionality is to compute the difference between two columns and plot the resulting time series. Computing the difference between two NumPy arrays is also very easy, and since it is common for our task, we write yet another function to do the job:

```
In [29]: def delta(first, second):
    ...:     """
    ...:     Returns an array of deltas for the two arrays.
    ...:     """
    ...:     first = list(first)
    ...:     years = yrange(first)
    ...:     first = np.array(list(d[1] for d in first), dtype="f8")
    ...:     second = np.array(list(d[1] for d in second), dtype="f8")
    ...:     if first.size != second.size:
    ...:         first = np.insert(first, [0,0,0,0], [None, None,
None,None])
    ...:     diff = first - second
    ...:     return zip(years, diff)
    ...:
```

Furthermore, the following is an appropriate helper function:

```
In [30]: def yrange(data):
    ...:     """
    ...:     Get the range of years from the dataset
    ...:     """
    ...:     years = set()
    ...:     for row in data:
    ...:         if row[0] not in years:
    ...:             yield row[0]
    ...:         years.add(row[0])
```

This function once again creates NumPy arrays from each dataset, casting the datatype to floats. Note that we need to get the list of years from one of the datasets, so we gather it from the first dataset.

5. We also need to keep in mind that `first.size` needs to be the same as `second.size`, for example, that each array shares the same dimensionality. The difference is computed and the years are once again zipped to the data to form a time series:

```
In [31]: def capital_gains_lift(source):
    ...: """
    ...: Computes capital gains lift in top income percentages over
time chart
    ...: """
    ...: columns = (
    ...: ("Top 10% income share-including capital gains",
    ...: "Top 10% income share"),
    ...: ("Top 5% income share-including capital gains",
    ...: "Top 5% income share"),
    ...: ("Top 1% income share-including capital gains",
    ...: "Top 1% income share"),
    ...: ("Top 0.5% income share-including capital gains",
    ...: "Top 0.5% income share"),
    ...: ("Top 0.1% income share-including capital gains",
    ...: "Top 0.1% income share"),
    ...: ("Top 0.05% income share-including capital gains",
    ...: "Top 0.05% income share"),
    ...: )
    ...: source = list(dataset(source))
    ...: series = [delta(timeseries(source, a),
timeseries(source,b))
    ...: for a, b in columns]
    ...: return linechart(series,labels=list(col[1] for col in
    ...: columns),
    ...: ,
    ...: ylabel="Percentage Difference")
    ...: capital_gains_lift(data_file)
    ...: plt.show()
    ...:
```

The preceding code stores the columns as tuples of two columns-first and second-and then uses the delta function to compute the difference between the two. Like our previous graphs, it then creates a line chart as shown here:

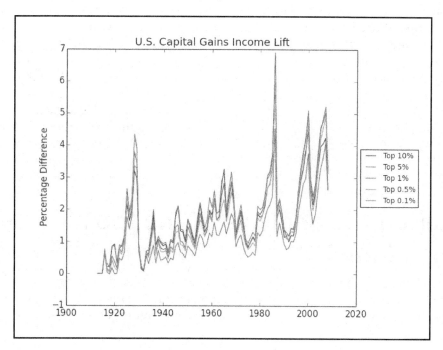

This is interesting as the graph shows the volatility of the capital gains income over time. If you are familiar with U.S. financial history, you can see the effect on the capital gains income of the well-known stock market booms and busts in this chart.

How it works...

The easiest way to perform operations on big datasets is to use NumPy's `array` class. As we've already seen, this class allows us to perform common operations, including basic mathematical operations between a scalar and an array. Converting the generator to an array, however, requires us to load the data into memory. Python's built-in `list` function takes an iterator and returns a list. This is required because the NumPy array must know the length of the data in order to allocate the correct amount of memory. With the array, it is easy enough to calculate the mean and then perform the divide equals scalar operation across the entire array. This broadcasts the division operation so that each element in the array is divided by the mean. We are, in essence, normalizing the elements of the array by their mean. We can then zip together our years with the newly computed data and return the time series.

Furthering the analysis of the top income groups of the US

So far in this chapter, we have focused on the analysis of income percentages over time. Next, we will continue our analysis by taking a look at some of the other interesting figures that we have in our dataset, specifically the actual income figures and income categories that comprise these figures.

Getting ready

If you've completed the previous recipe, *Analyzing and visualizing the top income data of the US*, you should have everything you need to continue.

How to do it...

With the following steps, we will dive deeper into the dataset and examine additional income figures:

1. The dataset also contains the average incomes by year of the different groups. Let's graph these and see how they have changed over time, relative to each other:

```
In [32]: def average_incomes(source):
    ...:     """
```

```
...: Compares percentage average incomes
...: """
...: columns = (
...: "Top 10% average income",
...: "Top 5% average income",
...: "Top 1% average income",
...: "Top 0.5% average income",
...: "Top 0.1% average income",
...: "Top 0.05% average income",
...: )
...: source = list(dataset(source))
...: return linechart([timeseries(source, col) for col in
...: columns], labels=columns, ,
...: ylabel="2008 US Dollars")
...: average_incomes(data_file)
...: plt.show()
```

Since we have the foundation in place to create line charts, we can immediately analyze this new dataset with the tools we already have. We simply choose a different collection of columns and then customize our chart accordingly! The following is the resulting graph:

The results shown by this graph are quite fascinating. Until the 1980s, the wealthy have been about $1-1.5 million richer than the lower income groups. From the 1980s forward, the disparity has increased dramatically.

2. We can also use the `delta` functionality to see how much richer the rich are than the average American:

```
In [33]: def average_top_income_lift(source):
   ...:     """
   ...:     Compares top percentage avg income over total avg
   ...:     """
   ...:     columns = (
   ...:     ("Top 10% average income", "Top 0.1% average income"),
   ...:     ("Top 5% average income", "Top 0.1% average income"),
   ...:     ("Top 1% average income", "Top 0.1% average income"),
   ...:     ("Top 0.5% average income", "Top 0.1% average income"),
   ...:     ("Top 0.1% average income", "Top 0.1% average income"),
   ...:     )
   ...:     source = list(dataset(source))
   ...:     series = [delta(timeseries(source, a), timeseries(source,
   ...:     b)) for a, b in columns]
   ...:     return linechart(series, labels=list(col[0] for col in
columns),
   ...:     ,ylabel="2008 US Dollars")
   ...:
```

We still haven't written new code other than the selection of our columns and utilization of the functionality that we have already added to our project. This reveals the following:

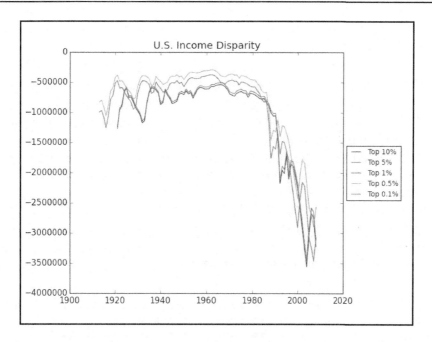

3. In our last analysis, we'll show off a different kind of chart to look at the composition of the income of the wealthiest americans. Since the composition is a percentage-based time series, a good chart for this task is a stacked area. Once again, we can utilize our time series code and simply add a function to create stacked area charts as follows:

```
In [34]: def stackedarea(series, **kwargs):
    ...: fig = plt.figure()
    ...: axe = fig.add_subplot(111)
    ...: fnx = lambda s: np.array(list(v[1] for v in s),
dtype="f8")
    ...: yax = np.row_stack(fnx(s) for s in series)
    ...: xax = np.arange(1917, 2008)
    ...: polys = axe.stackplot(xax, yax)
    ...: axe.margins(0,0)
    ...: if 'ylabel' in kwargs:
    ...: axe.set_ylabel(kwargs['ylabel'])
    ...: if 'labels' in kwargs:
    ...: legendProxies = []
    ...: for poly in polys:
    ...: legendProxies.append(plt.Rectangle((0, 0), 1, 1,
    ...: fc=poly.get_facecolor()[0]))
    ...: axe.legend(legendProxies, kwargs.get('labels'))
    ...: if 'title' in kwargs:
    ...: plt.title(kwargs['title'])
```

```
...: return fig
...:
```

The preceding function expects a group of time series, the total percentages of which add up to 100. We create a special, anonymous function that will convert each series into a NumPy array. The NumPy `row_stack` function creates a sequence of arrays stacked vertically; this is what will generate our stackplot using the `subplot.stackplot` function. The only other surprise in this function is the requirement to use a legend proxy to create rectangles with the fill color from the stackplot in the legend.

4. Now, we can take a look at the income composition of the wealthiest Americans:

```
In [35]: def income_composition(source):
    ...:     """
    ...:     Compares income composition
    ...:     """
    ...:     columns = (
    ...:     "Top 10% income composition-Wages, salaries andpensions",
    ...:     "Top 10% income composition-Dividends",
    ...:     "Top 10% income composition-Interest Income",
    ...:     "Top 10% income composition-Rents",
    ...:     "Top 10% income composition-Entrepreneurial income",
    ...:     )
    ...:     source = list(dataset(source))
    ...:     labels = ("Salary", "Dividends", "Interest",
"Rent","Business")
    ...:     return stackedarea([timeseries(source, col) for col in
columns],
    ...:     labels=labels, ,
    ...:     ylabel="Percentage")
    ...:
```

The preceding code generates the following plot:

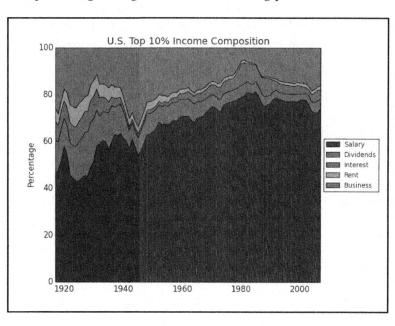

As you can see, the top 10 percent of American earners make most of their money from a salary income; however, business income also plays a large role. Dividends played a bigger role earlier in the century than they do towards the end of the century, which is true for interest and rent as well. Interestingly, for the first part of the 20th century, the percentage of income that is related to entrepreneurial income declines, until the 1980s, when it starts to grow again, possibly because of the technology sector.

How it works...

This recipe really helps to demonstrate the value of the application-oriented approach. We continue to abstract out portions of code that perform singular tasks and use them as functions. As our library of functions increases, our analysis, often filled with repeated but slightly different tasks, becomes more composition than creation. Even better, these individual pieces are much easier to test and evaluate. Over time, with additional analyses, we will build a rich and fully customized library of tools that will drastically speed up future investigations.

This recipe also reveals how Python code can be created to construct more R-like analyses. As we performed further evaluations, we leveraged functions and tools that we had already built for our dataset and created new ones, such as the stacked area function that built off our older tools. However, unlike an analysis-oriented approach, these tools now exist in a data-specific library of code that can be used to build applications and reports, as we'll see in the next recipe.

Reporting with Jinja2

Visualizations and graphs are excellent for identifying obvious patterns in the dataset. However, as trends emerge from multiple sources, more in-depth reporting is required, as well as descriptions of the techniques used for those not directly involved in the project. Instead of creating these reports by hand, application-oriented analyses make use of template languages to dynamically construct documents at the time of analysis. Jinja2 is a Python library that is used to generate documents by combining a template-usually an HTML file, but it can be any kind of text file-with a context, a data source that is used to fill in the template. This combination is ideal to report on the analyses that we're performing.

Getting ready

The Jinja2 template library should be installed and ready to use.

How to do it...

The following steps will walk us through using the **Jinja2** templating library to create flexible and appealing reporting output:

1. Jinja2 is simple and has familiar Python-esque syntax (though it is not Python). Templates can include logic or control flow, including iteration, conditionals, and formatting, which removes the need to have the data adapt to the template. A simple example is as follows:

```
In [36]: from jinja2 import Template
    ...: template = Template(u'Greetings, {{ name }}!')
    ...: template.render(name='Mr. Praline')
Out[36]: 'Greetings, Mr. Praline!'
```

2. However, we should decouple our templates from our Python code, and instead, store the templates as text files on our system. Jinja2 provides a central `Environment` object, which is used to store configurations and global objects to load templates either from the filesystem or other Python packages:

```
In [37]: from jinja2 import Environment, PackageLoader,
FileSystemLoader
     ...: # 'templates' should be the path to the templates folder
     ...: # as written, it is assumed to be in the current directory
     ...: jinjaenv = Environment(loader =
FileSystemLoader('templates'))
     ...: template = jinjaenv.get_template('report.html')
```

Here, the Jinja2 environment is configured to look for template files in the templates directory of our Python module. Another recommended loader is `FileSystemLoader`, which should be provided as a search path to look for template files. In this case, the template called `report.html` is fetched from the Python module and is ready to be rendered.

Rendering can be as simple as `template.render(context)`, which will return a unicode string of generated output. The context should be a Python dictionary whose keys are the variable names that will be used in the template. Alternatively, the context can be passed in as keyword arguments; `template.render({'name':'Terry'})` is equivalent to `template.render(name='Terry')`. However, for large templates (and large datasets) it is far more efficient to use the `template.stream` method; it does not render the entire template at once, but evaluates each statement sequentially and yields it as a generator.

3. The stream can then be passed to a file-like object to be written to disk or serialized over the network:

```
template.stream(items=['a', 'b',
'c'],name='Eric').dump('report-2013.html')
```

This seemingly simple technique is incredibly powerful, especially when combined with the JSON module. JSON data can be dumped directly into JavaScript snippets for interactive charting and visualization libraries on the web, such as **D3**, **Highcharts**, and **Google Charts**.

4. Let's take a look at a complete example using the world's top incomes dataset:

```
In [38]: import csv

    ...: import json
    ...: from datetime import datetime
    ...: from jinja2 import Environment, PackageLoader,
FileSystemLoader
    ...: from itertools import groupby
    ...: from operator import itemgetter
    ...:

In [39]: def dataset(path, include):
    ...: column = 'Average income per tax unit'
    ...: with open(path, 'r') as csvfile:
    ...: reader = csv.DictReader(csvfile)
    ...: key = itemgetter('Country')
    ...: # Use groupby: memory efficient collection by country
    ...: for key, values in groupby(reader, key=key):
    ...: # Only yield countries that are included
    ...: if key in include:
    ...: yield key, [(int(value['Year']),
    ...: float(value[column]))
    ...: for value in values if value[column]]
    ...:
    ...:

In [40]: def extract_years(data):
    ...: for country in data:
    ...: for value in country[1]:
    ...: yield value[0]
    ...:
    ...: datetime.now().strftime("%Y%m%d")
    ...: jinjaenv = Environment(loader =
FileSystemLoader('templates'))
    ...: template = jinjaenv.get_template('report.html')
    ...: template.stream(context).dump(path)
    ...:

In [41]: def write(context):
    ...: path = "report-%s.html" %datetime.now().strftime("%Y%m%d")
    ...: jinjaenv = Environment(loader =
FileSystemLoader('templates'))
    ...:     template = jinjaenv.get_template('report.html')
    template.stream(context).dump(path)
In [40]: def main(source):
    ...: # Select countries to include
    ...: include = ("United States", "France", "Italy",
```

```
      ...: "Germany", "South Africa", "New Zealand")
      ...: # Get dataset from CSV
      ...: data = list(dataset(source, include))
      ...: years = set(extract_years(data))
      ...: # Generate context
      ...: context = {
      ...: 'title': "Average Income per Family, %i - %i"
      ...: % (min(years), max(years)),
      ...: 'years': json.dumps(list(years)),
      ...: 'countries': [v[0] for v in data],
      ...: 'series': json.dumps(list(extract_series(data, years))),
      ...: }
      ...:
      ...:

In [42]: write(context)
      ...: if __name__ == '__main__':
      ...: source = '../data/income_dist.csv'
      ...: main(source)
```

This is a lot of code, so let's go through it step by step. The dataset function reads our CSV file for the Average income column and filters based on a set of included countries. It uses a functional iteration `helper`, `groupby`, which collects the rows of our CSV file by the country field, which means that we get a dataset per country. Both the `itemgetter` and `groupby` functions are common, memory-safe helper functions in Python that do a lot of heavy lifting during large-scale data analyses.

After we extract the dataset, we have two helper methods. The first, `extract_years`, generates all the year values from every country. This is necessary because not all countries have values for every year in the dataset. We'll also use this function to determine the range of years for our template. This brings us to the second function, `extract_series`, which normalizes the data, replacing empty years with None values to ensure our time series is correct.

The `write()` method wraps the template-writing functionality. It creates a file called `report-{date}.html`, adding the current date for reference. It also loads the Environment object, finds the report template, and writes the output to disk. Finally, the main method gathers all the data and context together and connects the functions.

5. The report template is as follows:

```html
<html>
<head>
    <title>{{ title }}</title>
</head>
<body>
    <div class="container">
        <h1>{{ title }}</h1>
        <div id="countries">
            <ul>
            {% for country in countries %}
                <li>{{ country }}<li>
            {% endfor %}
            </ul>
        </div>
        <div id="chart"></div>
    </div>

    <script type="text/javascript"
src="http://codeorigin.jquery.com/jquery-
2.0.3.min.js"></script>
    <script src="http://code.highcharts.com/highcharts.js">
    </script>
    <script type="text/javascript">
        $.noConflict();
        jQuery(document).ready(function($) {
            $('#chart').highcharts({
                xAxis: {
                    categories: JSON.parse('{{ years }}'),
                    tickInterval: 5,
                },
                yAxis: {
                    title: {
                        text: "2008 USD"
                    }
                },
                plotOptions: {
                    line: {
                        marker: {
                            enabled: false
                        }
                    }
                },
                series: JSON.parse('{{ series }}')
            });
        });
    </script>
```

```
        </body>
        </html>
```

The preceding template fills in the title in the correct spot, and then creates an unordered list of the countries included in our dataset. Additionally, it uses Highcharts to create an interactive chart. Highcharts is an option-based, JavaScript chart library. Note that we're using `JSON.parse` to parse the JSON data that we dumped in Python. This will ensure that there are no conflicts when converting Python datatypes to JavaScript ones. When you open up the report in a browser, it should look something like the following screenshot:

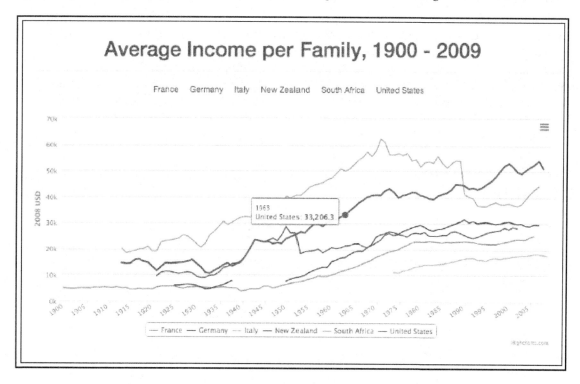

How it works...

Performing analytics and data mining in Python parallels R closely, especially when using the NumPy library. NumPy, like R, is designed for scientific computing and has a similar set of functionality when dealing with multidimensional arrays. However, as a general rule, Python takes more lines of code, especially when creating charts with matplotlib. This is caused by Python's generic approach to data, particularly because it is used in many problem domains, not specifically statistical analyses, and this is also Python's strength.

In particular, data analyses with Python tend to have an application-oriented approach, typically involving live or streaming data that is routinely updated, rather than analyses on a single dataset. This usually means that analyses performed in Python leverage fast prototyping and statistical exploration with tools such as NumPy, but then leverage an extremely inclusive standard library to handle the data in all phases of the data pipeline.

There's more...

There are several different Python template languages, each with a different approach to combining a predefined template with data to form human-readable output. Many of these template languages are intended as the backbone of web application frameworks, such as Django and Flask that are used to construct dynamic web pages from a database. Since these languages are well suited to generate HTML, reporting with these tools creates an easy transition, from one-off reporting to scheduled reporting, to on-demand reporting from a web application. Jinja2 is the primary template language for Flask and has a Django-like syntax, making it an excellent choice for future implementations.

See also

- For the data source, go to
  `http://topincomes.g-mond.parisschoolofeconomics.eu/`
- The *Templating in Python* article at `https://wiki.python.org/moin/Templating`
- The *What is Data Science?* article at
  `http://radar.oreilly.com/2010/06/what-is-data-science.html`
- The Setting up Python and Matplotlib in OSX Mountain Lion article at `http://ww w.tapir.caltech.edu/~dtsang/python.html`

Repeating the analysis in R

This brief survey session is intended to replicate most of the data analysis discussed in the preceding section using the R software. The section is self-contained in the sense that there is no dependency on any R package.

Getting ready

The functions available in the R default version suffice to perform the analysis done earlier in the chapter. The income_dist.csv file needs to be present in the current working directory.

How to do it...

A step-by-step approach to perform the analysis related to the income_dist.csv file can be easily carried out as shown in the next program.

1. Load the dataset income_dist.csv using the read.csv function and use the functions nrow, str, length, unique, and so on to get the following results:

```
id <- read.csv("income_dist.csv",header=TRUE)
nrow(id)
str(names(id))
length(names(id))
ncol(id) # equivalent of previous line
unique(id$Country)
levels(id$Country) # alternatively
min(id$Year)
max(id$Year)
id_us <- id[id$Country=="United States",]
```

The data is first stored in the R object ID. We see that there are 2180 observations/rows in the dataset. The dataset has 354 variables and a few are seen with the use of two functions, str and names. The number of variables is also verified using the ncol and length functions. The data related to United States is selected through the code id[id$Country=="United States",]. Now, we first use the plot function to get a first view of the average income tax, which is a poor plot.

2. Using the plot function, we obtain a simple display as follows:

```
plot(id_us$Year , id_us$Average.income.per.tax.unit) 0
```

The output is not given here as we intend to improvise it. Instead of a plot, we now use the barplot function.

3. An elegant display is obtained using the `barplot` function along with a suitable choice of labels:

```
barplot(id_us$Average.income.per.tax.unit,ylim=c(0,60000),

        ylab="Income in USD",col="blue",main="U.S. Average Income
1913-2008",
        names.arg=id_us$Year)
```

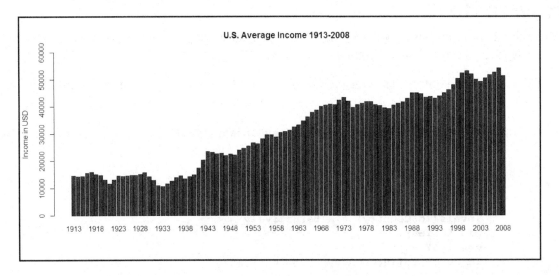

It is always a good practice to use options of a graphical function. For instance, we specified the range of the y-variable through `ylim`, the y-axis label through `ylab`, and a caption for the graph through main.

For further analyses, we continue to focus on the United States region only:

1. The analysis for the top income data of the US, as in the earlier recipe, *Analyzing and visualizing the top income data of the US,* is reproduced in R in the following program. After subsetting on the US region, we select the specific variables of 10%, 5%, 1%, 0.5%, and 0.1% using the subsetting as in [. The new R object is `id2_us2`:

```
id2 <- read.csv("income_dist.csv",header=TRUE,check.names = F)
# using the check.names=F option to ensure special characters in
colnames
id2_us <- id2[id$Country=="United States",]
id2_us2 <- id2_us[,c("Top 10% income share",
                "Top 5% income share",
                "Top 1% income share",
```

```
            "Top 0.5% income share",
            "Top 0.1% income share")]
row.names(id2_us2) <- id2_us$Year
```

2. The R object `id2_us2` is converted into a time series object with the `ts` function. Now, for this specific choice of the data, we visualize it year-on-year with the next chunk of R code:

```
id2_us2 <- ts(id2_us2,start=1913,frequency = 1)
windows(height=20,width=10)
plot.ts(id2_us2,plot.type="single",ylab="Percentage",frame.plot=TRU
E,
        col=c("blue","green","red","blueviolet","purple"))
legend(x=c(1960,1980),y=c(45,30),c("Top 10%","Top 5%","Top 1%","Top
0.5%","Top 0.1%"),
        col = c("blue","green","red","blueviolet","purple"),pch="-")
```

Note that the object `id2_us2` has five time series objects. We plot all of them in a single frame using the option `plot.type="single"`. Legends and colors are used to enhance the aesthetics of the graphical display. The resulting graphical output is given as follows:

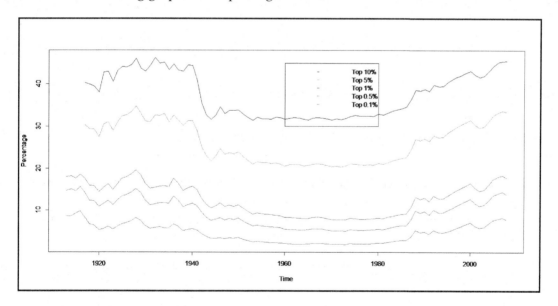

3. The preceding exercise is repeated with scaled data:

```
id2_scale <- scale(id2_us2)
windows(height=20,width=10)
plot.ts(id2_scale,plot.type="single",ylab="Percentage",frame.plot=T
RUE,
        col=c("blue","green","red","blueviolet","purple"))
legend(x=c(1960,1980),y=c(2,1),c("Top 10%","Top 5%","Top 1%","Top
0.5%","Top 0.1%"), col =
c("blue","green","red","blueviolet","purple"),pch="-")
```

The output is as follows:

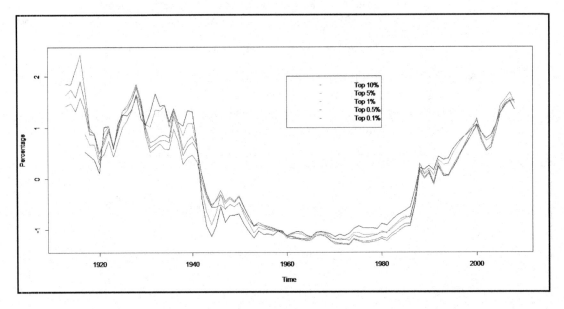

4. Note that this display makes the comparison between the five time series easier.
5. To replicate the Python analyses in the *Furthering the analysis of the top income groups of the US,* recipe in R, we give the R code and output in the final chunk of the code:

```
id2_us3 <- id2_us[,c("Top 10% income share-including capital
gains",
                     "Top 10% income share",
                     "Top 5% income share-including capital gains",
                     "Top 5% income share",
                     "Top 1% income share-including capital gains",
                     "Top 1% income share",
                     "Top 0.5% income share-including capital
```

```
gains",
                        "Top 0.5% income share",
                        "Top 0.1% income share-including capital
gains",
                        "Top 0.1% income share",
                        "Top 0.05% income share-including capital
gains",
                        "Top 0.05% income share")
                ]
id2_us3[,"Top 10% capital gains"] <- id2_us3[,1]-id2_us3[,2]
id2_us3[,"Top 5% capital gains"] <- id2_us3[,3]-id2_us3[,4]
id2_us3[,"Top 1% capital gains"] <- id2_us3[,5]-id2_us3[,6]
id2_us3[,"Top 0.5% capital gains"] <- id2_us3[,7]-id2_us3[,8]
id2_us3[,"Top 0.1% capital gains"] <- id2_us3[,9]-id2_us3[,10]
id2_us3[,"Top 0.05% capital gains"] <- id2_us3[,11]-id2_us3[,12]
id2_us3 <- ts(id2_us3,start=1913,frequency = 1)
windows(height=20,width=10)
plot.ts(id2_us3[,13:18],plot.type="single",ylab="Percentage",frame.
plot=TRUE,
        col=c("blue","green","red","blueviolet","purple","yellow"))
legend(x=c(1960,1980),y=c(7,5),c("Top 10%","Top 5%","Top 1%","Top
0.5%",
                                "Top 0.1%","Top 0.05%"),
        col =
c("blue","green","red","blueviolet","purple","yellow"),pch="-")
```

The graphical output is given as follows:

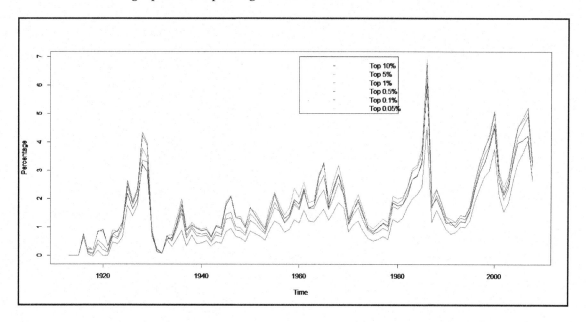

There's more...

R and Python are two of the most competing, compelling, and complete software. In most cases, it is possible to replicate the Python analysis in R, and vice versa. It goes without saying that it would not be possible to get exact answers of one software in another. However, that is not the purpose of this recipe.

4
Modeling Stock Market Data

In this chapter, we will cover:

- Acquiring stock market data
- Summarizing the data
- Cleaning and exploring the data
- Generating relative valuations
- Screening stocks and analyzing historical prices

Introduction

This chapter will walk you through a financial analysis project where you will analyze stock market data, determine whether stocks are over or under-valued, use this information to identify a list of target stocks that may make good investments, and visually analyze the price histories of the target stocks.

We must caution that the goal of this chapter is not to make you an expert in stock market analysis or to make you rich. Quants on Wall Street study engineering models that perform significantly more sophisticated operations than those we will touch upon here. Entire books have been written on stock market models and financial engineering, but we only have a single chapter to dedicate to this topic. So given the time and format constraints, the goals of this chapter will be:

- To get a basic understanding of the data that we will work with
- To find useful and interesting ways to analyze and model this data
- To learn how to leverage data science tools and techniques to perform the types of analytical tasks that we need to perform on the data

The data we will use for this chapter consists of current data for stocks tracked by the website `finviz.com` and daily histories of stock prices obtained from **Yahoo! Finance**.

As in previous chapters, the tool we will rely on for this project will be the R statistical programming language. As you've probably noticed by now, R has strong packages available that can assist us in the needed analytical tasks; we will be leveraging some of these packages in this chapter. Additionally, the recipes in this chapter will roughly follow the data science pipeline, which we will adapt to the type of data we are working with and the types of analysis we would like to conduct on the data.

Requirements

For this chapter, you will need a computer with access to the internet. You will also need to have R installed and the following packages installed and then loaded:

```
install.packages("XML")
install.packages("ggplot2")
install.packages("plyr")
install.packages("reshape2")
install.packages("zoo")

library(XML)
library(ggplot2 ,quietly=TRUE)
library(plyr ,quietly=TRUE)
library(reshape2 ,quietly=TRUE)
library(zoo ,quietly=TRUE)
```

The XML package will assist us with acquiring data from the internet, `ggplot2` will let us create beautiful graphs and visualizations from our data, `plyr` and `reshape2` will help us with summarizing our data, and the `zoo` package will allow us to calculate moving averages.

You will also want to set a working directory where some of the charts that we generate will be saved:

```
setwd("path/where/you/want/to save/charts")
```

Acquiring stock market data

If you look on the internet for stock market data, you will quickly find yourself inundated with sources providing stock quotes and financial data. An important and often overlooked factor when acquiring data is the efficiency of getting the data. All else being equal, you don't want to spend hours piecing together a dataset that you could have acquired in far less time. Taking this into consideration, we will try to obtain the largest amount of data from the least number of sources. This not only helps to keep the data as consistent as possible, but it also improves the repeatability of the analysis and the reproducibility of the results.

How to do it...

The first piece of data we want to obtain is a snapshot of the stocks we want to analyze. One of the best ways to do this is to download data from one of the many stock screener applications that exist. Our favorite screener to download stock data from belongs to `http://finviz.com`.

Let's acquire the stock market data that we will use for this chapter with the help of the following steps:

1. First, let's pull up **finviz** stock screener available at `http://finviz.com/screene
r.ashx`:

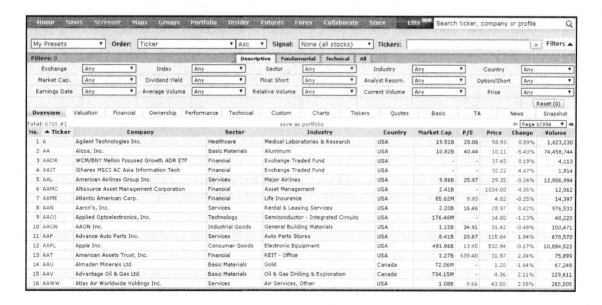

As you can see, the site has multiple fields that can be filtered. If you click on the **All** tab, you can see all of the fields that can be displayed.

2. For this project, we want to export all the fields for all the companies in the screener. You can either customize the screener by checking 69 check-boxes, at the time of writing, or you can use the following URL to make all the fields show up automatically:

```
http://finviz.com/screener.ashx?v=152&c=
0,1,2,3,4,5,6,7,8,9,10,11,12,13,14,15,16,17,18,19,20,21,22,23,
24,25,26,27,28,29,30,31,32,33,34,35,36,37,38,39,40,41,42,43,44
,45,46,47,48,49,50,51,52,53,54,55,56,57,58,59,60,61,62,63,64,6
5,66,67,68
```

You should now see the screener with all the available fields.

3. If you scroll all the way to the bottom right of the screen, there should be an **export** link. Click on this link and save the CSV file as `finviz.csv`.

4. Finally, we will launch **RStudio,** read the `finviz.csv` file from the path where we saved it, and assign it to a data frame, as follows:

```
finviz <- read.csv("path/finviz.csv")
```

In data analysis, it is always better for each step that is performed to be in code instead of as a series of point-and-click actions that require human intervention. This way, it is much easier and faster to reproduce your results.

5. After going through *steps 1 to 4* for the first time (and some clever reading of URLs from our browser), we can replace the previous lines of code with the following two commands:

```
url_to_open <-
'http://finviz.com/export.ashx?v=152&c=0,1,2,3,4,5,6,7,8,9,10,
11,12,13,14,15,16,17,18,19,20,21,22,23,24,25,26,27,28,29,30,31
,32,33,34,35,36,37,38,39,40,41,42,43,44,45,46,47,48,49,50,51,5
2,53,54,55,56,57,58,59,60,61,62,63,64,65,66,67,68'

finviz <- read.csv(url(url_to_open))
```

Note the structure of the URL in *step 2*; it contains a comma-separated list of the check-boxes we wish to select. You can programmatically generate this URL to easily select whichever combination of companies' data you want to download.

If you want to avoid typing the numbers 0 through 68, you can use a combination of the sprintf and paste commands to accomplish the same thing:

```
url_to_open <-
sprintf("http://finviz.com/export.ashx?v=152&c=%s",
paste(0:68, collapse = ","))
```

Summarizing the data

Now that we have acquired our stock data, let's use a couple of commands to find out what fields our data contains and get some useful information about the values contained in these fields.

Getting ready

You will need the data downloaded from the previous recipe, *Acquiring stock market data*, to begin the summary.

How to do it...

The following steps will walk you through a quick summary of the data:

1. Take a look at the fields you imported using the following command:

    ```
    > head(finviz[,1:4])
    ```

This command will show you the first six rows of your data, as shown in the following snippet, so that you can see what fields are in your data and also examples of possible values for the fields. In this example, we can also see that there is some missing data, identified by NA:

```
   No.   Ticker                            Company            Sector
1  1      A                Agilent Technologies Inc.        Healthcare
2  2      AA                         Alcoa, Inc.       Basic Materials
3  3     AADR     WCM/BNY Mellon Focused Growth ADR ETF      Financial
4  4     AAIT     iShares MSCI AC Asia Information Tech      Financial
5  5     AAL                American Airlines Group Inc.      Services
6  6     AAMC    Altisource Asset Management Corporation     Financial
```

2. The next command will return a summary of each field. For numeric fields, it will tell you what the min, max, mean, median, and quartiles are, and for character fields, it will tell you which appear most often:

```
> summary(finviz[,1:4])
      No.              Ticker           Company                   Sector
 Min.    :   1    A      :   1    Banco Bradesco S.A.       :   2    Financial      :2915
 1st Qu. :1677    AA     :   1    Banco Santander-Chile     :   2    Technology     : 867
 Median  :3354    AADR   :   1    Berkshire Hathaway Inc.   :   2    Services       : 864
 Mean    :3354    AAIT   :   1    Embotelladora Andina S.A. :   2    Basic Materials: 608
 3rd Qu. :5030    AAL    :   1    First Bancorp             :   2    Healthcare     : 578
 Max.    :6706    AAMC   :   1    Gray Television Inc.      :   2    Consumer Goods : 375
                  (Other):6700    (Other)                   :6694    (Other)        : 499
```

How it works...

Now that we've taken an initial glance at the data, it's important to take some time out to identify the fields that will be most important to us, and understand what these fields mean.

The first few fields contain identifying information about the company.

The ticker (sometimes also called the symbol) is the identifier for the stock of a company. No two companies will have the exact same ticker symbol. So AA is always Alcoa, AAPL is always Apple, and so forth.

Next, we have the company name, sector, industry, and home country of the company. The sector and industry details serve as ways to classify stocks to inform us of each company's primary line of business; sector is more general (higher level), and industry is more specific (lower level). For example, Apple Inc. (AAPL) is in the Consumer Goods sector and primarily produces consumer goods in the Electronic Equipment industry.

There's more...

Once we get past these fields, most of the other fields in our dataset are numeric. Let's define some of the most important ones:

- **Price**: This indicates the ongoing dollar value to purchase one share of a company's stock.
- **Volume**: This indicates the most recent number of shares of the stock transacted in a day.
- **Shares Outstanding**: This is the total number of stock shares the company has issued.
- **P/E**: The Price to Earnings ratio is the price of the company's stock divided by the company's earnings per share outstanding.
- **PEG**: The P/E Growth ratio is the company's P/E ratio divided by its annual growth rate, and it gives you a sense of the valuation of the company's earnings relative to its growth.
- **EPS growth next year**: This is the expected rate at which the company's earnings per share will grow in the next year.
- **Total Debt/Equity**: The total debt to equity is used as a measure of financial health calculated by dividing the dollar value of the company's total debt with the equity in the company. This gives you a sense of how the company has been financing its growth and operations. Debt is more risky than equity, so a high ratio will be cause for concern.
- **Beta**: This is a measure of the stock's volatility (swings in its price) relative to the overall stock market. A beta of 1 means the stock is as volatile as the market. A beta more than 1 means it's more volatile, while a beta less than 1 means it's less volatile.

- **RSI**: The Relative Strength Index is a metric based on stock price activity, which uses the number of days a stock has closed higher than its opening price and the number of days a stock has closed lower than its opening price within the last two weeks to determine a score between 0 and 100. A higher index value indicates that the stock might be overvalued, and therefore, the price might drop soon; a lower value indicates that the stock might be undervalued, so the price might rise soon.

If you want to know the definitions of some of the other fields, `http://investopedia.com` is a great place to find definitions of financial and investment terms.

Cleaning and exploring the data

Now that we've acquired the data and learned a little about what the fields mean, the next step is to clean up the data and conduct some exploratory analysis.

Getting ready

Make sure you have the packages mentioned at the beginning of this chapter under the *Requirements* section installed and you have successfully imported the `FINVIZ` data into R using the steps in the previous sections.

How to do it...

To clean and explore the data, closely follow the ensuing instructions:

1. Imported numeric data often contains special characters such as percentage signs, dollar signs, commas, and so on. This causes R to think that the field is a character field instead of a numeric field. For example, our `FINVIZ` dataset contains numerous values with percentage signs that must be removed. To do this, we will create a `clean_numeric` function that will strip away any unwanted characters using the `gsub` command. We will create this function once and then use it multiple times throughout the chapter:

```
clean_numeric <- function(s){
  s <- gsub("%|\\$|,|\\)|\\(", "", s)
  s <- as.numeric(s)
}
```

2. Next, we will apply this function to the numeric fields in our `finviz` data frame:

```
finviz <- cbind(finviz[,1:6],apply(finviz[,7:68], 2,
clean_numeric))
```

3. If you look at the data again, all the pesky percentage signs will be gone, and the fields will all be numeric.

> In this command, and throughout the rest of this chapter, there will be many instances where we reference columns by their column number. If the number of columns changes for some reason, the numbers referenced will need to be adjusted accordingly.

4. Now we are ready to really start exploring our data! The first thing to do is take a look at how the prices are distributed in order to get a visual sense of what is a high stock price, what is a low stock price, and where the prices of most stocks fall:

```
hist(finviz$Price, breaks=100, main="Price Distribution",
xlab="Price")
```

You will get the following graph as output:

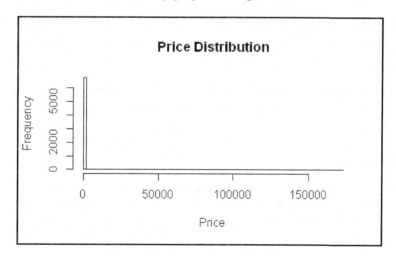

Here, we encounter our first problem. Outlier stocks with a very high price causes R to scale the **x** axis of the histogram in such a way as to make the graph useless. We simply cannot see what the distribution for the more normally priced stocks looks like. This is a very common issue when producing a histogram.

5. Let's put a cap on the **x** axis of *$150* and see what that produces for us:

```
hist(finviz$Price[finviz$Price<150], breaks=100, main=
"Price Distribution", xlab="Price")
```

You will get the following graph as output:

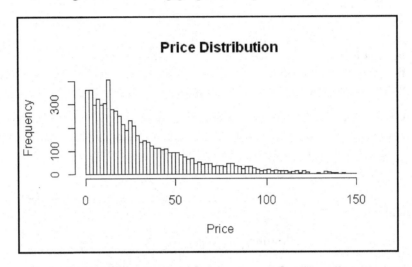

This is much better! It shows that the majority of stocks in our dataset are priced under $50. So, in absolute terms, a stock that was priced at $100 would be considered expensive.

6. But of course things aren't so simple. Perhaps different sectors and industries have different price levels. So, theoretically a $100 stock might be cheap if all the other stocks in its industry are priced in the $120 to $150 range. Let's get the average prices by sector and see how they compare. Note that we are not excluding any stocks:

```
sector_avg_prices <- aggregate(Price~Sector,data=finviz,FUN="mean")
colnames(sector_avg_prices)[2] <- "Sector_Avg_Price"
ggplot(sector_avg_prices, aes(x=Sector, y=Sector_Avg_Price,
fill=Sector)) + geom_bar(stat="identity") + ggtitle("Sector Avg
Prices") + theme(axis.text.x = element_text(angle = 90, hjust = 1))
```

You will get the following graph as output:

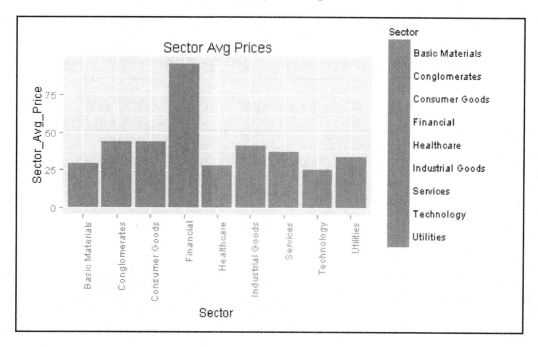

This is interesting. Stocks in the financial sector seem to have a significantly higher average price than stocks in other sectors. I'm willing to bet that this is due to some of the outliers that messed up our distribution earlier.

7. Let's get to the bottom of this! Let's find out which industries and companies are responsible for making the average price of the financial sector so much higher than all the others.

First, we create a summary of the average prices by industry:

```
industry_avg_prices <-
aggregate(Price~Sector+Industry,data=finviz,FUN="mean")
industry_avg_prices <- industry_avg_prices[order(
industry_avg_prices$Sector,industry_avg_prices$Industry),]
colnames(industry_avg_prices)[3] <- "Industry_Avg_Price"
```

Then, we isolate the industries in the financial sector:

```
industry_chart <- subset(industry_avg_prices,Sector=="Financial")
```

Finally, we create a chart showing the average price of each industry in the financial sector:

```
ggplot(industry_chart, aes(x=Industry, y=Industry_Avg_Price,
fill=Industry)) + geom_bar(stat="identity") +
theme(legend.position="none") + ggtitle("Industry Avg Prices") +
theme(axis.text.x = element_text(angle = 90, hjust = 1))
```

You will get the following graph as output:

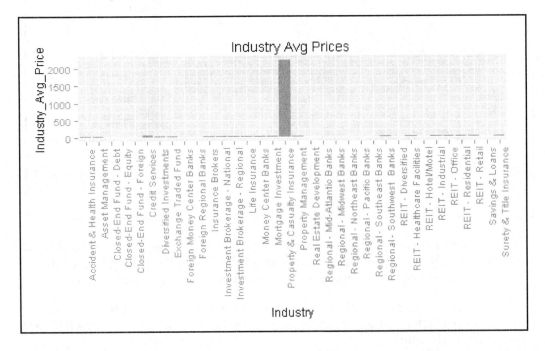

From this graph, it looks like the **Property & Casualty Insurance** industry is the main culprit that is driving the average prices up.

8. Next, we will drill down further into the `Property & Casualty Insurance` industry to identify which companies are the outliers:

```
company_chart <- subset(finviz,Industry=="Property & Casualty
Insurance")

ggplot(company_chart, aes(x=Company, y=Price, fill=Company)) +
  geom_bar(stat="identity") + theme(legend.position="none") +
  ggtitle("Company Avg Prices") +
  theme(axis.text.x = element_text(angle = 90, hjust = 1))
```

You will get the following graph as output:

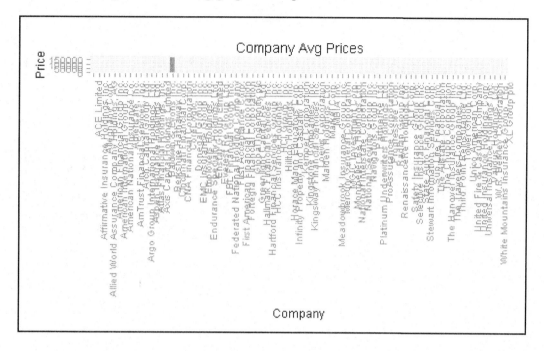

It's hard to see because there are so many companies, but if you zoom in on the graph, it is clear that the outlier company is **Berkshire Hathaway**, where the stock price is currently over $172,000 per share.

9. Since their stock price is so extreme, let's remove them from our dataset and then re-average the sectors so that we have a more realistic average price for the financial sector:

```
finviz <- subset(finviz, Ticker!="BRK-A")
sector_avg_prices <- aggregate(Price~Sector,data=finviz,FUN="mean")
colnames(sector_avg_prices)[2] <- "Sector_Avg_Price"
ggplot(sector_avg_prices, aes(x=Sector, y=Sector_Avg_Price,
fill=Sector)) + geom_bar(stat="identity") + ggtitle("Sector Avg
Prices") + theme(axis.text.x = element_text(angle = 90, hjust = 1))
```

You will get the following graph as output:

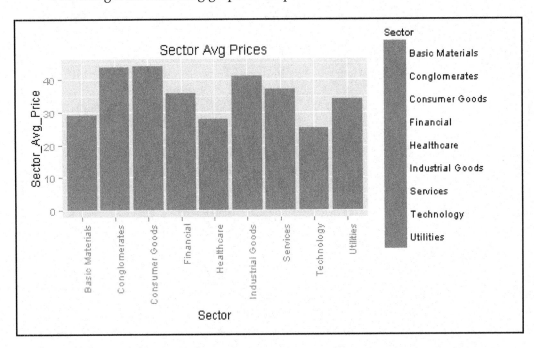

Now our averages look much better and we have a decent basis to compare stock prices to their industry and sector averages.

How it works...

In this section, we used the `aggregate` command to summarize our data. Here's a reminder of the code we used:

```
sector_avg_prices <- aggregate(Price~Sector,data=finviz,FUN="mean")
```

An alternative way to do this is with the `ddply` command that is part of the `plyr` package:

```
sector_avg_prices <- ddply(finviz, "Sector", summarise,
  Price=mean(Price, na.rm=TRUE))
```

Wherever you see the `aggregate` command used in this chapter, feel free to challenge yourself by also trying to summarize the data, using the `ddply` command.

See also

- The `gsub` command at
  http://stat.ethz.ch/R-manual/R-devel/library/base/html/grep.html
- The `cbind` command at http://stat.ethz.ch/R-manual/R-devel/library/base/html/cbind.html
- The `plyr` documentation at
  http://cran.r-project.org/web/packages/plyr/plyr.pdf
- The `aggregate` command at
  http://stat.ethz.ch/R-manual/R-devel/library/stats/html/aggregate.html

Generating relative valuations

One of the most interesting things that you can do with stock market data is come up with a valuation model. The ultimate goal is to arrive at a decision about whether the stock might be overvalued or undervalued. There are two main ways to do this. Intrinsic valuation is generally more time consuming because it involves digging into the financial statements of a company to arrive at a valuation decision. The alternative method is relative valuation which will quickly provide a sense of how the stock is valued, but does not take into account a comprehensive set of factors. The basic idea is that it compares a stock's price and valuation ratios to similar stocks to arrive at a conclusion. In this section, we will value stocks using the simpler relative valuation method.

Getting ready

This recipe requires the data downloaded and cleaned in the previous recipes.

How to do

We will essentially do three major things in this section. First, we calculate sector averages for fields that we can use in our relative valuation efforts. Then, we do the same at the industry level. Finally, we compare the stocks' statistics to the averages to arrive at an index value for each stock that indicates whether it might be undervalued. The following steps will guide you:

1. In order to calculate averages in multiple columns in R, we first need to melt the data. This will make every column after `Sector` a row and then display its value, essentially making the data long instead of wide. Take a look at the following screenshot for the different steps in this recipe to better understand how the data changes shape. It goes from being wide to long, and then back to wide again, but in summary form:

Sector	Industry	Country	Market.Cap	P.E	Forward.P.E	PEG	P.S	P.B	P.Cash
Healthcare	Medical Laboratories & Research	USA	19823.59	28.52	16.78	2.97	2.92	3.75	7.41
Basic Materials	Aluminum	USA	12062.38	NA	19.33	NA	0.52	1.15	8.39
Financial	Exchange Traded Fund	USA	NA	NA	NA	NA	NA	NA	NA
Financial	Exchange Traded Fund	USA	NA	NA	NA	NA	NA	NA	NA
Services	Major Airlines	USA	11645.76	30.67	6.61	0.87	0.46	NA	1.72
Financial	Asset Management	USA	2348.00	NA	NA	NA	78.27	671.14	23.00
Financial	Life Insurance	USA	83.71	8.73	NA	NA	0.52	0.86	2.24
Services	Rental & Leasing Services	USA	2297.49	17.15	15.81	2.34	1.02	1.85	7.43
Technology	Semiconductor - Integrated Circuits	USA	159.82	NA	13.24	NA	2.17	NA	21.89
Industrial Goods	General Building Materials	USA	1035.39	31.31	24.94	3.13	3.18	6.39	47.28
Services	Auto Parts Stores	USA	9090.47	22.56	15.17	1.46	1.42	6.19	16.02
Consumer Goods	Electronic Equipment	USA	480222.89	13.29	11.60	0.68	2.76	3.70	11.80
Financial	REIT - Office	USA	1296.44	651.20	95.76	132.90	5.11	1.99	19.73
Basic Materials	Gold	Canada	99.68	NA	NA	NA	332.28	2.27	6.83
Basic Materials	Oil & Gas Drilling & Exploration	Canada	520.70	NA	NA	NA	2.19	0.53	NA
Services	Air Services, Other	USA	789.65	7.96	8.05	3.07	0.48	0.62	2.70
Financial	Exchange Traded Fund	USA	NA	NA	NA	NA	NA	NA	NA
Financial	Asset Management	USA	2176.37	17.35	13.70	2.17	14.53	1.53	NA
Healthcare	Diagnostic Substances	USA	857.43	50.66	41.31	2.89	4.77	4.59	8.41
Industrial Goods	Industrial Equipment & Components	Switzerland	58963.99	20.54	15.88	1.77	1.42	3.35	12.61
Healthcare	Drug Manufacturers - Major	USA	81300.48	19.67	14.20	1.47	4.33	22.77	8.47
Services	Drugs Wholesale	USA	15598.96	43.42	15.76	3.13	0.16	6.94	44.89
Financial	Regional - Mid-Atlantic Banks	USA	480.18	26.65	10.90	3.33	3.80	1.66	1.69
Services	Education & Training Services	USA	91.80	NA	NA	NA	0.61	NA	1.71
Services	Business Services	USA	2150.47	93.64	41.22	5.70	4.41	6.95	27.61
Services	Trucking	USA	828.76	54.47	12.45	5.45	0.36	1.59	5.87
Services	Auto Dealerships	USA	1469.79	14.83	10.95	0.95	0.28	3.12	1130.61

We will use the following command to perform this action:

```
sector_avg <- melt(finviz, id="Sector")
```

2. Next, we need to filter so that the data frame contains only the fields we want to average:

```
sector_avg <- subset(sector_avg,variable %in%
c("Price","P.E","PEG","P.S", "P.B"))
```

Now your `sector_avg` data frame should look like this:

Sector	variable	value
Healthcare	P.E	28.52
Services	P.E	30.67
Financial	P.E	8.73
Services	P.E	17.15
Industrial Goods	P.E	31.31
Services	P.E	22.56
Consumer Goods	P.E	13.29
Financial	P.E	651.2
Services	P.E	7.06
Financial	P.E	17.35
Healthcare	P.E	50.66
Industrial Goods	P.E	20.54
Healthcare	P.E	19.67
Services	P.E	43.42
Financial	P.E	26.65

Each column heading (variable) is now listed vertically alongside its value. This allows us to do some grouping later to get the averages for each variable.

3. Not all stocks in our original dataset had all of these values; where the values were null, we wanted to remove the records. We also wanted to make sure all of our values are numeric:

```
sector_avg <- (na.omit(sector_avg))
sector_avg$value <- as.numeric(sector_avg$value)
```

4. The next step is to cast the data to make it wide again. This will produce a column for each of the fields we filtered, and will now contain the average by sector. We will also rename the columns so that we know they are sector averages:

```
sector_avg <- dcast(sector_avg, Sector~variable, mean)
colnames(sector_avg)[2:6] <-
c("SAvgPE","SAvgPEG","SAvgPS","SAvgPB", "SAvgPrice")
```

You will get the following plot as output:

	Sector	SAvgPE	SAvgPEG	SAvgPS	SAvgPB	SAvgPrice
1	Basic Materials	42.87945	5.390194	35.677311	10.203838	29.22257
2	Conglomerates	20.79571	1.045000	1.532000	58.426316	40.11000
3	Consumer Goods	30.29197	3.446652	1.380000	4.712809	42.40154
4	Financial	32.88929	5.403305	12.335628	4.465120	35.38289
5	Healthcare	38.44733	12.175091	184.600614	9.349106	27.94912
6	Industrial Goods	32.73892	3.314206	1.856246	3.765014	40.78930
7	Services	44.43990	3.927596	1.992289	33.536609	36.45865
8	Technology	59.85766	4.749591	9.386424	4.697576	24.87183
9	Utilities	27.20184	97.133068	7.979917	2.030339	34.01273

5. We will now do the exact same thing at the industry level:

```
industry_avg <- melt(finviz, id=c("Sector","Industry"))
industry_avg <- subset(industry_avg,variable %in%
c("Price","P.E","PEG","P.S","P.B"))
industry_avg <- (na.omit(industry_avg))
industry_avg$value <- as.numeric(industry_avg$value)
industry_avg <- dcast(industry_avg, Sector+Industry~variable, mean)
industry_avg <- (na.omit(industry_avg))
colnames(industry_avg)[3:7] <-
 c("IAvgPE","IAvgPEG","IAvgPS","IAvgPB","IAvgPrice")
```

6. We will now add the sector and industry average columns to our original `finviz` dataset:

```
finviz <- merge(finviz, sector_avg, by.x="Sector", by.y="Sector")
finviz <- merge(finviz, industry_avg, by.x=c("Sector","Industry"),
by.y=c("Sector","Industry"))
```

You might have noticed that the number of records in the `finviz` data frame decreased when we executed the last line of code. It removed all stock that didn't have an industry average from the dataset. This is fine since the overall goal is to narrow down the list of stocks, and we wouldn't have had sufficient information to generate a valuation for these stocks anyway.

7. Now it's time to put these new fields to use. First, we will add 10 placeholder fields that contain all 0. These will be used to track whether a stock is undervalued, based on being lower than the sector or industry average:

```
finviz$SPEUnder <- 0
finviz$SPEGUnder <- 0
finviz$SPSUnder <- 0
finviz$SPBUnder <- 0
finviz$SPriceUnder <- 0
finviz$IPEUnder <- 0
finviz$IPEGUnder <- 0
finviz$IPSUnder <- 0
finviz$IPBUnder <- 0
finviz$IPriceUnder <- 0
```

8. Next, we will replace the 0s with 1s wherever the respective value for the stock is less than the average to indicate that these stocks might be undervalued based on that metric:

```
finviz$SPEUnder[finviz$P.E<finviz$SAvgPE] <- 1
finviz$SPEGUnder[finviz$PEG<finviz$SAvgPEG] <- 1
finviz$SPSUnder[finviz$P.S<finviz$SAvgPS] <- 1
finviz$SPBUnder[finviz$P.B<finviz$SAvgPB] <- 1
finviz$SPriceUnder[finviz$Price<finviz$SAvgPrice] <- 1
finviz$IPEUnder[finviz$P.E<finviz$IAvgPE] <- 1
finviz$IPEGUnder[finviz$PEG<finviz$IAvgPEG] <- 1
finviz$IPSUnder[finviz$P.S<finviz$IAvgPS] <- 1
finviz$IPBUnder[finviz$P.B<finviz$IAvgPB] <- 1
finviz$IPriceUnder[finviz$Price<finviz$IAvgPrice] <- 1
```

9. Finally, we will sum these 10 columns to create a new column with the index value telling you, on a scale of 1 to 10, how undervalued the stock is based on the different dimensions that were considered:

```
finviz$RelValIndex <- apply(finviz[79:88],1,sum)
```

How it works...

Relative valuation involves comparing a stock's statistics with that of similar stocks in order to determine whether the stock is overvalued or undervalued. In an overly simplified example, a stock with a lower P/E ratio relative to the industry average *P/E* ratio for their industry (all else being equal) can be considered undervalued and might make a decent investment if the company has good financial health. Once we have this, we can filter for the stocks that look most promising, such as ones that have a `RelValIndex` of 8 or greater.

```
potentially_undervalued <- subset(finviz,RelValIndex>=8)
```

The `potentially_undervalued` data frame we just created should look this:

	row.names	Ticker	Company	RelValIndex
1	1	CGA	China Green Agriculture, Inc.	10
2	4	UAN	CVR Partners, LP	8
3	7	YONG	Yongye International, Inc.	8
4	8	AVD	American Vanguard Corp.	9
5	16	MOS	The Mosaic Company	8
6	27	ARSD	Arabian American Development Company	8
7	32	CE	Celanese Corporation	8
8	33	LNDC	Landec Corp.	10
9	36	ASH	Ashland Inc.	8
10	38	ACET	Aceto Corp.	10
11	40	DOW	The Dow Chemical Company	8
12	42	SQM	Chemical & Mining Co. of Chile Inc.	8
13	43	FF	FutureFuel Corp.	10

We admit that this is an overly simplistic approach. However, it provides a framework to expand into more complex calculations. For example, once comfortable with this process, you can:

- Add in customized criteria to assign a `1` to indicate that the stock is undervalued
- Weigh the values differently
- Add or remove criteria
- Create more precise index values than just 1s and 0s, and so on

The sky is the limit here, but the process is the same.

Screening stocks and analyzing historical prices

When we are looking for stocks to invest in, we need to have a way to narrow the list down. In other words, we need to eliminate stocks that we don't think will be good investments. The definition of a good investment varies from person to person, but in this section, we will use some basic criteria to reduce our master list of stocks to just a few that we think might make good prospects. Once comfortable with the process, we encourage you to modify the criteria based on your own opinion of what defines a stock worth investing in. Once we have our prospects, we will analyze their historical prices and see what conclusions we can draw from them.

Getting ready

We will start with the `finviz` dataset as it was at the end of the previous section, along with the sector and industry averages columns, the binary undervalued columns, and the index values that summed up the values in the binary columns.

In addition to the packages we have used so far in this chapter, we will also need the zoo package for this section. This will help us calculate moving averages for the historical stock prices that we will pull.

How to do it...

The steps that you are about to embark upon will allow you to screen stocks:

1. First, choose some stock screening criteria, that is, a way to select the stocks within the `finviz` dataset that we feel have the potential to be good investments. Here is some sample criteria to start with:
     - Only US companies
     - Price per share between $20 and $100
     - Volume greater than 10,000
     - Positive earnings per share currently and projected for the future
     - Total debt to equity ratio less than 1
     - Beta less than 1.5
     - Institutional ownership less than 30 percent
     - Relative valuation index value greater than 8

2. As mentioned, these are just examples. Feel free to remove criteria, add criteria, or make changes based on what you think will give you the best output. The goal is to narrow the list down to less than 10 stocks.

3. Next, we apply our criteria to subset the `finviz` data frame into a new data frame called `target_stocks`:

```
target_stocks <- subset(finviz, Price>20 & Price<100 & Volume>10000
&
                        Country=="USA" &
                        EPS..ttm.>0 &
                        EPS.growth.next.year>0 &
                        EPS.growth.next.5.years>0 &
                        Total.Debt.Equity<1 & Beta<1.5 &
                        Institutional.Ownership<30 &
                        RelValIndex>8)
```

At the time of writing, this produces a target list of six stocks, as shown in the following screenshot. You might get a different number or different stocks altogether if you pull updated data from the web:

	row.names	Ticker	Company	RelValIndex
1	1	CGA	China Green Agriculture, Inc.	10
2	4	UAN	CVR Partners, LP	8
3	7	YONG	Yongye International, Inc.	8
4	8	AVD	American Vanguard Corp.	9
5	16	MOS	The Mosaic Company	8
6	27	ARSD	Arabian American Development Company	8
7	32	CE	Celanese Corporation	8
8	33	LNDC	Landec Corp.	10
9	36	ASH	Ashland Inc.	8
10	38	ACET	Aceto Corp.	10
11	40	DOW	The Dow Chemical Company	8
12	42	SQM	Chemical & Mining Co. of Chile Inc.	8
13	43	FF	FutureFuel Corp.	10

4. Now, let's go out and get historical prices for our target list of stocks so that we can see how their prices have changed over time. We will use a `for` loop to iterate through the list of symbols and pull prices for each one, but we will break up the loop across several steps and explain what each chunk is doing:

```
counter <- 0
for (symbol in target_stocks$Ticker){
```

The preceding command initializes a counter to keep track of where we are in our list of target stocks. Immediately after, we begin the for loop by telling every symbol in our target list to do the following:

```
url <-
paste0("http://ichart.finance.yahoo.com/table.csv?s=",symbol,
"&a=08&b=7&c=1984&d=01&e=23&f=2014&g=d&ignore=.csv")
stock <- read.csv(url)
stock <- na.omit(stock)
colnames(stock)[7] <- "AdjClose"
stock[,1] <- as.Date(stock[,1])
stock <- cbind(Symbol=symbol,stock)
```

This code assigns a URL to the URL variable that has the current stock symbol embedded into it. Then, we read the data located at this URL and assign it to a data frame called `stock`. We then do some clean up and formatting by removing all null values from the data frame, renaming the last column, making sure the `Date` column is formatted as a date that R can recognize, and adding the stock's symbol to the first row of the data frame.

5. The next few lines of our `for` loop will calculate some moving averages so that we can compare them with the daily stock prices. For this step, make sure you have the `zoo` package mentioned at the beginning of this section installed and loaded.

   The first part will calculate both a 50-day moving average and a 200-day moving average:

```
maxrow <- nrow(stock)-49
ma50 <- cbind(stock[1:maxrow,1:2],rollmean(stock$AdjClose,
50,align="right"))
maxrow <- nrow(stock)-199
ma200 <-
cbind(stock[1:maxrow,1:2],rollmean(stock$AdjClose,200,align="right"
))
```

The second part will combine the moving average data frames with the data frame containing the historical stock prices so that everything is part of the same dataset:

```
stock <- merge(stock,ma50,by.x=c("Symbol","Date"),by.y=c("Symbol",
  "Date"), all.x=TRUE)
colnames(stock)[9] <- "MovAvg50"
stock <- merge(stock,ma200,by.x=c("Symbol","Date"),by.y=c("Symbol",
  "Date"),all.x=TRUE)
colnames(stock)[10] <- "MovAvg200"
```

6. Next, we will plot a historical chart for each stock that our `for` loop iterates through, and then save that plot:

```
price_chart <- melt(stock[,c(1,2,8,9,10)],id=c("Symbol","Date"))
qplot(Date, value, data=price_chart, geom="line", color=variable,
main=paste(symbol,"Daily Stock Prices"),ylab="Price")
ggsave(filename=paste0("stock_price_",counter,".png"))
```

The charts that get generated and saved should look like the following two charts:

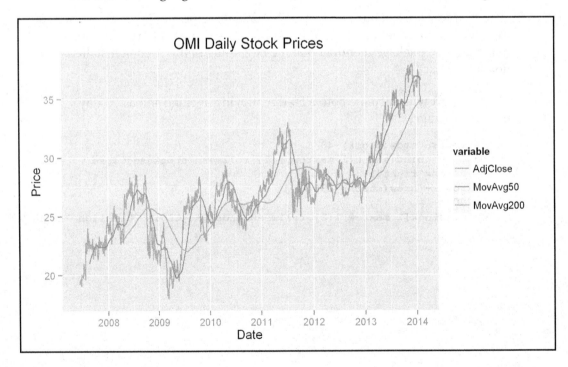

The next part of our loop summarizes the opening, high, low, and closing prices of the current stock:

```
price_summary <- ddply(stock, "Symbol", summarise,
open=Open[nrow(stock)],
high=max(High),low=min(Low),close=AdjClose[1])
```

Then, it accumulates the summarized opening, high, low, and closing prices in a data frame called stocks so that the different stocks can be compared later. Also, it separately accumulates all the daily historical prices for the stocks in a data frame called price summaries so that they can be compared as well:

```
if(counter==0){
    stocks <- rbind(stock)
    price_summaries <- rbind(price_summary)
}else{
    stocks <- rbind(stocks, stock)
    price_summaries <- rbind(price_summaries, price_summary)
}
```

At the end of the loop, we increment our counter by one, and then close our for loop with a curly bracket:

```
counter <- counter+1
}
```

We broke our loop into pieces in order to explain what each part of the loop does. If you want to see what the entire for loop should look like, check the accompanying code file for this chapter.

The complete code block is given here as an image:

```
#Pull historical prices
counter <- 0
for (symbol in target_stocks$Ticker){
  url <- paste0("http://ichart.finance.yahoo.com/table.csv?s=",symbol,
               ["&a=08&b=7&c=1984&d=01&e=23&f=2014&g=d&ignore=.csv")
  stock <- read.csv(url)
  stock <- na.omit(stock)
  colnames(stock)[7] <- "AdjClose"
  stock[,1] <- as.Date(stock[,1])
  stock <- cbind(Symbol=symbol,stock)
  maxrow <- nrow(stock)-49
  ma50 <- cbind(stock[1:maxrow,1:2],rollmean(stock$AdjClose,50,align="right"))
  maxrow <- nrow(stock)-199
  ma200 <- cbind(stock[1:maxrow,1:2],rollmean(stock$AdjClose,200,align="right"))
  stock <- merge(stock,ma50,by.x=c("Symbol","Date"),by.y=c("Symbol","Date"),all.x=TRUE)
  colnames(stock)[9] <- "MovAvg50"
  stock <- merge(stock,ma200,by.x=c("Symbol","Date"),by.y=c("Symbol","Date"),all.x=TRUE)
  colnames(stock)[10] <- "MovAvg200"
  price_chart <- melt(stock[,c(1,2,8,9,10)],id=c("Symbol","Date"))
  qplot(Date, value, data=price_chart, geom="line", color=variable,
       main=paste(symbol,"Daily Stock Prices"),ylab="Price")
  ggsave(filename=paste0("stock_price_",counter,".png"))
  price_summary <- ddply(stock, "Symbol", summarise, open=Open[nrow(stock)],
                        high=max(High),low=min(Low),close=AdjClose[1])
  #Compile prices and summaries for all symbols into a single data frame
  if(counter==0){
    stocks <- rbind(stock)
    price_summaries <- rbind(price_summary)
  }else{
    stocks <- rbind(stocks, stock)
    price_summaries <- rbind(price_summaries, price_summary)
  }
  counter <- counter+1
}
```

Once we have iterated through all the stock symbols, we are left with a data frame named `stocks` that contains the historical prices for all the symbols in our target list and a data frame named `price_summaries` that holds the summaries for all our stocks. Let's graph them and see what they look like.

9. First, we will graph the historical prices for all our stocks:

```
qplot(Date, AdjClose, data=stocks, geom="line", color=Symbol, main="Daily
Stock Prices")
ggsave(filename=("stock_price_combined.png"))
```

The preceding commands will produce the following graph:

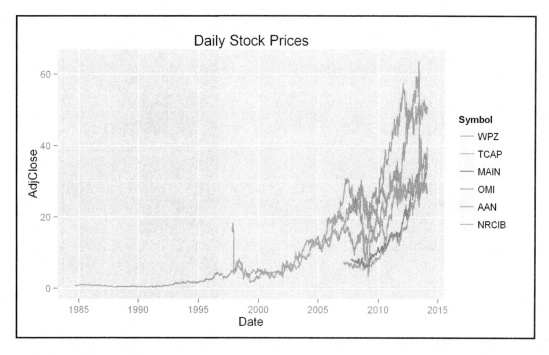

10. Then, let's visualize the price summaries:

```
summary <- melt(price_summaries,id="Symbol")
ggplot(summary, aes(x=variable, y=value, fill=Symbol)) +
geom_bar(stat="identity") + facet_wrap(~Symbol)
ggsave(filename=("stock_price_summaries.png"))
```

The resulting graph should look similar to this:

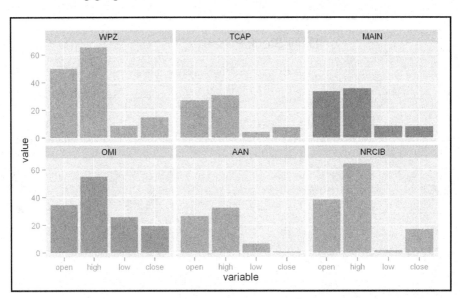

How it works...

Daily stock price charts are very *spiky* or volatile, and this sometimes makes them difficult to read. Moving averages smooth out the price fluctuations of a stock so that you can get a better sense of whether the stock is moving up or down over time.

Moving averages are also used to time investment in stocks. In other words, they are used as a guide to determine whether to invest in a stock now or to wait. There are varying opinions about what signals the best time, but one example is when the stock's 50-day moving average is below its 200-day moving average but is trending up. For more on moving averages, please see `http://www.investopedia.com/university/movingaverage/`.

The combined historical price chart we generated in this section shows us the degree to which our target stocks' prices move in tandem. If you are looking to invest in multiple stocks, it can be good to invest in ones where the prices are not too highly correlated. You can also visualize how volatile one stock has been when compared to another. In our graph, you can see that the symbols `WPZ` and `NRCIB` have been fairly volatile, while the other symbols have been somewhat less volatile.

Another way to look at the price comparisons is by examining the price summaries bar chart that we created. This chart shows the opening, high, low, and closing prices for the period analyzed. The opening price is the very first price the stock traded at, the closing price is the very last price the stock has traded at thus far, the high price is the highest price the stock has been at during the period, and the low price is the lowest price the stock has been at during the period. The volatility mentioned previously can be viewed in a different way on this graph, as you can clearly see the difference between the highs and the lows of our two most volatile stocks. This chart also lets you see where the stock's closing price is relative to its all-time high and all-time low, which might help to give you a clue of the fairness of its current valuation.

Visually Exploring Employment Data

5

In this chapter, we will cover:

- Preparing for analysis
- Importing employment data into R
- Exploring the employment data
- Obtaining and merging additional data
- Adding geographical information
- Extracting state- and county-level wage and employment information
- Visualizing geographical distributions of pay
- Exploring where the jobs are, by industry
- Animating maps for a geospatial time series
- Benchmarking performance for some common tasks

Introduction

This project will introduce you to the US employment data provided by the **Bureau of Labor Statistics (BLS)** of the United States government. The BLS is the federal agency responsible for measuring labor market activity and working conditions and prices in the US economy. Its mission is the collection, analysis, and dissemination of essential economic information to support public and private decision-making. In this project, we will use the aggregated annual data on employment and pay, stratified by geography and industry, from 2012, derived from the **Quarterly Census of Employment and Wages (QCEW)**.

This data can be downloaded as a compressed **comma-separated value (CSV)** file at `http://www.bls.gov/cew/data/files/2012/csv/2012_annual_singlefile.zip`, which contains the single file `2012.annual.singlefile.csv`. This file has 15 columns and about 3.5 million rows.

The **QCEW** is a quarterly collection of data, via the corporate tax collection system, related to employment and wages reported by employers. This census covers about 98 percent of the US civilian jobs, and excludes proprietors, unincorporated self-employed, unpaid family members, and some farm and domestic workers. The data is available as the aggregate data by county, metropolitan area (MSA), state, and national levels by industry. This government program has been in place since the 1930s in some form, and the current form has been in existence since 2003. The data is based on corporate reports to federal and local governments that are required by law, so it should be relatively free of reporting bias. This data gives a snapshot, in aggregate, of the wages and employment levels in the country by geography and industry.

The basic questions that we will address in this chapter are the geographical distribution of pay and employment in the US in 2012 and the last available full year of data at the time of writing. We will look at state and county levels as well as drill down to a few industries. We will also look at the temporal change in the geographical distribution of pay for the period 2003-2012 and what this reveals about the changing employment landscape in the US.

The goal of this chapter is to guide you through the data science pipeline using a step-by-step example, which, in this case, is the exploration of government employment data freely available at the US Government's BLS. We will work through ingesting the data into R, transforming and manipulating the data, creating subsets of the data, and generating visualizations that might provide some insight about patterns in the data. We hope that this example will serve as another exemplar that you can transfer to other projects for similar purposes.

Please be aware that the content in this chapter is more advanced than some of the previous chapters.

We assume that you have already gone through Chapter 1, *Preparing Your Data Science Environment*, and have RStudio readily available on the computer that you will use to complete the recipes in this chapter.

Preparing for analysis

This recipe will prepare the groundwork with the tools you need to complete this project. If you do not have R installed on your computer, please see the instructions in Chapter 1, *Preparing Your Data Science Environment*.

Getting ready

You need a computer with R installed and an internet connection.

How to do it...

The following steps will get you prepared for the remainder of this chapter by downloading the dataset from the BLS website and ensuring that we have the needed R packages:

1. Download the 76.8 MB compressed data from
   `http://www.bls.gov/cew/data/files/2012/csv/2012_annual_singlefile.zip`,
   and save it to a location that you will remember.
2. Uncompress the file by right-clicking on it in explorer or finder, and use the appropriate menu item.

   > If you are familiar with the command line in the Terminal in Linux/Mac OS X, you can easily uncompress the downloaded file using `unzip 2012_annual_singlefile.zip`.

3. Launch the RStudio IDE on your computer (or just plain R for purists).
4. Load the R packages that we will need for this project:

```
library(data.table)
library(plyr)
library(dplyr)
library(stringr)
library(ggplot2)
library(maps)
library(bit64)
library(RColorBrewer)
library(choroplethr)
```

If you do not have one of these packages installed on your machine, you can easily install it using the following command, exchanging `data.table` for the package name to be installed:

```
install.packages('data.table',repos='http://cran.r-project.org')
```

The R package repository, known as CRAN, has several mirrors around the world. A mirror, in this usage, is a duplicate copy of the software repository that is run on a server in a different region, providing faster access for individuals near the location. You can, and should, choose a mirror geographically closest to your location to speed up the package download. In the preceding code snippet, you change `http://cran.r-project.org` to the URL of your preferred CRAN mirror.

5. Finally, set your working directory to the path where you have saved the file. This will tell R where you want it to look for the file:

```
setwd('path')
```

How it works...

We will primarily use three different R packages that are extremely useful in importing, manipulating, and transforming large datasets.

The package `data.table` improves upon the `data.frame` object in R, making operations faster and allowing the specification of an index variable in a dataset, a concept familiar to database experts. It also allows the fast aggregation of large data, including very fast-ordered joins. We will primarily use the `data.table` package for its `fread` function, which allows (very) fast importing of large-structured datasets into R. We will also investigate the relative performance of functions in this package against other functions we use in the benchmarking recipe later in this chapter.

The `stringr` package provides tools for text and string manipulation. This package streamlines and syntactically unifies available string manipulation functionalities available in R, making tasks involving string search, manipulation, and extraction much easier. We will need these functionalities here.

The `dplyr` package is the next iteration of the popular package, `plyr`, by *Dr. Hadley Wickham*. It is targeted at rectangular data and allows very fast aggregation, transformation, summarization, column selection, and joins. It also provides syntactical sugar to allow commands to be strung together, piping the results of one command into the next. This will be our workhorse in this project.

The `ggplot2` package will be our visualization workhorse. It implements the **Grammar of Graphics** paradigm in R and provides a very flexible means of creating visualizations.

The `maps` package provides geographical information about the US that we will use in our visualizations.

See also

- Refer to the `dplyr` reference material available at
  `https://github.com/hadley/dplyr/blob/master/README.md`, which has links to vignettes and other reference materials
- Refer to the `ggplot2` reference manual available at
  `http://cran.r-project.org/web/packages/ggplot2/ggplot2.pdf`
- Refer to the `sqldf` reference materials available at
  `https://code.google.com/p/sqldf/`

Importing employment data into R

Our first step in this project is to import the employment data into R so that we can start assessing the data and perform some preliminary analysis.

Getting ready

You should be ready to go ahead after completing the previous recipe.

How to do it...

The following steps will guide you through two different ways of importing the CSV file:

1. We can directly load the data file into R (even from the compressed version) using the following command:

    ```
    ann2012 <- read.csv(unz('2012_annual_singlefile.zip',
      '2012.annual.singlefile.csv'), stringsAsFactors=F)
    ```

    However, you will find that this takes a very long time with this file. There are better ways.

2. We chose to import the data directly into R since there are further manipulations and merges that we will do later. We will use the `fread` function from the `data.table` package to do this:

    ```
    library(data.table)
    ann2012 <- fread('data/2012.annual.singlefile.csv')
    ```

    That's it. Really! It is also many times faster than the other method. It will not convert character variables to factors by default, so if you need factors later, you will have to convert them, which in our opinion is a desirable feature in any case.

How it works...

We were familiar with `read.csv` from Chapter 2, *Driving Visual Analysis with Automobile Data*. It basically reads the data line by line, separating columns by commas. As the data we are using for this project is 3.5 million rows, it is still small enough to fit into the memory of most modern personal computers, but will take quite some time to import using `read.csv()`.

The `fread` function from the `data.table` package uses an underlying C-level function to figure out from the file the length, number of fields, data types, and delimiters in the file, and it then reads the file using the parameters it has learned. As a result, it is significantly faster than `read.csv`. There is an extensive description of the details of `fread` in the R documentation.

There's more...

One of the limitations currently in R is that data imported into R needs to fit into the memory of the host computer. For large datasets, using an SQL-based database for data storage and manipulation takes advantage of the speed of the SQL-based database and circumvents R's memory limitation. Often, in enterprise environments, data is stored in Oracle, SAP, MySQL, or PostgreSQL databases.

The `sqldf` package is extremely useful if you are from an SQL background, and many entering the world of data science have such a background. This package allows you to use SQL commands and queries within R, and treats `data.frame` objects in R just as you would treat tables in an SQL database. It also allows you to connect with most SQL-based databases that you have access, including SQLite, MySQL, and PostgreSQL, among others.

As a demonstration, we can import data into an SQLite database, and then read and manipulate it there:

```
sqldf('attach blsdb as new')
read.csv.sql(file='2012.annual.singlefile.csv', sql='create table
main.ann2012 as select * from file', dbname='blsdb')
ann2012 <- sqldf("select * from main.ann2012", dbname='blsdb')
```

 You must have SQLite installed and available on your machine for the preceding code to work. We will leave the installation up to you.

This will also take some time, but you'll have the data in SQLite. The preceding command actually doesn't ingest the data into R, but just imports it into SQLite.

You can import the data into R using the following command:

```
ann2012 <- sqldf("select * from main.ann2012", dbname='blsdb')
```

You can also choose to do your manipulations using SQL within SQLite with `sqldf`. For some users it will be easier to manipulate the data using SQL and then merely import the munged data into R.

As the first part of this book is focused on R, we will not delve deeper into the use of `sqldf` beyond what was presented here. However, if you are more familiar with SQL, you are welcome to replicate the steps presented in R in the various recipes with SQL commands.

See also

- Refer to the SQLite documentation available at `http://www.sqlite.org`
- Refer to the `data.table` documentation available at `http://datatable.r-forge.r-project.org/`

Exploring the employment data

Now that the data is imported into R and we have learned some strategies to import larger datasets into R, we will do some preliminary analysis of the data. The purpose is to see what the data looks like, identify idiosyncrasies, and ensure that the rest of the analysis plan can move forward.

Getting ready

If you completed the last recipe, you should be ready to go.

How to do it...

The following steps will walk you through this recipe to explore the data:

1. First, let's see how large this data is:

   ```
   > dim(ann2012)
   [1] 3556289      15
   ```

   Good, it's only 15 columns.

2. Let's take a peek at the first few rows so that we can see what the data looks like:

   ```
   head(ann2012)
   ```

You can refer to the following screenshot:

```
Console  D:/Github/practical-data-science/two/
> head(ann2012)
   area_fips own_code industry_code agglvl_code size_code year qtr disclosure_code
1:     01000        0            10          50         0 2012   A
2:     01000        1            10          51         0 2012   A
3:     01000        1           102          52         0 2012   A
4:     01000        1          1021          53         0 2012   A
5:     01000        1          1022          53         0 2012   A
6:     01000        1          1023          53         0 2012   A
   annual_avg_estabs_count annual_avg_emplvl total_annual_wages taxable_annual_wages
1:                  116233           1828248       3.792883e-313         6.632697e-314
2:                    1252             56031       2.072269e-314         0.000000e+00
3:                    1252             56031       2.072269e-314         0.000000e+00
4:                     599             11734       3.555500e-315         0.000000e+00
5:                       2                13       2.155134e-318         0.000000e+00
6:                      17               161       6.053830e-317         0.000000e+00
   annual_contributions annual_avg_wkly_wage avg_annual_pay
1:          2.07203e-315                  808          41990
2:          0.00000e+00                 1440          74857
3:          0.00000e+00                 1440          74857
4:          0.00000e+00                 1179          61330
5:          0.00000e+00                  662          34437
6:          0.00000e+00                 1468          76343
> |
```

What are the variables `own_code`, `industry_code`, and so on, and what do they mean? We might need more data to understand this data.

3. There is also a weird idiosyncrasy in this data. Some of the values for `total_annual_wages`, `taxable_annual_wages`, and `annual_contributions` look impossibly small. A peek at the actual data shows that these numbers don't appear to be correct. However, `fread` actually gives an indication of what is going on:

```
ann2012 <- fread('data/2012.annual.singlefile.csv', sep=',',
colClasses=c('character', 'integer', 'integer', 'integer',
'integer', 'integer', 'character',rep('integer',8)))
```

You can refer to the following screenshot:

```
> ann2012 <- fread('data/2012.annual.singlefile.csv', sep=',',
+               colClasses=c('character','integer','integer','integer','integer',
+                            'integer','character',rep('integer',8)))
Read 3556289 rows and 15 (of 15) columns from 0.191 GB file in 00:00:04
Warning message:
In fread("data/2012.annual.singlefile.csv", sep = ",", colClasses = c("character",  :
  Some columns have been read as type 'integer64' but package bit64 isn't loaded. Those column
s will display as strange looking floating point values. There is no need to reload the data. Ju
st require(bit64) to obtain the integer64 print method and print the data again.
```

4. This points to the fact that the `bit64` package might be needed to properly display these large numbers. Installing and loading this package, and then re-importing the data corrects the problem, as seen in the following command lines:

```
install.packages('bit64')
library('bit64')
ann2012 <- fread('data/2012.annual.singlefile.csv', sep=',',
  colClasses=c('character', 'integer', 'integer', 'integer',
  'integer', 'integer', 'character',rep('integer',8)))
```

You can refer to the following screenshot:

```
> head(ann2012)
   area_fips own_code industry_code agglvl_code size_code year qtr disclosure_code
1:    01000        0            10          50         0 2012   A
2:    01000        1            10          51         0 2012   A
3:    01000        1           102          52         0 2012   A
4:    01000        1          1021          53         0 2012   A
5:    01000        1          1022          53         0 2012   A
6:    01000        1          1023          53         0 2012   A
   annual_avg_estabs_count annual_avg_emplvl total_annual_wages taxable_annual_wages
1:                  116233           1828248          76768801894          13424728725
2:                    1252             56031           4194319351                    0
3:                    1252             56031           4194319351                    0
4:                     599             11734            719641114                    0
5:                       2                13               436204                    0
6:                      17               161             12253089                    0
   annual_contributions annual_avg_wkly_wage avg_annual_pay
1:             419383612                  808          41990
2:                     0                 1440          74857
3:                     0                 1440          74857
4:                     0                 1179          61330
5:                     0                  662          34437
6:                     0                 1468          76343
```

How it works...

The `head` command displays the first few lines (the default is the top six lines) of a data frame. We notice that some of the headings are self-explanatory, but some allude to codes that we currently don't have access to. We will have to obtain additional data in order to make a meaningful analysis. We could have looked at the data without importing it into R. The UNIX command, `less`, and the **Windows PowerShell** command, `type`, could have shown us the same thing as `head` did.

See also

- Refer to the documentation for the dataset available at
  `http://www.bls.gov/cew/doc/layouts/csv_annual_layout.htm`

Obtaining and merging additional data

In the previous recipe, we found that additional data was needed to understand what the data in the CSV file actually represents, and this recipe will directly address this need.

Getting ready

We can find additional data on the BLS website at `http://www.bls.gov/cew/datatoc.htm` under the header **Associated Codes and Titles**. There are five files there, which we will download to our computer. They are as follows:

- `agglevel_titles.csv`
  (`http://www.bls.gov/cew/doc/titles/agglevel/agglevel_titles.csv`)
- `area_titles.csv`
  (`http://www.bls.gov/cew/doc/titles/area/area_titles.csv`)
- `industry_titles.csv`
  (`http://www.bls.gov/cew/doc/titles/industry/industry_titles.csv`)
- `ownership_titles.csv`
  (`http://www.bls.gov/cew/doc/titles/ownership/ownership_titles.csv`)
- `size_titles.csv`
  (`http://www.bls.gov/cew/doc/titles/size/size_titles.csv`)

We download them to our computer, remembering where we stored them. We need to get ready to import them into R and merge them with our original data.

How to do it...

The following steps will lead you through loading these files into R and joining them into a larger data frame:

1. We will now import these data files into R using the following command lines:

```
for(u in c('agglevel','area','industry', 'ownership','size')){
assign(u,read.csv(paste('data/',u,'_titles.csv',sep=''),strings
AsFactors=
F))
}
```

   This is an example of code that makes it easier for us to do repeated tasks.

2. Each of these datasets has exactly one variable (column header) in common with our original data ann2012 as shown in the following screenshot:

```
> intersect(names(agglevel),names(ann2012))
[1] "agglvl_code"
> intersect(names(industry), names(ann2012))
[1] "industry_code"
> intersect(names(area), names(ann2012))
[1] "area_fips"
> intersect(names(ownership),names(ann2012))
[1] "own_code"
> intersect(names(size), names(ann2012))
[1] "size_code"
```

3. Hence it should be fairly easy to combine the datasets together. We'll join four of these datasets with ann2012 now, and save area, that is, the data from area_titles.csv, for the next recipe, since we want to manipulate it a bit:

```
codes <- c('agglevel','industry','ownership','size')
ann2012full <- ann2012
for(i in 1:length(codes)){
  eval(parse(text=paste('ann2012full <- left_join(ann2012full,
',codes[i],')', sep='')))
}
```

The end result is shown in the following screenshot:

```
> head(ann2012full)
  area_fips own_code industry_code agglvl_code size_code year qtr disclosure_code
1     01000        0            10          50         0 2012   A
2     01000        1            10          51         0 2012   A
3     01000        1           102          52         0 2012   A
4     01000        1          1021          53         0 2012   A
5     01000        1          1022          53         0 2012   A
6     01000        1          1023          53         0 2012   A
  annual_avg_estabs_count annual_avg_emplvl total_annual_wages taxable_annual_wages
1                  116233           1828248         76768801894          13424728725
2                    1252             56031          4194319351                    0
3                    1252             56031          4194319351                    0
4                     599             11734           719641114                    0
5                       2                13              436204                    0
6                      17               161            12253089                    0
  annual_contributions annual_avg_wkly_wage avg_annual_pay
1            419383612                  808          41990
2                    0                 1440          74857
3                    0                 1440          74857
4                    0                 1179          61330
5                    0                  662          34437
6                    0                 1468          76343
                              agglvl_title                         industry_title
1                      State, Total Covered                 Total, all industries
2      State, Total -- by ownership sector                 Total, all industries
3     State, by Domain -- by ownership sector                  Service-providing
4 State, by Supersector -- by ownership sector Trade, transportation, and utilities
5 State, by Supersector -- by ownership sector                       Information
6 State, by Supersector -- by ownership sector              Financial activities
                own_title           size_title
1      Total Covered All establishment sizes
2 Federal Government All establishment sizes
3 Federal Government All establishment sizes
4 Federal Government All establishment sizes
5 Federal Government All establishment sizes
6 Federal Government All establishment sizes
```

How it works...

In *step 1* of the *How to do it...* section, we want to assign each dataset to its own object. We can write an individual line of code for each import, but this code allows us to do this much faster, and it will be easier to maintain in the future. The `assign` command takes two basic inputs: a variable name and a value to be assigned to the variable name. The `for` loop here doesn't iterate over numbers, but over objects. At the first iteration, `u` takes the value `agglevel`. The `assign` function takes the name `agglevel` and assigns it the result of the `read.csv` command. Within the `paste` command, we again use the value of `u`, since all the files we are importing have the same naming convention. It is this common naming convention that allows us to use this type of coding. Thus, the first iteration gives `assign('agglevel', read.csv('data/agglevel_title.csv'))`, and so forth.

In *step 2*, we join the datasets together. We first copy the original data to a new name, `ann2012full`, so that we can build up this new dataset without corrupting the original data in case something goes wrong. We then use a macro-like construct to join all the new datasets to the original one, iterating over numbers in the `for` loop and the indices of the vector code.

Let's work our way inside out in this complex command (a sound strategy to understand complex code in general). Within the `paste` command, we create the command we would like evaluated. We want to do a `left_join` (this is from the `dplyr` package), joining `ann2012full` with `agglevel` in the first iteration. The `left_join` ensures that all the rows of `ann2012full` are preserved, and the rows of `agglevel` are appropriately replicated to match the number of rows in `ann2012full`. Since there is only one common variable in the two datasets, `left_join` automatically chooses to join using this.

 In general, `left_join` will join the two datasets using all the variable names it finds common between the two. If you do not want this, you can specify which variables you want to use for the join by specifying, for example, `left_join(ann2012full, agglevel, by="agglvl_code")`.

The `eval` statement then evaluates the command we constructed using the `paste` command. We iterate over the names in code so that each of the four datasets gets joined with `ann2012full`.

A quick check will show that the number of rows in `ann2012full` after the joins, and in `ann2012`, is the same.

Adding geographical information

The main purpose of this chapter is to look at the geographical distribution of wages across the US. Mapping this out requires us to first have a map. Fortunately, maps of the US, both at the state and county-levels, are available in the `maps` package, and the data required to make the maps can be extracted. We will align our employment data with the map data in this recipe so that the correct data is represented at the right location on the map.

Getting ready

We already have the `area` dataset imported into R, so we are ready to go.

How to do it...

The following steps will guide you through the process of creating your first map in R:

1. Let's first look at the data in `area`:

```
head (area)
```

The output is shown in the following screenshot:

```
> head(area)
  area_fips                                    area_title
1    US000                                     U.S. TOTAL
2    USCMS    U.S. Combined Statistical Areas (combined)
3    USMSA U.S. Metropolitan Statistical Areas (combined)
4    USNMS U.S. Nonmetropolitan Area Counties (combined)
5    01000                           Alabama -- Statewide
6    01001                        Autauga County, Alabama
```

We see that there is something called `area_fips` here. **Federal Information Processing Standards (FIPS)** codes are used by the Census Bureau to designate counties and other geographical areas in the US.

2. We want to capitalize all the names, according to the conventions. We'll write a small function to do this:

```
simpleCap <-function(x){
  if(!is.na(x)){
    s <- strsplit(x,' ')[[1]]
    paste(toupper(substring(s,1,1)), substring(s,2), sep='',
collapse=' ')
  } else {NA}
}
```

3. The `maps` package contains two datasets that we will use; they are `county.fips` and `state.fips`. We will first do some transformations. If we look at `county.fips`, we notice that the FIPS code there is missing a leading `0` on the left for some of the codes. All the codes in our employment data comprise of five digits:

```
> data(county.fips)
> head(county.fips)
  fips          polyname
1 1001  alabama,autauga
2 1003  alabama,baldwin
3 1005  alabama,barbour
4 1007     alabama,bibb
5 1009   alabama,blount
6 1011  alabama,bullock
```

4. The `stringr` package will help us out here:

```
county.fips$fips <- str_pad(county.fips$fips, width=5, pad="0")
```

5. We want to separate the county names from the `polyname` column in `county.fips`. We'll get the state names from `state.fips` in a minute:

```
county.fips$polyname <- as.character(county.fips$polyname)
county.fips$county <- sapply(
  gsub('[a-z\ ]+,([a-z\ ]+)','\\1',county.fips$polyname),
simpleCap)
county.fips <- unique(county.fips)
```

6. The `state.fips` data involves a lot of details:

```
> data(state.fips)
```

The output is shown in the following screenshot:

```
> head(state.fips)
  fips ssa region division abb    polyname
1    1   1             3    6  AL     alabama
2    4   3             4    8  AZ     arizona
3    5   4             3    7  AR    arkansas
4    6   5             4    9  CA  california
5    8   6             4    8  CO    colorado
6    9   7             1    1  CT connecticut
```

7. We'll again pad the `fips` column with a `0`, if necessary, so that they have two digits, and capitalize the state names from `polyname` to create a new `state` column. The code is similar to the one we used for the `county.fips` data:

```
state.fips$fips <- str_pad(state.fips$fips, width=2, pad="0",
side='left')
state.fips$state <- as.character(state.fips$polyname)
state.fips$state <- gsub("([a-z\ ]+):[a-z\
\\']+",'\\1',state.fips$state)
state.fips$state <- sapply(state.fips$state, simpleCap)
```

8. We make sure that we have unique rows. We need to be careful here, since we only need to have uniqueness in the `fips` and `state` values, and not in the other code:

```
mystatefips <-unique(state.fips[,c('fips','abb','state')])
```

9. The `unique` function, when applied to a `data.frame` object, returns the unique rows of the object. You might be used to using `unique` on a single vector to find the unique elements in the vector.

10. We get a list of the lower 48 state names. We will filter our data to look only at these states:

```
lower48 <- setdiff(unique(state.fips$state),c('Hawaii','Alaska'))
```

The `setdiff` set operation looks for all the elements in the first set that are not in the second set.

11. We put all this information together into a single dataset, `myarea`:

```
myarea <- merge(area, county.fips, by.x='area_fips', by.y='fips',
all.x=T)
myarea$state_fips <- substr(myarea$area_fips, 1, 2)
myarea <- merge(myarea, mystatefips,by.x='state_fips',by.y='fips',
all.x=T)
```

12. Lastly, we join the geographical information with our dataset, and filter it to keep only data on the lower 48 states:

```
ann2012full <- left_join(ann2012full, myarea)
ann2012full <- filter(ann2012full, state %in% lower48)
```

13. We now store the final dataset in an R data (`rda`) file on disk. This provides an efficient storage mechanism for R objects:

```
save(ann2012full, file='data/ann2014full.rda',compress=T)
```

How it works...

The 12 steps of this recipe covered quite a bit of material, so let's dive into some of the details, starting with step 2. The `simpleCap` function is an example of a function in R. We use functions to encapsulate repeated tasks, reducing code duplication and ensuring that errors have a single point of origin. If we merely repeat code, changing the input values manually, we can easily make errors in transcription, break hidden assumptions, or accidentally overwrite important variables. Furthermore, if we want to modify the code, we have to do it manually at every duplicate location. This is tedious and error-prone, and so we make functions, a best practice that we strongly encourage you to follow.

The `simpleCap` function uses three functions: `strsplit, toupper,` and `substring`. The `strsplit` function splits strings (or a vector of strings) whenever it finds the string fragment to split on (in our case, `' '`, or a space). The `substring` function extracts substrings from strings between the character locations specified. Specifying only one character location implies extracting from this location to the end of the string. The `toupper` function changes the case of a string from lowercase to uppercase. The reverse operation is done by `tolower`.

From *step 3*, packages often have example data bundled with them. `county.fips` and `state.fips` are examples of datasets that have been bundled into the `maps` package.

The `stringr` package, used in *step 4*, is another package by *Dr. Wickham*, which provides string manipulation functions. Here, we use `str_pad`, which pads a string with a character (here, `0`) to give the string a particular width.

In step 5, we use the inbuilt regular expression (regex) capabilities in R. We won't talk about regular expressions too much here. The `gsub` function looks for the first pattern and substitutes the second pattern in the string specified as third. Here, the pattern we're looking for comprises of one or more letters or spaces (`[a-z\ ]+`), then a comma, and then one or more letters or spaces. The second set of letters and spaces is what we want to keep, so we put parentheses around it. The `1` pattern says to replace the entire pattern with the first pattern we used parentheses around. This replacement happens for every element of the `polyname` field.

Since we want capitalization for every element in `polyname`, we can use a `for` loop, but choose to use the more efficient `sapply` instead. Every element in `polyname` is passed through the `simpleCap` function, and is thus capitalized in *step 7*.

In step 10, we join the `area`, `county.fips`, and `mystatefips` datasets together. We use the `merge` function rather than `left_join`, since the variables we want to join on have different names for different `data.frame` objects. The `merge` function in the R standard library allows this flexibility. To ensure a left join, we specify `all.x=TRUE`.

In step 11, we join the `myarea` data frame to our `ann2014full` dataset. We then use the **filter** function to subset the data, restricting it to data from the lower 48 states. The `filter` function is from the `dplyr` package. We'll speak about the functionalities in `dplyr` in the next recipe.

See also

- Read about regular expressions in R at
  `http://stat.ethz.ch/R-manual/R-patched/library/base/html/regex.html`
- Refer to information about the **stringr** library available at
  `http://journal.r-project.org/archive/2010-2/RJournal_2010-2_Wickham.pd`
  `f`

Extracting state- and county-level wage and employment information

So far, we worked to get the data into shape for analysis. We'll now start with looking at the geographical distribution of the average annual pay per state and per county.

Getting ready

If you have thoroughly followed the recipes in this chapter until now, you will have the data in a form from where you can extract information at different levels. We're good to go!

How to do it...

We will first extract data from `ann2014full` at the state-level. We need to perform the following steps:

1. We look at the `aggregate` state-level data. A peek at `agglevel` tells us that the code for the level of data that we want is `50`. Also, we only want to look at the average annual pay (`avg_annual_pay`) and the average annual employment level (`annual_avg_emplvl`), and not the other variables:

   ```
   d.state <- filter(ann2014full, agglvl_code==50)
   d.state <- select(d.state, state, avg_annual_pay,
   annual_avg_emplvl)
   ```

2. We create two new variables, `wage` and `empquantile`, which discretizes the `pay` and `employment` variables:

   ```
   d.state$wage <- cut(d.state$avg_annual_pay,
   quantile(d.state$avg_annual_pay, c(seq(0,.8, by=.2), .9, .95, .99,
   1)))
   d.state$empquantile <- cut(d.state$annual_avg_emplvl,
    quantile(d.state$annual_avg_emplvl,
   c(seq(0,.8,by=.2),.9,.95,.99,1))))
   ```

3. We also want the levels of these discretized variables to be meaningful. So we run the following commands:

   ```
   x <- quantile(d.state$avg_annual_pay, c(seq(0,.8,by=.2),.9, .95,
   .99, 1))
   xx <- paste(round(x/1000),'K',sep='')
   Labs <- paste(xx[-length(xx)],xx[-1],sep='-')
   levels(d.state$wage) <- Labs
   x <- quantile(d.state$annual_avg_emplvl, c(seq(0,.8,by=.2),.9, .95,
   .99, 1))
   xx <- ifelse(x>1000, paste(round(x/1000),'K',sep=''), round(x))
   Labs <- paste(xx[-length(xx)],xx[-1],sep='-')
   levels(d.state$empquantile) <- Labs
   ```

The 0, 0.2, 0.4, 0.6, 0.8, 0.9, 0.95, 0.99, and 1 quantiles of annual average pay is obtained, and it is then obtained per thousand number. The task is then repeated for the annual average employment.

4. We repeat this process at the county-level. We will find that the appropriate aggregation level code is 70 (`agglvl_code==70`). Everything else will be the same. Let's try to be a bit smarter this time around. First of all, we will discretize our variables the same way, and then change the labels to match. A function might be a good idea! The following command lines depict this:

```
Discretize <- function(x, breaks=NULL){
    if(is.null(breaks)){
        breaks <- quantile(x, c(seq(0,.8,by=.2),.9, .95, .99, 1))
        if (sum(breaks==0)>1) {
          temp <- which(breaks==0, arr.ind=TRUE)
          breaks <- breaks[max(temp):length(breaks)]
        }
    }
    x.discrete <- cut(x, breaks, include.lowest=TRUE)
    breaks.eng <- ifelse(breaks > 1000,
                         paste0(round(breaks/1000),'K'),
                         round(breaks))
    Labs <- paste(breaks.eng[-length(breaks.eng)], breaks.eng[-
1],
                      sep='-')
    levels(x.discrete) <- Labs
    return(x.discrete)
}
```

5. We alluded to the syntactic sugar of `dplyr` before; now, we see it in action. The `dplyr` package allows you to string together different operations, piping the results of one operation as input for the next, using the %.% operator. We'll describe the main operations of `dplyr` in the next recipe. Using some function encapsulation, the following code achieves everything that we spent significantly more lines of code to achieve in steps *1-3*:

```
d.cty <- filter(ann2012full, agglvl_code==70)%.%
select(state,county,abb, avg_annual_pay, annual_avg_emplvl)%.%
mutate(wage=Discretize(avg_annual_pay),
empquantile=Discretize(annual_avg_emplvl))
```

We now have the basic datasets that we need to visualize the geographic patterns in the data.

How it works...

The preceding five steps covered a lot of R code, so let's start breaking things down. The two functions, `filter` and `select`, are from `dplyr`. The `dplyr` package provides five basic functions, which are as follows:

- `filter`: This creates subsets of the data based on specified criteria
- `select`: This selects columns or variables from the dataset
- `mutate`: This creates new columns or variables in a dataset, which are derived from other variables in the dataset
- `group_by`: This splits the data by a variable or set of variables, and subsequent functions operate on each component defined by a unique variable value or combination
- `arrange`: This rearranges the data (or sorts it) according to variable(s) in the dataset

Each of these functions can operate on a `data.frame`, `data.table`, or `tbl` object, which is part of `dplyr`.

The `cut` function discretizes a continuous variable based on specified breakpoints or thresholds. Here, we specify the thresholds based on quantiles of the variable. We specify which quantiles we want by a sequence of fractions:

```
c(seq(0, .8, by=.2), .9, .95, .99, 1)
```

This is done using the `seq` function to create a regular sequence of numbers with a start value, an end value, and the difference between two successive values.

In step 3, we take the specified thresholds and format them. Numbers above 1,000 are truncated at the thousands place and appended with a `K`, as is conventionally seen. Using `round` without specifying the number of decimal places implies no decimal places.

Further, in step 3, we want our labels to represent a range. So we need to create the labels by putting a dash (–) between successive values of our formatted thresholds. One way of doing this is to create two copies of the vector of thresholds, one without the last element and another without the first element. We then paste them together with –. Notice that this trick allows successive thresholds to be aligned and pasted together. If you're not convinced, print out `xx[-length(xx)]` and `xx[-1]`, and see for yourself.

The `Discretize` function encapsulates the work we were doing in discretizing our outcomes and formatting their labels.

This code snippet uses the syntax of `dplyr` to string together functions. We first subset the original data, keeping only data that has `agglvl_code=50` (note the `==` in the code). We then pipe the resulting reduced data into the second function, `select`, which keeps only the four variables we're interested in. This further reduces data, and it is then inputted into the `mutate` function, which then creates two new variables in the data object. This final object is then stored with the variable name `d.cty`.

See also

- Get more details about `dplyr` at
  `http://blog.rstudio.org/2014/01/17/introducing-dplyr/`

Visualizing geographical distributions of pay

We created datasets that contain the data we need to visualize average pay and employment by county and state. In this recipe, we will visualize the geographical distribution of pay by shading the appropriate areas of the map with a color that maps to a particular value or range of values. This is commonly referred to as a chloropleth map; this visualization type has become increasingly popular over the last few years as it has become much simpler to make such maps, especially online. Other geographic visualizations will overlay a marker or some other shape to denote data; there is no need to fill specific shapes with geographically meaningful boundaries.

Getting ready

After the last recipe, you should be ready to use the datasets we created to visualize geographical distributions. We will use the ggplot2 package to generate our visualizations. We will also use the RColorBrewer package, which provides palettes of colors that are visually appealing. If you don't currently have RColorBrewer, install it using install.packages('RColorBrewer', repos='http://cran.r-project.org').

How to do it...

The following steps walk you through the creation of this geospatial data visualization:

1. We first need to get some data on the map itself. The ggplot2 package provides a convenient function, map_data, to extract this from data bundled in the maps package:

   ```
   library(ggplot2)
   library(RColorBrewer)
   state_df <- map_data('state')
   county_df <- map_data('county')
   ```

2. We now do a bit of transforming to make this data conform to our data:

   ```
   transform_mapdata <- function(x){
      names(x)[5:6] <- c('state','county')
      for(u in c('state','county')){
        x[,u] <- sapply(x[,u],simpleCap)
      }
      return(x)
   }
   state_df <- transform_mapdata(state_df)
   county_df <- transform_mapdata(county_df)
   ```

3. The `data.frame` objects, `state_df` and `county_df`, contain the latitude and longitude of points. This is our primary graphical data and it needs to be joined with the data we created in the previous recipe, which contains what is in effect the color information for the map:

```
chor <- left_join(state_df, d.state, by='state')
ggplot(chor, aes(long,lat,group=group))+
geom_polygon(aes(fill=wage))+geom_path(color='black',size=0.2) +
scale_fill_brewer(palette='PuRd') +
theme(axis.text.x=element_blank(),
axis.text.y=element_blank(), axis.ticks.x=element_blank(),
axis.ticks.y=element_blank())
```

This gives us the following figure that depicts the distribution of average annual pay by state:

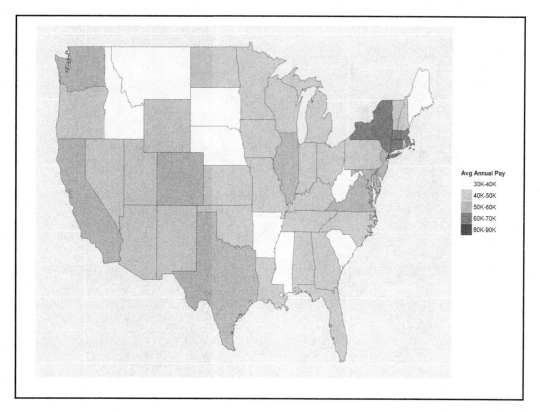

4. We can similarly create a visualization of the average annual pay by county, which will give us more granular information about the geographical distribution of wages:

```
chor <- left_join(county_df, d.cty)
ggplot(chor, aes(long,lat, group=group))+
  geom_polygon(aes(fill=wage))+
  geom_path( color='white',alpha=0.5,size=0.2)+
  geom_polygon(data=state_df, color='black',fill=NA)+
  scale_fill_brewer(palette='PuRd')+
  labs(x='',y='', fill='Avg Annual Pay')+
  theme(axis.text.x=element_blank(), axis.text.y=element_blank(),
axis.ticks.x=element_blank(), axis.ticks.y=element_blank())
```

This produces the following figure showing the geographical distribution of average annual pay by county:

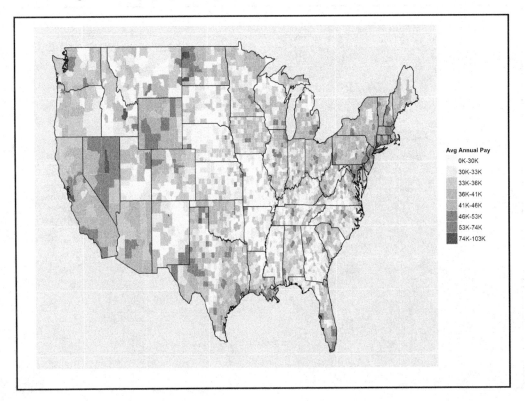

It is evident from the preceding figure that there are well-paying jobs in western North Dakota, Wyoming, and northwestern Nevada, most likely driven by new oil exploration opportunities in these areas. The more obvious urban and coastal areas also show up quite nicely.

How it works...

Let's dive into the explanation of how the preceding 4 steps work. The `map_data` function is provided by `ggplot2` to extract map data from the `maps` package. In addition to county and state, it can also extract data for the `france`, `italy`, `nz`, `usa`, `world`, and `world2` maps provided by the `maps` package.

The columns that contain state and county information in `county_df` and `state_df` are originally named `region` and `subregion`. In step 2, we need to change their names to `state` and `county`, respectively, to make joining this data with our employment data easier. We also capitalize the names of the states and counties to conform to the way we formatted the data in our `employment` dataset.

For the creation of the map in step 3, we create the plotting dataset by joining `state_df` and `d.state` using the name of the state. We then use `ggplot` to draw the map of the US and fill in each state with a color corresponding to the level of wage and the discretized average annual pay created in the previous recipe. To elaborate, we establish that the data for the plot comes from `chor`, and we draw polygons (`geom_polygon`) based on the latitude and longitude of the borders of each state, filling them with a color depending on how high wage is, and then we draw the actual boundaries of the states (`geom_path`) in black. We specify that we will use a color palette that starts at white, goes through purple, and has red corresponding to the highest level of wage. The remainder of the code is formatted by specifying labels and removing axis annotations and ticks from the plot.

For step 4, the code is essentially the same as step 3, except that we draw polygons for the boundaries of the counties rather than the states. We add a layer to draw the state boundaries in black (`geom_polygon(data=state_df, color='black', fill=NA)`), in addition to the county boundaries in white.

See also

- Refer to the `ggplot2` documentation available at `http://www.ggplot2.org`

Exploring where the jobs are, by industry

In the previous recipe, we saw how to visualize the top-level aggregate data on pay. The employment dataset has more granular data, divided by public/private sectors and types of jobs. The types of jobs in this data follow a hierarchical coding system called **North American Industry Classification System** (**NIACS**). In this recipe, we will consider four particular industries and look at visualizing the geographical distribution of employment in these industries, restricted to private sector jobs.

We will look at four industrial sectors in this recipe:

- Agriculture, forestry, fishing, and hunting (NIACS 11)
- Mining, quarrying, and oil and gas extraction (NIACS 21)
- Finance and insurance (NIACS 52)
- Professional and technical services (NIACS 54)

How to do it...

We need to create a subset of the employment data, including the data for industrial sectors, but restricting it to the private sector, by performing the following steps:

1. We start by filtering the data by the conditions we are imposing on the industry and private sectors, and keeping only the relevant variables:

```
d.sectors <- filter(ann2012full, industry_code %in%
c(11,21,54,52),
own_code==5, # Private sector
agglvl_code == 74 # county-level
) %.%
select(state,county,industry_code, own_code,agglvl_code,
       industry_title, own_title, avg_annual_pay,
       annual_avg_emplvl)%.%
mutate(wage=Discretize(avg_annual_pay),
emplevel=Discretize(annual_avg_emplvl))
d.sectors <- filter(d.sectors, !is.na(industry_code))
```

 Here, our selection is based on a set of industry codes, and we restrict ourselves to county-level data. This code is different from before since we're now looking at industry-specific data.

2. We now create the visualization using `ggplot2`. This visualization will be an array of four panels, one for each industrial sector. Each panel will have a county-level map of the US, with colors signifying the level of employment in each county in 2012 in each particular industry. We will also choose a blue-dominated palette for this visualization:

```
chor <- left_join(county_df, d.sectors)
ggplot(chor, aes(long,lat,group=group))+
  geom_polygon(aes(fill=emplevel))+
  geom_polygon(data=state_df, color='black',fill=NA)+
  scale_fill_brewer(palette='PuBu')+
  facet_wrap(~industry_title, ncol=2, as.table=T)+
  labs(fill='Avg Employment Level',x='',y='')+
  theme(axis.text.x=element_blank(),
  axis.text.y=element_blank(),
 axis.ticks.x=element_blank(),
 axis.ticks.y=element_blank())
```

This produces the following visualization, showing geographical distribution of employment by industry:

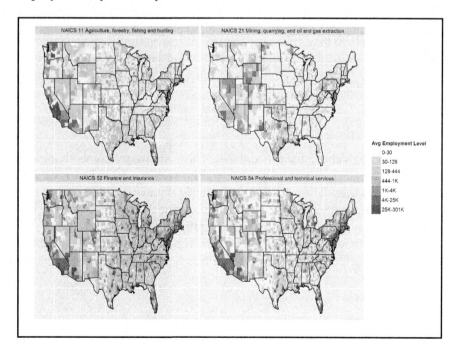

How it works...

In this recipe, we used the dplyr functions for data munging. One of our filter criteria was that the industry_code variable should have one of the values out of 11, 21, 52, or 54. This was achieved by the %in% operator, which is a set operation. It asks if an element on the left is a member of the set on the right. We have multiple criteria in the filter statement, separated by commas. This implies an AND relationship in that all of the criteria must be satisfied in order for the data to pass the filter.

We noticed that there were some missing values in the industry code. This resulted in an extra panel in the visualization, corresponding to data where the industry code was missing. We didn't want this, so we filtered out this data in this first step.

In the second step, the command to create the visualization is essentially the same as in the previous recipe, except for the following line:

```
facet_wrap(~industry_title, ncol=2)
```

This command splits the data up by the value of industry_title, creates separate visualizations for each value of industry_title, and puts them back onto a grid with two columns and an appropriate number of rows. We also used industry_title instead of industry_code here (they give the same visualization) so that the labeling of the panels is understandable, rather than comprising just some numbers that require the reader to look up their meaning.

There's more...

This recipe is the tip of the iceberg for this dataset. There are many levels that can be explored with this data, both in terms of private/public sectors and in terms of drilling down into different industries. The additional quarterly data from 2012 is also available and can shed light on temporal patterns. The annual and quarterly data is available from 1990 onwards. Further analyses are possible by the association of temporal patterns of employment with other socioeconomic events. The choroplethr and rMaps packages provide ways of creating animations over time for this type of data.

See also

- Read about the `rMaps` package at `http://rmaps.github.io` and `http://rmaps.github.io/blog/posts/animated-choropleths/`
- Read about the `choroplethr` package at `https://github.com/trulia/choroplethr`
- Have a look at the `choropleth` challenge results at `http://blog.revolutionanalytics.com/2009/11/choropleth-challenge-resul t.html`
- Look at examples of animated maps at `http://www.r-bloggers.com/animated-choropleths-using-animation-ggplot2 -rcharts-googlevis-and-shiny-to-visualize-violent-crime-rates-in- different-us-states-across-5-decades/`

Animating maps for a geospatial time series

One of the real interests in this project is to see how wage patterns, as a surrogate for income patterns, changed over time. The QCEW site provides data from 2003 to 2012. In this recipe, we will look at the overall average annual pay by county for each of these years and create an animation that displays the changes in the pay pattern over this period.

Getting ready

For this recipe, we need to download the annual data for the years 2003 to 2011 from the BLS website, at `http://www.bls.gov/cew/datatoc.htm`. You will need to download the files corresponding to these years for the QCEW NIACS-based data files in the column `CSVs Single Files-Annual Averages`. Store these files (which are compressed `.zip` files) in the same location as the zipped 2012 data that you downloaded at the beginning of this project. Don't unzip them! You must also download and install the `choroplethr` package using `install.packages('chloroplethr')`, if you haven't already done so.

> Note that this recipe is relatively memory-intensive. Those running on 32-bit machines might face out-of-memory issues.

How to do it...

What we need to do is import the data for all the years from 2003 through 2012 and extract data for the county-level (`agglvl_code==70`) average annual pay (`avg_annual_pay`) for each county, plot it, and then string the pay values together in an animation. Since we basically need to do the same thing for each year's data, we can do this in a `for` loop, and we can create functions to encapsulate the repeated actions. We start by writing code for a single year, performing the following steps:

1. We import the data from the ZIP file that we call `zipfile` in this prototype code. In reality, the filenames are of the pattern `2003_annual_singlefile.zip`, and the CSV files in them are of the pattern `2003.annual.singlefile.csv`. We will use the common patterns in the ZIP and CSV files in our code to automate the process. For me, the data lies in a folder called `data`, which is reflected in the following code:

```
unzip(file.path('data',zipfile), exdir='data') # unzips the file
csvfile <- gsub('zip','csv', zipfile) # Change file name
csvfile <- gsub('_','.',csvfile) # Change _ to . in name
dat <- fread(file.path('data', csvfile)) # read data
```

2. We now join the employment data with the geographical data from `myarea`:

```
dat <- left_join(dat, myarea)
```

3. We then use the `dplyr` functions to extract the county-level aggregate pay data, keeping the state and county information:

```
dat <- filter(dat, agglvl_code==70) %.% # County-level aggregate
select(state, county, avg_annual_pay) # Keep variables
```

4. We then encapsulate the actions in steps 1 through 3 in a function:

```
get_data <- function(zipfile){
  unzip(file.path('data',zipfile), exdir='data') # unzips the file
  csvfile <- gsub('zip','csv', zipfile) # Change file name
  csvfile <- gsub('_','.',csvfile) # Change _ to . in name
  dat <- fread(file.path('data', csvfile)) # read data
  dat <- left_join(dat, myarea)
  dat <- filter(dat, agglvl_code==70) %.% # County-level aggregate
  select(state, county, avg_annual_pay) # Keep variables
  return(dat)
}
```

5. We now have to repeat this for each of the 10 years and store the data. For this type of data, a list object usually makes sense:

```
files <- dir('data', pattern='annual_singlefile.zip') # file names
n <- length(files)
dat_list <- vector('list',n) # Initialize the list
for(i in 1:n){
  dat_list[[i]]<- get_data(files[i])  # ingest data
  names(dat_list)[i] <- substr(files[i],1,4) #label list with years
}
```

6. Next, we start creating the visualizations. Since we are essentially creating 10 visualizations, the colors need to mean the same thing on all of them for comparison purposes. So the discretization needs to be the same for all the years:

```
annpay <- ldply(dat_list) # puts all the data together
breaks <- quantile(annpay$avg_annual_pay,
c(seq(0,.8,.2),.9,.95,.99,1)) # Makes a common set of breaks
```

7. We will create the same visualization for each year, using the same breaks. Let's create a function for this common visualization to be produced. We will use ggplot2 for the visualizations. The input values are the data that we create using get_data, and the output is a plot object that can create the visualization:

```
mychoro <- function(d, fill_label=''){
  # d has a variable "outcome" that
  # is plotted as the fill measure
  chor <- left_join(county_df, d)
  plt <- ggplot(chor, aes(long,lat, group=group))+
  geom_polygon(aes(fill=outcome))+
  geom_path(color='white',alpha=0.5,size=0.2)+
  geom_polygon(data=state_df, color='black',fill=NA)+
  scale_fill_brewer(palette='PuRd')+
  labs(x='',y='', fill=fill_label)+
  theme(axis.text.x=element_blank(),
  axis.text.y=element_blank(),
  axis.ticks.x=element_blank(),axis.ticks.y=element_blank())
  return(plt)
}
```

8. We now create `plot` objects for each year using a **for** loop. We store these objects in a list, with each element corresponding to each year. In the process, we create a new variable, `outcome`, which is the discretized pay variable, using the common breaks. This variable needs to be called `outcome` because of the way we designed the `mychoro` function:

```
plt_list <- vector('list',n)
for(i in 1:n){
   dat_list[[i]] <- mutate(dat_list[[i]],
   outcome=Discretize(avg_annual_pay,breaks=breaks))
   plt_list[[i]] <-
   mychoro(dat_list[[i]])+ggtitle(names(dat_list)[i])
}
```

9. The `choroplethr` package has the utility function, `choroplethr_animate`, which takes a list of `plot` objects created with **ggplot2** and makes a web page with an animated GIF, layering the plots we created in order. The default web file is `animated_choropleth.html`:

```
library(choroplethr)
choroplethr_animate(plt_list)
```

We extract three panels from this animation here to give you a flavor of what the animation looks like:

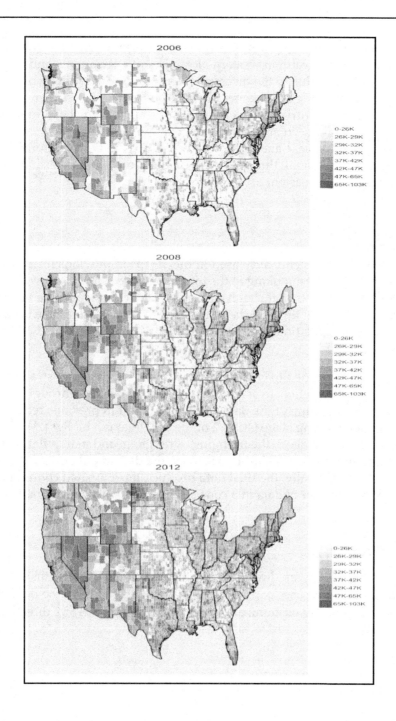

Even from this limited view of the data, we can see the striking growth of employment and wealth in western North Dakota, Wyoming, and northeast Nevada, probably due to the discovery, exploration, and mining of shale oil in this region. We can also see that generally, over the eight years shown here, pay has risen across the country; however, regions throughout the heart of the continental United States have seen almost no change in average pay over this period. We also see a clear increase and expansion of high pay in both California and the northeast. Recall that all three plots are on the same color scale, and so, the interpretation is consistent across them.

How it works...

We covered the individual functionality used in this recipe in previous recipes and so we will not repeat them. However, looking at the big picture here shows us two key points worth noting. First, we had to run through a common set of steps multiple times to create a single image. As we had to go through the same steps to create each image used in the final animation, we started to operationalize the code a bit, refactoring repeated code blocks into functions.

Secondly, the set of steps needed to create each image is another demonstration of the stages of the data science pipeline. In stage one, we acquire the data through the ingestion of CSV files. Our understanding of the dataset has been built in previous recipes, so the exploration and understanding stage (stage 2 of the pipeline) is a bit light. We join disparate datasets and filter them for stage 3, the munging, wrangling, and manipulation stage. For stage 4, analysis and modeling, we simply discretize the data and then map it to a particular but consistent color scale. Finally, the final data product, the animated choropleth, is used to communicate the vast amount of data in a concise and quickly understandable fashion.

There is more...

The R package `choroplethr` can directly create the individual choropleths using the `choropleth` function, which uses `ggplot2`. However, we didn't like the default appearance of the output, and customization was easier using `ggplot2` directly.

Dr. Vaidyanathan, the creator of the popular **rCharts** package, also created the `rMaps` package. It creates choropleths from R using JavaScript visualization libraries for presentation on the Web, and it can also create animated choropleths using the function `ichoropleth`. However, the package is still in development at the time of writing, so we didn't have the facility to create county-level maps. An example with state-level maps is shown in the `rMaps` blog at `http://rmaps.github.io/blog/posts/animated-choropleths/`.

Benchmarking performance for some common tasks

R and its package ecosystem often provide several alternative ways of performing the same task. R also promotes users to create their own functions for particular tasks. When execution time is important, benchmarking performance is necessary to see which strategy works best. We will concentrate on speed in this recipe. The two tasks we will look at are loading the data into R and joining two data objects based on a common variable. All tests are done on a Windows 7 desktop running a 2.4 GHz Intel processor with 8 GB of RAM.

Getting ready

We will use the `ann2012full` and `industry` data objects for our performance experiments here, along with the 2012 annual employment data CSV file for data loading. Since you already have these, you are good to go. If you don't, you will need to install the two functions, `rbenchmark` and `microbenchmark`, using the `install.packages()` command.

How to do it...

The following steps will walk us through benchmarking two different tasks in R:

1. Our first task is to load the employment data into R. The `2012.annual.singlefile.csv` file has *3,556,289* lines of data and 15 columns. While we used `fread` in this chapter, there are many other possible ways of importing this data, which are as follows:

The first and most standard way is to use `read.csv` to read the CSV file. You can also unzip the original `2012_annual_singlefile.zip` data file on the fly and read the data using `read.csv`. We can save the data to an `RData` file the first time we load it, and also subsequent times we load this file, to import the data into R

2. The most basic way to benchmark speed is using the `system.time` function, which measures the time (both elapsed and actual computing time) taken for the task to be performed:

```
> system.time(fread('data/2012.annual.singlefile.csv'))
   user   system elapsed
 14.817   0.443   15.23
```

Note that the times you see will be different than those listed in the preceding command.

3. However, there are packages in R that make benchmarking and comparing different functions much easier. We will introduce the `rbenchmark` package, which provides the `benchmark` function that allows the simultaneous comparison of different functions:

```
library(rbenchmark)
opload <- benchmark(
  CSV=read.csv('data/2012.annual.singlefile.csv',
  stringsAsFactors=F),
  CSVZIP=read.csv(unz('data/2012_annual_singlefile.zip',
   '2012.annual.singlefile.csv'), stringsAsFactors=F),
  LOAD = load('data/ann2012full.rda'),
  FREAD = fread('data/2012.annual.singlefile.csv'),
  order='relative', # Report in order from shortest to longest
  replications=5
)
```

You can refer to the following screenshot for the output of the preceding commands:

```
> opload
  test replications elapsed relative user.self sys.self user.child sys.child
4 FREAD            5   16.29    1.000     15.85     0.43         NA         NA
3 LOAD             5   79.67    4.891     79.10     0.50         NA         NA
1 CSV              5  189.30   11.621    160.82     2.54         NA         NA
2 CSVZIP           5  212.02   13.015    182.46     1.55         NA         NA
```

Note that the results are ordered, and the relative times are recorded under the `relative` column. This shows that `fread` is quite a bit faster than reading using `read.csv`. The very interesting thing is that, on an average, it is four times faster than loading the data from an `RData` file, which is the usual storage method for R data. It is apparently faster to load the data from the file using `fread` than storing the data in R's own serialized format!

4. Our second task is to perform a left outer join of two data objects. We'll look at a task that we have already performed-a left join of the employment data with the industry codes. A left join ensures that the rows of data on the *left* of the operation will be preserved through the operation, and the other data will be expanded by repetition or missing data to have the same number of rows. We used `left_join` in this chapter, but there are three other strategies that we can take, which are as follows:

   - The `merge` function available in R's standard library
   - The `join` function from the `plyr` package
   - The `merge` function from the `data.table` package, first transforming the data into `data.table` objects

5. We will again use the `benchmark` function to compare these strategies with `left_join`:

```
ann2012full_dt <- data.table(ann2012full, key='industry_code')
industry_dt <- data.table(industry, key='industry_code')
op <- benchmark(
    DT = data.table::merge(ann2012full_dt, industry_dt,
            by='industry_code', all.x=T),
    PLYR = plyr::join(ann2012full, industry,
          by='industry_code',type='left'),
    DPLYR = dplyr::left_join(ann2012full, industry),
    DPLYR2 = dplyr::left_join(ann2012full_dt, industry_dt),
    MERGE = merge(ann2012full, industry,
            by='industry_code', all.x=T),
    order='relative',
    replications=5
)
```

You can refer to the following screenshot for the output of the preceding commands:

```
> op
    test replications elapsed relative user.self sys.self user.child sys.child
1     DT            5    0.41    1.000      0.41     0.00         NA         NA
4 DPLYR2            5    4.90   11.951      4.24     0.63         NA         NA
3  DPLYR            5    5.40   13.171      4.52     0.86         NA         NA
2   PLYR            5   97.70  238.293     95.46     1.67         NA         NA
5  MERGE            5  207.14  505.220    204.14     2.54         NA         NA
```

Here, we see that the `data.table` method is a lot faster than any other strategy. Using `dplyr` is about 12 times slower for this particular task, `plyr` is about 100 times slower, and the standard `merge` method is 200 times slower. There is a bit of overhead in converting the `data.frame` objects to `data.table` objects, but the margin of advantage in this task overcomes this overhead.

How it works...

The basic workhorse of time benchmarking in R is the `system.time` function. This function records the time when evaluation of an expression starts, runs the expression, and then notes the time when it finishes. It then reports the difference of the two times. By default, garbage collection takes place before each evaluation so that the results are more consistent and maximal memory is freed for each evaluation.

The `benchmark` function in the `rbenchmark` package provides additional flexibility. It wraps the `system.time` function and allows several expressions to be evaluated in a single run. It also does some basic computations, such as relative times, to simplify reporting.

In terms of our tasks here, `fread` uses a powerful optimized C function to read the data, resulting in a high degree of speed optimization. The `read.csv` function just reads the data file line by line and parses the fields by the comma separator. We can get some speed improvements in our experiments by specifying the column types in `read.csv`, using the `colClasses` option, since determining data types consumes some execution time. The `load` function reads the data from the **RData** files created using the `save` function, which stores binary representations of R objects. It compresses the size of the data a lot, but we see that there are more efficient ways of reading data than loading the **RData** file.

The second task we set ourselves to benchmark is a left outer join of the employment data `ann2014full`, with the data object of the `industry` industry codes. The former has 3,556,289 rows and 15 columns, and the latter has 2,469 rows and two columns. They are merged based on the common variable, `industry_code`. In a left join, all the rows of `ann2014full` will be preserved. For this, the `merge` commands will use the `all.x=T` option. The `join` function has the `type='left'` option for a left join. For the **data.table** merge, we first convert the `data.frame` objects to `data.table` objects, specifying that each has the same key variable, (think index in a database) `industry_code`. The `data.table` objects are then merged using this key variable.

There is a bit of new code formatting in this code snippet. We use `plyr::join` and `dplyr::left_join`, rather than just `join` and `left_join`. This style of coding explicitly specifies that we are using a particular function from a particular package to avoid confusion. Sometimes, this style of coding is useful when you have functions with the same name in two different packages that are both loaded in R.

There's more...

The `data.table` package provides very fast tools for data loading, munging, and joining. The `data.table` object is a derivative object of the `data.frame` package, and many of the functions in R that input `data.frame` objects can also import `data.table` objects. It is for this reason that the `data.table` object becomes your default container for rectangular data.

See also

- Hadley Wickham has a very nice exposition on benchmarking that is part of his online book, available at `http://adv-r.had.co.nz/Performance.html`. He promotes the `microbenchmark` package for benchmarking purposes.

6
Driving Visual Analyses with Automobile Data

In this chapter, we will cover:

- Getting started with Jupyter
- Exploring Jupyter Notebook
- Preparing to analyze automobile fuel efficiencies
- Exploring and describing fuel efficiency data with Python
- Analyzing automobile fuel efficiency over time with Python
- Investigating the makes and models of automobiles with Python

Introduction

In the first chapter on R (Chapter 2, *Driving Visual Analysis with Automobile Data with R*), we walked through an analysis project that examined automobile fuel economy data using the R statistical programming language. This dataset, available at http://www.fueleconomy.go v/feg/epadata/vehicles.csv.zip, contains fuel efficiency performance metrics over time for all makes and models of automobiles in the United States of America. This dataset also contains numerous other features and attributes of the automobile models other than fuel economy, providing an opportunity to summarize and group the data so that we can identify interesting trends and relationships.

Unlike the first chapter on R, we will perform the entire analysis using Python. However, we will ask the same questions and follow the same sequence of steps as before, again following the data science pipeline. With study, this will allow you to see the similarities and differences between the two languages for a mostly identical analysis.

Here we used mostly pure Python with some help from NumPy and SciPy, either straight from the Python command line-also known as **Read-Eval-Print Loop** (REPL)-or from executable script files. In this chapter, we will take a very different approach using Python as a scripting language in an interactive fashion that is more similar to R. We will introduce the reader to the unofficial interactive environment of Python, IPython, and the Jupyter notebook, showing how to produce readable and well-documented analysis scripts. Furthermore, we will leverage the data analysis capabilities of the relatively new, but powerful Pandas library and the invaluable data frame data type that it offers. Pandas often allows us to complete complex tasks with fewer lines of code. The drawback to this approach is that while you don't have to reinvent the wheel for common data manipulation tasks, you do have to learn the API of a completely different package, which is Pandas.

The goal of this chapter is not to guide you through an analysis project that you have already completed, but to show you how that project can be completed in another language. More importantly, we want to get you, the reader, to become more introspective with your own code and analysis. Think not only about how something is done, but why something is done that way in that particular language. How does the language shape the analysis?

Getting started with IPython

IPython is the interactive computing shell for Python that will change the way you think about interactive shells. It brings to the table a host of very useful functionalities that will most likely become part of your default toolbox, including magic functions, tab completion, easy access to command-line tools, and much more. We will only scratch the surface here and strongly recommend that you keep exploring what can be done with IPython, see `http s://ipython.org/` for more details and options.

Getting ready

If you have completed the installation instructions in the first chapter, you should be ready to tackle the following recipes. Note that IPython 6.1, a major release, was launched in May 2017. The IPython session had been run in March 2017 on an earlier release of the interactive software.

How to do it...

The following steps will get you up and running with the IPython environment:

1. Open up a Terminal window on your computer and type `ipython`. You should be immediately presented with the following:

```
IPython: home/pranathi
pranathi@pranathi-Aspire-ES1-521:~$ ipython
Python 3.6.1 |Anaconda 4.4.0 (64-bit)| (default, May 11 2017, 13:09:58)
Type "copyright", "credits" or "license" for more information.

IPython 5.3.0 -- An enhanced Interactive Python.
?         -> Introduction and overview of IPython's features.
%quickref -> Quick reference.
help      -> Python's own help system.
object?   -> Details about 'object', use 'object??' for extra details.

In [1]:
```

Note that your version might be slightly different than what is shown in the preceding command-line output.

2. Just to show you how great IPython is, type in `ls`, and you would be greeted with the directory listing! Yes, you have access to common Unix commands straight from your Python prompt inside the Python interpreter.

3. Now, let's try changing directories. Type `cd` at the prompt, hit space, and now hit *Tab*. You should be presented with a list of directories available from within the current directory. Start typing the first few letters of the target directory, and then, hit *Tab* again. If there is only one option that matches, hitting the *Tab* key automatically will insert that name. Otherwise, the list of possibilities will show only those names that match the letters that you have already typed. Each letter that is entered acts as a filter when you press *Tab*.

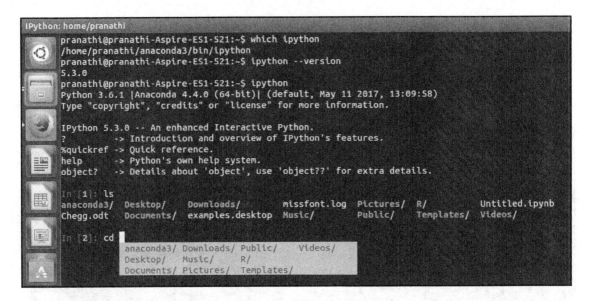

4. Now, type ?, and you will get a quick introduction to and an overview of IPython's features.

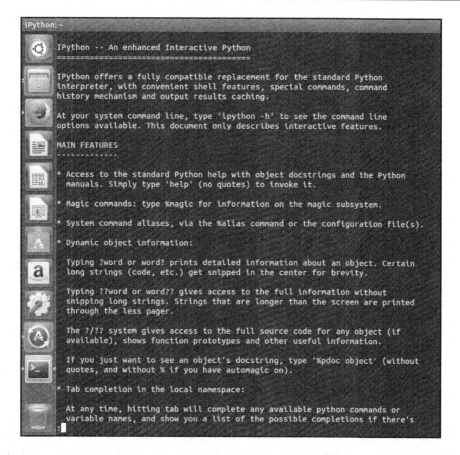

```
IPython: ~

IPython -- An enhanced Interactive Python
=========================================

IPython offers a fully compatible replacement for the standard Python
interpreter, with convenient shell features, special commands, command
history mechanism and output results caching.

At your system command line, type 'ipython -h' to see the command line
options available. This document only describes interactive features.

MAIN FEATURES
-------------

* Access to the standard Python help with object docstrings and the Python
  manuals. Simply type 'help' (no quotes) to invoke it.

* Magic commands: type %magic for information on the magic subsystem.

* System command aliases, via the %alias command or the configuration file(s).

* Dynamic object information:

  Typing ?word or word? prints detailed information about an object. Certain
  long strings (code, etc.) get snipped in the center for brevity.

  Typing ??word or word?? gives access to the full information without
  snipping long strings. Strings that are longer than the screen are printed
  through the less pager.

  The ?/?? system gives access to the full source code for any object (if
  available), shows function prototypes and other useful information.

  If you just want to see an object's docstring, type '%pdoc object' (without
  quotes, and without % if you have automagic on).

* Tab completion in the local namespace:

  At any time, hitting tab will complete any available python commands or
  variable names, and show you a list of the possible completions if there's
:
```

5. Let's take a look at the magic functions. These are special functions that IPython understands and will always start with the % symbol. The %paste function is one such example and it is amazing for copying and pasting Python code into IPython without losing proper indentation. A simple illustration is to type 2+3 in any text editor and copy it and then execute %paste in IPython.

6. We will try the %timeit magic function that intelligently benchmarks Python code. Enter the following commands:

```
In [2]: n=10000
   ...: %timeit range(n)
   ...:
```

We should get an output like this:

```
The slowest run took 4.74 times longer than the fastest. This could
mean that an intermediate result is being cached.
1000000 loops, best of 3: 1.83 mus per loop
```

Note that the range function in Python 3.x version is the `xrange` function from the earlier Python 2.x versions.

7. You can also easily run system commands by prefacing the command with an exclamation mark. Try the following command:

```
In [3]: !ping www.google.com
```

You should see the following output:

```
Pinging www.google.com [216.239.32.20] with 32 bytes of data:
Reply from 216.239.32.20: bytes=32 time=35ms TTL=57
Reply from 216.239.32.20: bytes=32 time=34ms TTL=57
Reply from 216.239.32.20: bytes=32 time=33ms TTL=57
Reply from 216.239.32.20: bytes=32 time=35ms TTL=57

Ping statistics for 216.239.32.20:
Packets: Sent = 4, Received = 4, Lost = 0 (0% loss),
Approximate round trip times in milli-seconds:
Minimum = 33ms, Maximum = 35ms, Average = 34ms
```

8. Finally, IPython provides an excellent command history. Simply press the up arrow key to access the previously entered command. Continue to press the up arrow key to walk backwards through the command list of your session and the down arrow key to come forward. Also, the magic `%history` command allows you to jump to a particular command number in the session. Type the following command to see the first command that you entered:

```
In [4]: %history 1
```

The complete screenshot of the IPython session is given below:

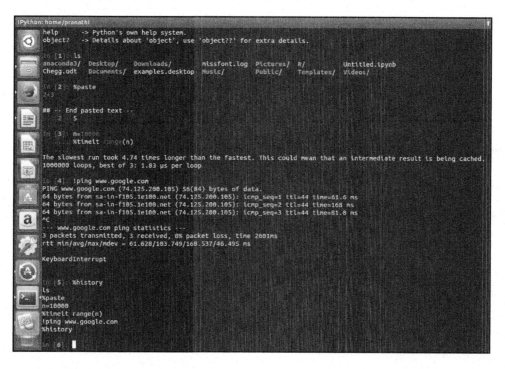

Now, type `exit` to drop out of IPython and back to your system Command Prompt.

How it works...

There isn't much to explain here and we have just scratched the surface of what IPython can do. Hopefully, we have gotten you interested in diving deeper, especially with the wealth of new features offered by IPython 6.0, including dynamic and user-controllable data visualizations.

See also

- IPython at `http://ipython.org/`
- The *IPython Cookbook* at
  `https://github.com/ipython/ipython/wiki?path=Cookbook`
- *IPython: A System for Interactive Scientific Computing* at
  `http://fperez.org/papers/ipython07_pe-gr_cise.pdf`

- *Learning IPython for Interactive Computing and Data Visualization, Cyrille Rossant, Packt Publishing,* available at `http://www.packtpub.com/learning-ipython-for-interactive-computing-and -data-visualization/book`
- The future of IPython at `http://www.infoworld.com/print/236429`

Exploring Jupyter Notebook

Jupyter Notebook is the perfect complement to Python. In practice, Jupyter Notebook allows you to intersperse your code with comments and images and anything else that might be useful. You can use Jupyter Notebooks for everything from presentations (a great replacement for PowerPoint) to an electronic laboratory notebook or a textbook.

Getting ready

If you have completed the installation instructions in the first chapter, you should be ready to tackle the following recipes.

How to do it...

These steps will get you started with exploring the incredibly powerful Jupyter Notebook environment. We urge you to go beyond this simple set of steps to understand the true power of the tool:

1. Create a folder at the terminal, say test, with `mkdir test`, and move into that folder with `cd test`.
2. Type `jupyter notebook` in the command prompt. You should see some text quickly scroll by in the terminal window, and then, the following screen should load in the default browser (for me, this is Firefox). Note that the URL should be `localhost:8888/tree`, indicating that the browser is connected to a server running on the local machine at port `8888`.

3. You should not see any notebooks listed in the browser (note that Jupyter Notebook files have a `.ipynb` extension) as Jupyter Notebook searches the directory you launched it from for notebook files. Let's create a notebook now. Click on the drop down **New** to find option of Notebook and click on the Python 3 option (it might be different for you though):

4. A new browser tab or window should open up, showing you something similar to the following screenshot:

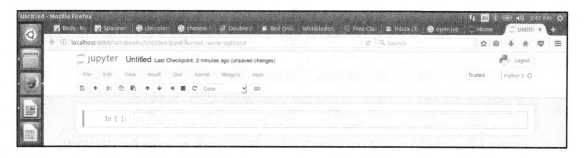

5. From the top down, you can see the text-based menu followed by the toolbar for issuing common commands, and then, your very first cell, which should resemble the command prompt in IPython.

6. Place the mouse cursor in the first cell and type 5+5. Next, either navigate to **Cell | Run** or press *Shift + Enter* as a keyboard shortcut to cause the contents of the cell to be interpreted. You should now see something similar to the following screenshot. Basically, we just executed a simple Python statement within the first cell of our first Jupyter Notebook.

7. Click on the second cell, and then, navigate to **Cell | Cell Type | Markdown**. Now, you can easily write `markdown` in the cell for documentation purposes.

8. Close the two browser windows or tabs (the notebook and the notebook browser).

9. Go back to the terminal in which you typed `jupyter notebook`, hit *Ctrl + C*, then hit *Y*, and press *Enter*. This will shut down the Jupyter Notebook server.

How it works...

For those of you coming from either more traditional statistical software packages, such as **Stata**, **SPSS**, or **SAS**, or more traditional mathematical software packages, such as MATLAB, Mathematica, or Maple, you are probably used to the very graphical and feature-rich interactive environments provided by the respective companies. From this background, Jupyter Notebook might seem a bit foreign, but hopefully much more user friendly and less intimidating than the traditional Python prompt. Furthermore, Jupyter Notebook offers an interesting combination of interactivity and sequential workflow that is particularly well suited for data analysis, especially during the prototyping phases. R has a library called `Knitr` (http://yihui.name/knitr/) that offers the report-generating capabilities of Jupyer Notebook.

When you type in `jupyter notebook`, you are launching a server running on your local machine, and Jupyter Notebook itself is really a web application that uses server-client architecture. The Jupyter Notebook server, as per `ipython.org`, uses two-process kernel architecture with **ZeroMQ** (http://zeromq.org/) and **Tornado**. ZeroMQ is an intelligent socket library for high-performance messaging, helping Jupyter manage distributed compute clusters among other tasks. Tornado is a Python web framework and asynchronous networking module that serves Jupyter Notebook's HTTP requests. The project is open source and you can contribute to the source code if you are so inclined.

Jupyter Notebook also allows you to export your notebooks, which are actually just text files filled with JSON, to a large number of alternative formats using the command-line tool called `nbconvert` (http://ipython.org/ipython-doc/rel-1.0.0/interactive/nbconvert.html). Available export formats include HTML, LaTex, `reveal.js` HTML slideshows, Markdown, simple Python scripts, and `reStructuredText` for the **Sphinx** documentation.

Finally, there is Jupyter Notebook Viewer (`nbviewer`), which is a free web service where you can both post and go through static, HTML versions of notebook files hosted on remote servers (these servers are currently donated by **Rackspace**). Thus, if you create an amazing `.ipynb` file that you want to share, you can upload it to `http://nbviewer.jupyter.org/` and let the world see your efforts.

There's more...

We will try not to sing too loudly the praises of Markdown, but if you are unfamiliar with the tool, we strongly suggest that you try it out. Markdown is actually two different things: a syntax for formatting plain text in a way that can be easily converted to a structured document and a software tool that converts said text into HTML and other languages. Basically, Markdown enables the author to use any desired simple text editor (**VI**, **VIM**, **Emacs**, **Sublime** editor, **TextWrangler**, **Crimson Editor**, or Notepad) that can capture plain text yet still describe relatively complex structures such as different levels of headers, ordered and unordered lists, and block quotes as well as some formatting such as bold and italics. Markdown basically offers a very human-readable version of HTML that is similar to JSON and offers a very human-readable data format.

See also

- Jupyter Notebook at `http://jupyter.org`
- The Jupyter Notebook documentation at `jupyter.readthedocs.io/en/latest/install.html`

Preparing to analyze automobile fuel efficiencies

In this recipe, we are going to start our Python-based analysis of the automobile fuel efficiencies data.

Getting ready

If you completed the first chapter successfully, you should be ready to get started.

How to do it...

The following steps will see you through setting up your working directory and IPython for the analysis for this chapter:

1. Create a project directory called `fuel_efficiency_python`.
2. Download the automobile fuel efficiency dataset from `http://fueleconomy.gov/feg/epadata/vehicles.csv.zip` and store it in the preceding directory. Extract the `vehicles.csv` file from the zip file into the same directory.
3. Open a terminal window and change the current directory (cd) to the `fuel_efficiency_python` directory.
4. At the terminal, type the following command:

   ```
   jupyter notebook
   ```

5. Once the new page has loaded in your web browser, click on New Notebook.
6. Click on the current name of the notebook, which is untitled0, and enter in a new name for this analysis (mine is `fuel_efficiency_python`).
7. Let's use the top-most cell for import statements. Type in the following commands:

   ```
   In [5]: import pandas as pd
      ...: import numpy as np
      ...: from ggplot import *
      ...: %matplotlib inline
   ```

Then, hit *Shift + Enter* to execute the cell. This imports both the `pandas` and `numpy` libraries, assigning them local names to save a few characters while typing commands. It also imports the `ggplot` library. Please note that using the `from ggplot import *` command line is not a best practice in Python and it pours the `ggplot` package contents into our default namespace. However, we are doing this so that our `ggplot` syntax resembles most closely the R `ggplot2` syntax, which is strongly not Pythonic. Finally, we use a magic command to tell Jupyter Notebook that we want `matploblib` graphs to render in the notebook.

8. In the next cell, let's import the data and look at the first few records:

```
In [6]: vehicles = pd.read_csv("vehicles.csv")
```

However, notice that a red warning message appears as follows:

```
C:\Users\prabhanjan.tattar\AppData\Local\Continuum\Anaconda3\lib\si
te-packages\IPython\core\interactiveshell.py:2717: DtypeWarning:
Columns (70,71,72,73,74,76,79) have mixed types. Specify dtype
option on import or set low_memory=False.
```

This tells us that columns $70, 71, 72, 73, 74, 76,$ and 79 contain mixed data types. Let's find the corresponding names using the following commands:

```
In [7]: column_names = vehicles.columns.values

   ...: column_names[[70,71,72,73,74,76,79]]

   ...:

Out[7]: array(['cylinders', 'displ', 'fuelType2', 'rangeA',
'evMotor', 'mfrCode'], dtype=object)
```

Mixed data types sounds like it could be problematic, so make a mental note of these column names. Remember, data cleaning and wrangling often consume 90 percent of project time.

How it works...

With this recipe, we are simply setting up our working directory and creating a new Jupyter Notebook that we will use for the analysis. We have imported the Pandas library and very quickly read the `vehicles.csv` data file directly into a data frame. Speaking from experience, pandas' robust data import capabilities will save you a lot of time.

Although we imported data directly from a comma-separated value file into a data frame, pandas is capable of handling many other formats, including Excel, HDF, SQL, JSON, Stata, and even the clipboard using the reader functions. We can also write out the data from data frames in just as many formats using writer functions accessed from the data frame object.

Using the bound method `head` that is part of the `Data Frame` class in pandas, we have received a very informative summary of the data frame, including a per-column count of

non-null values and a count of the various data types across the columns.

There's more...

The data frame is an incredibly powerful concept and data structure. Thinking in data frames is critical for many data analyses yet also very different from thinking in array or matrix operations (say, if you are coming from MATLAB or C as your primary development languages).

With the data frame, each column represents a different variable or characteristic and can be a different data type, such as floats, integers, or strings. Each row of the data frame is a separate observation or instance with its own set of values. For example, if each row represents a person, the columns could be `age` (an integer) and `gender` (a category or string). Often, we will want to select the set of observations (rows) that match a particular characteristic (say, all males) and examine this subgroup. The data frame is conceptually very similar to a table in a relational database.

See also

- Data structures in pandas at
  `http://pandas.pydata.org/pandas-docs/stable/dsintro.html`
- Data frames in R at `http://www.r-tutor.com/r-introduction/data-frame`

Exploring and describing fuel efficiency data with Python

Now that we have imported the automobile fuel efficiency dataset into Jupyter and witnessed the power of pandas, the next step is to replicate the preliminary analysis performed in R from the earlier chapter, getting your feet wet with some basic Pandas functionality.

Getting ready

We will continue to grow and develop the Jupyer Notebook that we started in the previous recipe. If you've completed the previous recipe, you should have everything you need to continue.

How to do it...

1. First, let's find out how many observations (rows) are in our data using the following command:

   ```
   In [8]: len(vehicles)
       ...:
   Out[8]: 38120
   ```

   If you switch back and forth between R and Python, remember that in R, the function is `length` and in Python, it is `len`.

2. Next, let's find out how many variables (columns) are in our data using the following command:

   ```
   In [9]: len(vehicles.columns)
       ...:
   Out[9]: 83
   Let's get a list of the names of the columns using the following
   command:
   In [10]: print(vehicles.columns)
       ...:
   Index(['barrels08', 'barrelsA08', 'charge120', 'charge240',
   'city08',
   'city08U', 'cityA08', 'cityA08U', 'cityCD', 'cityE', 'cityUF',
   'co2',
   'co2A', 'co2TailpipeAGpm', 'co2TailpipeGpm', 'comb08', 'comb08U',
   ```

```
'combA08', 'combA08U', 'combE', 'combinedCD', 'combinedUF',
'cylinders',
'displ', 'drive', 'engId', 'eng_dscr', 'feScore', 'fuelCost08',
'fuelCostA08', 'fuelType', 'fuelType1', 'ghgScore', 'ghgScoreA',
'highway08', 'highway08U', 'highwayA08', 'highwayA08U',
'highwayCD',
'highwayE', 'highwayUF', 'hlv', 'hpv', 'id', 'lv2', 'lv4', 'make',
'model', 'mpgData', 'phevBlended', 'pv2', 'pv4', 'range',
'rangeCity',
'rangeCityA', 'rangeHwy', 'rangeHwyA', 'trany', 'UCity', 'UCityA',
'UHighway', 'UHighwayA', 'VClass', 'year', 'youSaveSpend',
'guzzler',
'trans_dscr', 'tCharger', 'sCharger', 'atvType', 'fuelType2',
'rangeA',
'evMotor', 'mfrCode', 'c240Dscr', 'charge240b', 'c240bDscr',
'createdOn', 'modifiedOn', 'startStop', 'phevCity', 'phevHwy',
'phevComb'],
dtype='object')
```

The u letter in front of each string indicates that the strings are represented in Unicode (http://docs.python.org/2/howto/unicode.html)

3. Let's find out how many unique years of data are included in this dataset and what the first and last years are using the following command:

```
In [11]: len(pd.unique(vehicles.year))
   ...:
Out[11]: 34

In [12]: min(vehicles.year)
   ...:
Out[12]: 1984

In [13]: max(vehicles["year"])
   ...:
Out[13]: 2017
```

Note that again, we have used two different syntaxes to reference individual columns within the vehicles data frame.

4. Next, let's find out what types of fuel are used as the automobiles' primary fuel types. In R, we have the `table` function that will return a count of the occurrences of a variable's various values. In pandas, we use the following:

```
In [14]: pd.value_counts(vehicles.fuelType1)
   ...:
Out[14]:
```

```
Regular Gasoline 26533
Premium Gasoline 10302
Diesel 1014
Electricity 134
Midgrade Gasoline 77
Natural Gas 60
Name: fuelType1, dtype: int64
```

5. Now if we want to explore what types of transmissions these automobiles have, we immediately try the following command:

```
In [15]: pd.value_counts(vehicles.trany)
```

However, this results in a bit of unexpected and lengthy output:

```
Out[15]:
Automatic 4-spd 11042
Manual 5-spd 8323
Automatic 3-spd 3151
Automatic (S6) 2684
Manual 6-spd 2448
Automatic 5-spd 2191
Manual 4-spd 1483
Automatic 6-spd 1447
Automatic (S8) 981
Automatic (S5) 827
Automatic (variable gear ratios) 702
Automatic 7-spd 675
Automatic (S7) 270
Auto(AM-S7) 266
Automatic 8-spd 259
Automatic (S4) 233
Auto(AM7) 166
Auto(AV-S6) 153
Automatic (A1) 125
Auto(AM6) 120
Automatic 9-spd 105
Auto(AM-S6) 87
Auto(AV-S7) 80
Manual 3-spd 77
Manual 7-spd 73
Automatic (S9) 29
Auto(AV-S8) 28
Manual 4-spd Doubled 17
Auto(AM5) 12
Automatic (AV-S6) 11
Automatic (S10) 8
Auto(AM-S8) 6
```

```
Auto(AM8)  5
Automatic  (AV)  4
Automatic  (A6)  4
Manual(M7)  3
Auto(L3)  2
Auto(L4)  2
Automatic  (AM5)  2
Auto  (AV)  2
Auto  (AV-S8)  1
Manual 5 spd 1
Auto  (AV-S6)  1
Auto(AM-S9)  1
Automatic  6spd  1
Automatic  (AM6)  1
Name: trany, dtype: int64
```

What we really want to know is the number of cars with automatic and manual transmissions. We notice that the trany variable always starts with the letter A when it represents an automatic transmission and M for manual transmission. Thus, we create a new variable, trany2, which contains the first character of the trany variable, which is a string:

```
In [16]: vehicles["trany2"] = vehicles.trany.str[0]
    ...: pd.value_counts(vehicles.trany2)
    ...:
```

The preceding command yields the answer that we wanted or twice as many automatics as manuals:

```
Out[16]:
A 25684
M 12425
Name: trany2, dtype: int64
```

How it works...

In this recipe, we looked at some basic functionality in Python and pandas. We have used two different syntax's (vehicles['trany'] and vehicles.trany) to access variables within the data frame. We have also used some of the core pandas functions to explore the data, such as the incredibly useful unique and the value_counts function.

There's more...

In terms of the data science pipeline, we have touched on two stages in a single recipe: data cleaning and data exploration. Often, when working with smaller datasets where the time to complete a particular action is quite short and can be completed on our laptop, we will very quickly go through multiple stages of the pipeline and then loop back, depending on the results. In general, the data science pipeline is a highly iterative process. The faster we can accomplish steps, the more iterations we can fit into a fixed time, and often, we can create a better final analysis.

See also

- The pandas API overview at
  `http://pandas.pydata.org/pandas-docs/stable/api.html`

Analyzing automobile fuel efficiency over time with Python

In this recipe, we are going to look at some of the fuel efficiency metrics over time and in relation to other data points. To do so, we are going to have to replicate the functionality of two very popular R libraries, which are `plyr` and `ggplot2`, in Python. The split-apply-combine data analysis capabilities that are so handily covered by the `plyr` R library are handled equally well, but in a slightly different fashion by pandas right out of the box. The data visualization abilities of `ggplot2`-an R library implementation of the grammar of graphics-are not handled as readily, as we shall see in this recipe.

Getting ready

If you've completed the previous recipe, you should have almost everything you need to continue. However, we are going to use a Python clone of the `ggplot2` library for R, which is conveniently named `ggplot`. If you didn't complete the entire setup chapter and haven't yet installed the `ggplot` package, open up a terminal and type the following:

```
pip install ggplot (or sudo pip install ggplot)
```

This works on the Windows machines as well. Wait for the installation to complete. After you do this, you will have to restart the IPython Notebook server to be able to import this newly installed ggplot library.

How to do it...

We will dive into the analysis stage with the following steps:

1. Let's start by looking at whether there is an overall trend of how mpg changes over time on average. We first want to group the data by year:

   ```
   In [17]: grouped = vehicles.groupby("year")
   ```

2. Next, we want to compute the mean of three separate columns by the previous grouping:

   ```
   In [18]: averaged = grouped['comb08',
   'highway08','city08'].agg([np.mean])
   ```

   This produces a new data frame with three columns containing the mean of comb08, highway08, and city08 variables, respectively. Notice that we are using the mean function supplied by NumPy (np).

3. To make life easier, we will rename the columns and then create a new column named year, which contains the data frame's index:

   ```
   In [19]: averaged.columns =
   ['comb08_mean','highway08_mean','city08_mean']
   ...: averaged['year'] = averaged.index
   ```

   Note how easy renaming columns is compared to what we had to do in R! The columns attribute of the data frame contains the name of the columns and what we need to modify in order to rename the columns.

4. Finally, we want to plot the results as a scatter plot using the new ggplot package for the Python library:

   ```
   In [20]: ggplot(averaged, aes('year', 'comb08_mean')) + geom_point(
   ...: color='steelblue') + xlab("Year") + ylab("Average MPG"
   ...: ) + ggtitle("All cars")
   ```

Refer to the following graph:

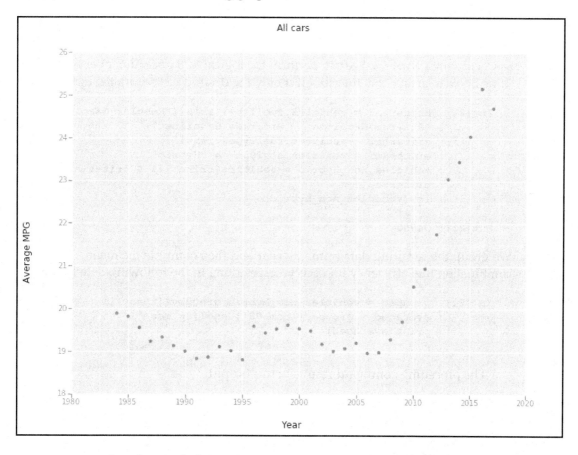

This plot might be misleading as hybrid cars with excellent mileage have recently become more popular. Let's see whether we can screen out these automobile makes. Astute observers will recognize that this figure does not include the `geom_smooth()` method of the matching image in the R chapter. While the current `ggplot` library (0.4.7 as of *February 11, 2014*) has the potentially equivalent `stat_smooth()` method, the current version still has some bugs that caused erroneous results to be plotted (and not shown).

5. To remove hybrid cars, we create three Boolean arrays. The `criteria1` array selects those rows of the data frame where `fuelType1` is `Regular Gasoline`, `Premium Gasoline`, or `Midgrade Gasoline`. The `criteria2` array makes sure that the rows contain a null for `fuelType2`, and `criteria3` ensures that the `atvType` is not `Hybrid`. We can perform the logical AND operation over these three Boolean arrays together to select only the desired rows from the data frame:

```
In [21]: criteria1 = vehicles.fuelType1.isin(["Regular Gasoline",
    ...: "Premium Gasoline", "Midgrade Gasoline"])
    ...: criteria2 = vehicles.fuelType2.isnull()
    ...: criteria3 = vehicles.atvType != "Hybrid"
    ...: vehicles_non_hybrid = vehicles[criteria1 & criteria2 &
    ...: criteria3]
    ...: len(vehicles_non_hybrid)
    ...:
Out [21]: 34990
```

6. We group the resulting data frame by year and then compute the mean combination fuel efficiency for each year, resulting in the following data frame:

```
In [22]: grouped = vehicles_non_hybrid.groupby(['year'])
    ...: averaged = grouped['comb08'].agg([np.mean])
    ...: print(averaged)
    ...:
```

The preceding command results in this output:

```
mean
year
1984 19.121622
1985 19.394686
1986 19.320457
1987 19.164568
1988 19.367607
1989 19.141964
1990 19.031459
1991 18.838060
1992 18.861566
1993 19.137383
1994 19.092632
1995 18.872591
1996 19.530962
1997 19.368000
1998 19.329545
1999 19.239759
2000 19.169345
2001 19.075058
```

```
2002 18.950270
2003 18.761711
2004 18.967339
2005 19.005510
2006 18.786398
2007 18.987512
2008 19.191781
2009 19.738095
2010 20.466736
2011 20.838219
2012 21.407328
2013 22.228877
2014 22.279835
2015 22.424555
2016 22.749766
2017 22.804085
```

Based on the preceding data, we see that there is still a marked rise in the average miles per gallon even after eliminating hybrids.

7. The next question that we can ask is whether there have been fewer cars with large engines built more recently? If this is true, it could explain the increase in average miles per gallon. First, let's verify that larger engine cars have poorer miles per gallon. To look at this, we need to dig into the displ variable that represents the engine displacement in liters. Remember, pandas gave us a warning about this variable containing multiple data types, so let's compute the unique displ values:

```
In [23]: pd.unique(vehicles_non_hybrid.displ)
   ...:
Out[23]:
array([ 2. , 4.9, 2.2, 5.2, 1.8, 1.6, 2.3, 2.8, 4. , 5. , 3.3,
       3.1, 3.8, 4.6, 3.4, 3. , 5.9, 2.5, 4.5, 6.8, 2.4, 2.9,
       5.7, 4.3, 3.5, 5.8, 3.2, 4.2, 1.9, 2.6, 7.4, 3.9, 1.5,
       1.3, 4.1, 8. , 6. , 3.6, 5.4, 5.6, 1. , 2.1, 1.2, 6.5,
       2.7, 4.7, 5.5, 1.1, 5.3, 4.4, 3.7, 6.7, 4.8, 1.7, 6.2,
       8.3, 1.4, 6.1, 7. , 8.4, 6.3, nan, 6.6, 6.4, 0.9])
```

8. We see that there are some values that might not be numeric, including the nan value. Let's remove all rows from the vehicles_non_hybrid data frame that have nandispl values and then do the same for the comb08 variable. In the process, let's use the astype method to ensure that each value is of type float, just in case:

```
In [24]: criteria = vehicles_non_hybrid.displ.notnull()
   ...: vehicles_non_hybrid = vehicles_non_hybrid[criteria]
```

```
   ...: vehicles_non_hybrid.displ =
vehicles_non_hybrid.displ.astype('float')
   ...:

In [25]: criteria = vehicles_non_hybrid.comb08.notnull()
   ...: vehicles_non_hybrid = vehicles_non_hybrid[criteria]
   ...: vehicles_non_hybrid.comb08 =
vehicles_non_hybrid.comb08.astype('float')
```

9. Finally, we will produce a scatter plot of the results again using the `ggplot` library:

```
In [26]: ggplot(vehicles_non_hybrid, aes('displ', 'comb08')) +
geom_point(
   ...: color='steelblue') + xlab("Engine Displacement") +ylab(
   ...: "Average MPG") + ggtitle("Gasoline cars")
```

Refer to the following graph:

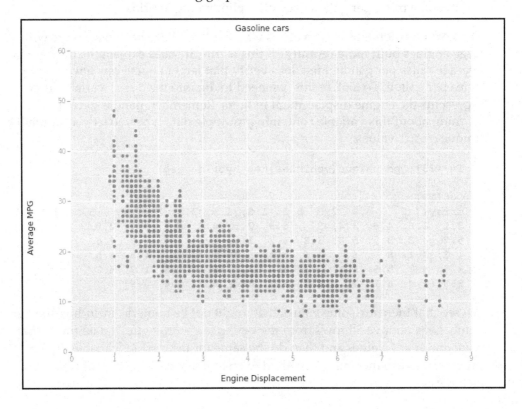

The preceding plot seems to confirm a negative relationship between fuel economy and engine displacement.

Now, have there been fewer cars with large engines made recently?

10. Let's see whether smaller cars were made in later years on average:

```
In [27]: grouped_by_year = vehicles_non_hybrid.groupby(['year'])
    ...: avg_grouped_by_year = grouped_by_year['displ',
    ...: 'comb08'].agg([np.mean])
```

11. Next, let's plot both the average `displ` value and the average `comb08` value by year on the same plot to look for trends. To do this, we need to reshape the `avg_grouped_by_year` data frame to convert it from the wide format to the long format:

```
In [28]: avg_grouped_by_year['year'] = avg_grouped_by_year.index
    ...: melted_avg_grouped_by_year =
pd.melt(avg_grouped_by_year,id_vars='year')
```

Then, let's create our faceted plot:

```
In [29]: p = ggplot(aes(x='year', y='value', color = 'variable_0'),
    ...: data=melted_avg_grouped_by_year)
    ...: p + geom_point() + facet_wrap("variable_0")
```

Refer to the following graph:

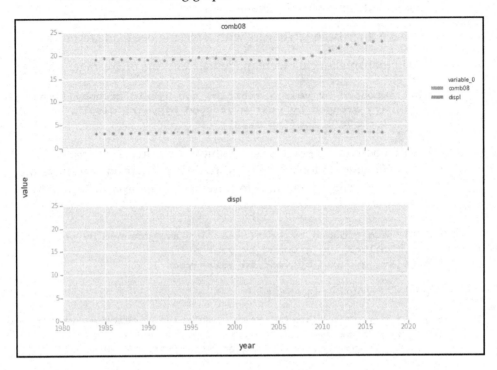

How it works...

Let's ignore the actual findings of the analysis, as they are the same as the ones in the chapter using R. The truly interesting part is the numerous important data analysis techniques that were used in this chapter. Let's break each technique down individually.

First and foremost, let's take a look at the general data analysis pattern known as split-apply-combine, which was previously mentioned in the companion R chapter. When analyzing a dataset, it is often desirable to group the data by one or more characteristics, perform an operation on the grouped subsets of data, and then put the results together. In this chapter, we grouped our data by year, computed averages on different variables, and then combined these results. In the previous chapter, we used the `plyr` package by Hadley Wickham. With `plyr`, we called the `ddply` function passing in the data frame to be analyzed, the characteristic or set of characteristics to group by, and then the functions to be used on the group data. The `ddply` function then returns the resulting data frame. One line of code performs the split-apply-combine pattern.

The Pandas library in Python takes a slightly different approach and splits up the functionality that is subsumed in a single function call in `plyr`. First, we can group a pandas object such as a data frame by a specified characteristic as in this line of code-`grouped_by_year = vehicles_non_hybrid.groupby(['year'])`-where we are grouping the rows of the `vehicles_non_hybrid` data frame by the `year` variable. Note that we are not limited to grouping by a single variable and can create groupings with multiple characteristics (year and car company, for example).

Once we have the `grouped_by_year` object, we can iterate through the groups if we wanted to:

```
for (name, group) in grouped_by_year:
  print name
  print group
```

This will print out each group name and the resulting data frame. Next, we use the `aggregrate` method on the `GroupBy` object using the `mean` function from the NumPy library (`np.mean`). In the following code, we are choosing to only aggregate a single variable, which is `comb08`, from the `grouped_by_year` data frame:

```
averaged = grouped['comb08'].agg([np.mean])
```

In pandas, this very robust split-apply-combine functionality is built into the library, and we have only scratched the surface of what it is capable of.

There's more...

We have also used the `ggplot` package from yhat instead of the venerable matplotlib. *The Grammar of Graphics* offers a very concise, although highly non-Pythonic, way of describing graphs. The back cover of the seminal book, *The Grammar of Graphics, Leland Wilkinson, Springer* states that:

> "*The Grammar of Graphics presents a unique foundation for producing almost every quantitative graphic found in scientific journals, newspapers, statistical packages, and data visualization systems. While the tangible results of this work have been several visualization software libraries, this book focuses on the deep structures involved in producing quantitative graphics from data. What are the rules that underlie the production of pie charts, bar charts, scatterplots, function plots, maps, mosaics, and radar charts?*"

The `ggplot2` package in R is one of R's greatest assets, and Python now has a functioning `ggplot` clone. Unfortunately, as shown by some of the experiences in this chapter, the `ggplot` Python library is not quite feature-complete at this time.

As the Python `ggplot` library is still under development (and we had a few issues with the smoothing functionality), you might be interested to know that there is a Python library that allows you to use R from within your Python program. The `rpy2` package, at `http://rpy.sourceforge.net/rpy2.html`, offers both a low-level and a high-level interface to R from Python. The low-level interface is somewhat similar to R's C API. The high-level interface exposes R objects as instances of Python classes. In order to use `rpy2`, ensure that you have R installed on your system. Any packages that you call from Python must be available in R!

See also

- Pandas: indexing and selecting data at
  `http://pandas.pydata.org/pandas-docs/stable/indexing.html`
- The *Matplotlib and the Future of Visualization in Python* article at
  `http://jakevdp.github.io/blog/2013/03/23/matplotlib-and-the-future-of-visualization-in-python/`
- The home page of *Hadley Wickham* at `http://had.co.nz/`
- The `ggplot` package for Python at
  `http://blog.yhathq.com/posts/ggplot-for-python.html`
- More `ggplot` for Python at
  `http://blog.yhathq.com/posts/aggregating-and-plotting-time-series-in-python.html`
- The article *The Split-Apply-Combine Strategy for Data Analysis, Hadley Wickham, Journal of Statistical Software* at `http://www.jstatsoft.org/v40/i01/paper`

Investigating the makes and models of automobiles with Python

To continue our investigation of this dataset, we are going to examine the makes and models of the various automobiles more closely, repeating many of the steps from the previous chapter while translating from R to Python.

Getting ready

If you've completed the previous recipe, you should have everything you need in order to continue.

How to do it...

The following steps will lead us through our investigation:

1. Let's look at how makes and models of cars inform us about fuel efficiency over time. First, let's look at the frequency of makes and models of cars available in the U.S., concentrating on 4-cylinder cars. To select the 4-cylinder cars, we first make the `cylinders` variable unique to see what the possible values are:

   ```
   In [30]: pd.unique(vehicles_non_hybrid.cylinders)
      ...:
   Out[30]: array([ 4., 12., 8., 6., 5., 10., 2., 3., 16., nan])
   ```

   Both `4.0` and `4` are listed as unique values; this fact should raise your suspicion. Remember, when we imported the data, pandas warned us that several variables were mixed types, and one of these variables was `cylinders`.

2. Let's convert the `cylinders` variable to `float` so that we can then easily subset the data frame:

   ```
   In [31]: vehicles_non_hybrid.cylinders =
   vehicles_non_hybrid.cylinders.astype('float')
      ...: pd.unique(vehicles_non_hybrid.cylinders)
      ...:
   Out[31]: array([ 4., 12., 8., 6., 5., 10., 2., 3., 16., nan])
   In [32]: vehicles_non_hybrid_4 =
   vehicles_non_hybrid[(vehicles_non_hybrid.cylinders == 4.0)]
   ```

3. Now, let's look at the numbers of makes that have 4-cylinder cars over the time frame that is available:

   ```
   In [35]: grouped_by_year_4_cylinder =
   vehicles_non_hybrid_4.groupby(['year']).make.nunique()
      ...: fig = grouped_by_year_4_cylinder.plot()
      ...: fig.set_xlabel('Year')
      ...: fig.set_ylabel('Number of 4-Cylinder Makes')
      ...: print fig
   ```

Note that we have switched from `ggplot` to `matplotlib` as we are trying to plot a series object. In Python, it is considered bad form to have your code littered with random `import` statements. Therefore, we will move the `import` statement to the top of our IPython Notebook. Remember, if you restart your IPython Notebook, make sure that you execute the `import` statements at the top of the Notebook first so that the rest of your code will run. Refer to the following graph:

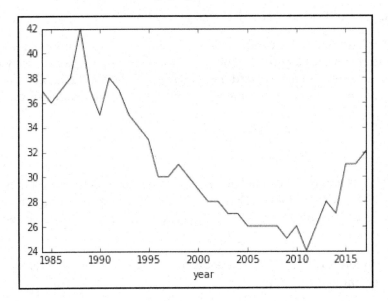

We can see in the preceding graph that there has been a decline in the number of makes with 4-cylinder engines available since 1980. However, as a caveat, this plot could be misleading, as we do not know if the total number of available makes per year has changed over the same period of time.

4. Can we look at the makes that have been available every year of this study? First, we want to find a list of the automobile makes with 4-cylinder engines that were present in every year of this study. To do this, we first compute the unique list of makes per model year:

```
In [36]: grouped_by_year_4_cylinder =
vehicles_non_hybrid_4.groupby(['year'])
     ...: from functools import reduce
     ...:
In [37]: unique_makes = []
     ...: for name, group in grouped_by_year_4_cylinder:
     ...: unique_makes.append(set(pd.unique(group['make'])))
```

```
    . . . :
    . . . :   unique_makes = reduce(set.intersection, unique_makes)
    . . . :   print(unique_makes)
    . . . :
{'Nissan', 'Chevrolet', 'Chrysler', 'Toyota', 'Honda', 'Dodge',
'Volkswagen', 'Jeep', 'Ford', 'Subaru', 'Mitsubishi', 'Mazda'}
```

We find that there are only 12 manufacturers that made 4-cylinder cars every year during this period.

5. Now, we ask the question of how these car manufacturers' models have performed over time in terms of fuel efficiency. To do this, we decide to take the long way. First, we create an empty list that will eventually be populated by Booleans. We then iterate over each row in the data frame using the `iterrows` generator that yields both an index and row (we choose to do nothing with the index in the loop). We then test whether the make of the current row is in the `unique_makes` set computed previously and append the Boolean to the `Boolean_mask` set. After the loop is completed, we subset the data frame to contain only rows with a make within the set of `unique_makes`:

```
In [38]: boolean_mask = []
    . . . :   for index, row in vehicles_non_hybrid_4.iterrows():
    . . . :   make = row['make']
    . . . :   boolean_mask.append(make in unique_makes)
    . . . :
    . . . :   df_common_makes = vehicles_non_hybrid_4[boolean_mask]
    . . . :
```

6. Next, we must group the data frame by both `year` and `make` and then compute the mean for each grouping:

```
In [39]: df_common_makes_grouped = df_common_makes.groupby(['year',
    . . . :   'make']).agg(np.mean).reset_index()
```

7. Finally, we display the results of our efforts using a faceted plot, courtesy of `ggplot`:

```
In [40]: ggplot(aes(x='year', y='comb08'), data =
    . . . :   df_common_makes_grouped) + geom_line() +
facet_wrap('make')
```

Refer to the following graph:

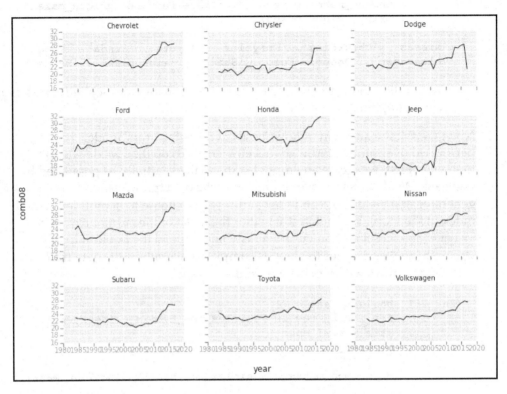

How it works...

A lot of the steps were spelled out in detail during the recipe itself, so we won't belabor the points here. However, there are a few things that are certainly worth pointing out. First, did you notice the `.reset_index()` call at the end of the last split-apply-combine step? The following command shows this:

```
df_common_makes.groupby(['year','make']).agg(np.mean).reset_index()
```

When performing the `groupby` step, pandas returns the key by which rows were grouped as an index and not as a simple data column. In the case of multiple grouping keys, pandas returns a multilevel index. Unfortunately, this will not work for `ggplot`, and we need to tell pandas to treat these indices as data columns with the `.reset_index()` method.

Second, we used a `for` loop, iterating over the rows of the data frame to determine whether the make was in the list of `unique_makes` of interest. If this block of code seemed a bit verbose, it is because it was. Pandas has an incredible amount of functionalities built in, and we could have performed the row selection using the `.isin()` method, as shown in the following command:

```
test =

vehicles_non_hybrid_4[vehicles_non_hybrid_4['make'].isin(unique_makes

)]
```

If there is a data analysis step that you wish to perform on your data frame, chances are that there is a method that has already been built to do this.

From a performance standpoint, we committed a very obvious sin in the `for` loop by appending the loop to a list, thus growing the size of the list with each iteration. To speed this up, we should have pre-allocated the list to the size of the number of rows in the data frame filled with false Boolean values. Preallocating arrays is a very general technique that speeds up code in most languages; this trick is especially powerful in `matplotlib`.

To perform the set intersection that we used in order to identify all of the makes present in every year of the data, we needed the `sets` Python package that is part of the Python distribution. Again, we would move this import statement to the top of our script in order to follow best Python practices.

See also

- The matplotlib home page at `http://matplotlib.org/`
- The `groupby` documentation at
  `http://pandas.pydata.org/pandas-docs/stable/groupby.html`

7
Working with Social Graphs

In this chapter, we will cover:

- Preparing to work with social networks in Python
- Importing networks
- Exploring subgraphs within a heroic network
- Finding strong ties
- Finding key players
- Exploring characteristics of entire networks
- Clustering and community detection in social networks
- Visualizing graphs
- Social networks in R

Introduction

Social networks have become a fixture of modern life, thanks to social networking sites such as Facebook and Twitter. Social networks themselves are not new, however. The study of such networks dates back to the early twentieth century, particularly in the fields of sociology and anthropology. It is their prevalence in mainstream applications that has moved these types of studies to the purview of data science.

It turns out that social networks are extremely interesting as models for human behavior. Human civilization stems from tribal societies and as a result, **Dunbar's number-a hypothesis** that at any given time we can only have 150 people in our extended social network-has famously been proven through the analysis of the most active networks. Latent social networks exist everywhere, not just in popular web 2.0 applications. We manage our lives through connections to various networks, and, because of that, we generate a lot of related, rich data that can be used to make predictions about ourselves and our relationships.

Networks, like the ones we'll discuss in this chapter, take a relationship-centered view of the world. By leveraging an existing data structure of people-to-people relationships (a social network), we can produce analyses about the larger network with clustering techniques to discover communities, reveal insights into the role of important members of the graph, and even generate behavioral predictions through relational inference. These analyses have a number of practical applications from law enforcement to election prediction and recommendations to application optimization.

The mathematical underpinnings of these analyses stem from graph theory. Therefore, the techniques for the analyses in this chapter will focus on the cardinality, traversal, and clustering of graphs. To introduce these techniques, we will make use of an excellent Python graph library, NetworkX. We'll go through several analyses at various levels of the network, such as pairwise comparisons at the individual level, community detection at the group level, and cohesion analyses at the network level. Finally, we'll look at visualizing and drawing our graphs and subgraphs with various tools.

Understanding graphs and networks

The basis for the analyses in this chapter comes from graph theory-the mathematical study of the application and properties of graphs, originally motivated by the study of games of chance. Generally speaking, this involves the study of network encoding and measuring properties of a graph. Graph theory can be traced back to Euler's work on the **Seven Bridges of Königsberg** problem in the year 1735. However, in recent decades, the rise of the social network has influenced the discipline and particularly with computer science graph data structures and databases.

Let's start with a point of contention. What is the difference between a network and a graph? The term graph can be used to imply visual representations of variables and functions, the mathematical concept of a set of nodes and edges, or the data structure based on that concept. Similarly, the term network has multiple definitions; it can be an interconnected system or a specialized type of mathematical graph. Therefore, either term, social network or social graph, is appropriate in this case, particularly as we are referring to the mathematical concept and data structure.

A graph is a symbolic representation of a network that is composed of a set of vertices (nodes) and their connections (relationships or edges). More formally, a graph can be defined as: $G = (V, E)$, an entity consisting of a finite set of nodes denoted by V (vertices) or $V(G)$ and a collection E (edges) or $E(G)$ of unordered pairs $\{u, v\}$ where $u, v \circledcirc V$. A visual example, as shown in the following figure, should be familiar to the reader:

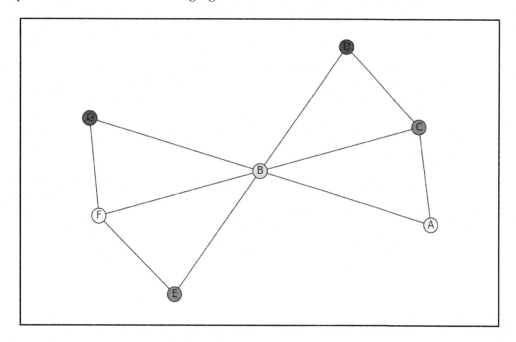

Graphs can be either directed or undirected. Directed graphs have ordered relationships; undirected graphs can be seen as bidirectional directed graphs. A directed graph in a social network tends to have directional semantic relationships, for example, friends, where Abe might be friends with Jane, but Jane might not reciprocate. Undirected social networks have more general semantic relationships, for example "knows". Any directed graph can easily be converted to the more general undirected graph. In this case, the adjacency matrix becomes symmetric, that is every relationship is reciprocal.

Adjacency matrices are two-dimensional graph representations, where each cell or element (i, j) is 1 if the ith node and jth node are connected; it is 0 otherwise. This is certainly not the most compact manner of storing information about graphs; a byte must be stored for every pair of nodes, even if the majority of nodes do not share an edge with most other nodes. However, this representation is computationally effective and is used for many graph algorithms. Consider that a node can be represented in this scheme as a vector of its edges. An example of a small adjacency matrix for an undirected graph with four nodes is shown in the following figure:

	A	B	C	D
A	-	1	1	0
B	1	-	1	0
C	1	1	-	1
D	0	0	1	-

A few final terms will help us in our discussion. The cardinality of vertices is called the order of the graph, whereas the cardinality of the edges is called the size. In the graph pictured in the preceding figure, the order is 7 and the size is 10. Two nodes are adjacent if they share an edge; if this is true, they are also called neighbors. The neighborhood of a vertex is the set of all vertices that the vertex is connected to. The degree of a vertex is the size of its neighborhood, the number of nodes that share an edge with the vertex.

With this in mind, graph problems generally fall into a few categories. Existence problems attempt to determine if a node, path, or subgraph exists, particularly if there is a constraint. Construction problems focus on the construction of a graph, given a set of nodes and paths, within given constraints. Enumeration problems attempt to determine the list of vertices and relationships within a set of constraints. Finally, optimization problems determine the shortest path between two nodes.

Preparing to work with social networks in Python

One of Python's key advantages that merits repeating is the number of excellent pre-made packages available for the language; fortunately for us, network analysis is no exception. This short recipe will walk you through installing the libraries you'll need for the rest of this chapter.

Getting ready

The required external libraries for the tasks in this chapter are as follows:

- NetworkX
- matplotlib
- python-louvain

How to do it...

We will use the following steps that should be familiar at this point to prepare for the remaining recipes:

1. Open a new Terminal or Command Prompt and change to your project directory.
2. If you are using a virtual environment, activate your virtual environment and type the following:

   ```
   pip install networkx
   ```

   If you are not using a virtual environment, you will most likely need to use sudo, as follows:

   ```
   sudo pip install networkx
   ```

3. Now, we must install the python-louvain package:

   ```
   pip install python-louvain
   ```

How it works...

NetworkX is a well-maintained Python library for the creation, manipulation, and study of the structure of complex networks. Its tools allow for the quick creation of graphs, and the library also contains many common graph algorithms. In particular, NetworkX complements Python's scientific computing suite of SciPy/NumPy, matplotlib, and Graphviz and can handle graphs in memory of 10M's of nodes and 100M's of links. NetworkX should be part of every data scientist's toolkit.

NetworkX and Python are the perfect combination to do social network analysis. NetworkX is designed to handle data at scale. The core algorithms that are included are implemented on extremely fast legacy code. Graphs are hugely flexible (nodes can be any hashable type), and there is an extensive set of native IO formats. Finally, with Python, you'll be able to access or use a myriad of datasources from databases on the Internet.

Python-louvain is a small Python library built for a singular purpose, which is to use the Louvain method for community detection, as described in the *Fast unfolding of communities in large networks* paper (*Journal of Statistical Mechanics: Theory and Experiment*, 2008 (10)). A C++ implementation is also available.

There's more...

While we will use NetworkX exclusively in this chapter, there are a number of excellent alternative social network analysis libraries that are worth mentioning. First, **igraph** (http://igraph.org/redirect.html) can be programmed and used from R, Python, and C/C++, with the underlying tools built in C/C++ for performance. The second library to take a look at is graph-tool (http://graph-tool.skewed.de/). Underneath its Python usability, it can also be implemented in C++, but with the added benefit of leveraging OpenMP for parallelization across multicore machines.

Importing networks

The dataset we will explore in this chapter is fun. It's the Marvel Universe Social Graph dataset constructed by *Cesc Rosselló, Ricardo Alberich*, and Joe Miro as part of their research on disordered systems and neural networks (http://bioinfo.uib.es/~joemiro/marvel.html). They created the network by compiling characters with the comic books in which they appear; as it turns out, the network actually mimics a real-world social network. Since then, there have been many visualizations of, and other mashups using this famous dataset (as well as extensions). In this recipe, we will import the needed data into our Python environment.

Getting ready

Once you have installed the needed libraries from the preceding recipe, you will need to use the dataset provided with the chapter.

How to do it...

Perform the following steps to import the data:

1. In order to get this graph into a NetworkX graph representation, iterate over the
   dataset and add edges (which automatically create the nodes) for each hero pair:

   ```python
   import networkx as nx
   import unicodecsv as csv

   def graph_from_csv(path):

       graph = nx.Graph(name="Heroic Social Network")

       with open(path, 'rU') as data:
           reader = csv.reader(data)
           for row in reader:
               graph.add_edge(*row)
       return graph
   ```

   Each row is a (hero, hero) tuple. Using the *row notation, we expand the
   tuple so that the function definition is actually graph.add_edge(hero,
   hero).

2. The dataset is large, weighing in at 21 MB, and takes a second or two to load into
   memory; you can compute the size and the order of the graph as follows:

   ```python
   >>> graph.order()  # graph.number_of_nodes()

   6426

   >>> graph.size()   # graph.number_of_edges()

   167219
   ```

   Keep this function handy; we'll need it to get the graph for most of the rest of
   the chapter!

3. The alternate dataset, from which the social network was derived, includes the comics in which the characters appeared. A slightly different graph generation mechanism is necessary for this format:

```python
def graph_from_gdf(path):
    graph = nx.Graph(name="Characters in Comics")
    with open(path, 'rU') as data:
        reader = csv.reader(data)
        for row in reader:
            if 'nodedef' in row[0]:
                handler = lambda row,G: G.add_node(row[0],
                    TYPE=row[1])
            elif 'edgedef' in row[0]:
                handler = lambda row,G: G.add_edge(*row)
            else:
                handler(row, graph)
    return graph
```

In this **tab-separated value (TSV)** file, there is a banner that says `nodedef` or `edgedef` before the rows of nodes or edge definitions. While we loop through each row, we create a handler function, `lambda`, depending on whether we've seen the banner. Then, for every row under the banner, we use the defined handler as we're in the section for either nodes or edges.

4. At this point, we can calculate some quick information for the graph using built-in methods from NetworkX:

```
>>> nx.info(graph)
Name: Heroic SociaL Network
Type: Graph
Number of nodes: 6426
Number of edges: 167219
Average degree:   52.0445
```

Note that the name for the graph was added when we instantiated `nx.Graph`, an optional feature that makes it easier to track multiple graphs in your code.

How it works...

Data import can be a challenge in any data science project and graph data can come in a variety of formats. For this recipe, the data is simple; it is a TSV file of hero-to-hero connections with the implied *knows* relationship.

There is also an alternate dataset that expands the knows relationship by including the source of their relationship, the comic book that the heroes appear in together. This expansion adds additional hops between the hero-to-hero network by expanding the comic-to-hero network via appears in relationships. This expanded network might allow us to compute the strength of the knows relationships; for example, the more comics that heroes appear in together, the better they probably know each other. It is interesting to note that this type of dataset has been shown to be effective at community discovery and relationship clustering.

The `graph_from_gdf` function determines whether we're reading edges or nodes, and it handles each line of the TSV file appropriately by implementing a new handler via a `lambda` function when it sees a row banner called `nodedef` or `edgedef`, indicating that the rows below it are nodes or edges, respectively. This function also gives us the opportunity to create a property graph.

A property graph extends our current graph definition with the inclusion of key/value pairs on nodes and edges, and even potentially on the graph itself. Property graphs are more expressive, and they are the basis of many graph databases because they can hold more information per node and per relationship (thus making it a possible replacement for traditional relational databases). NetworkX also allows you to specify additional properties for both nodes and edges.

Note the `add_node` method; additional keyword arguments are saved as a property. In this case, we set a `TYPE` property to determine whether the node is a comic book or a hero. NetworkX also allows the setting and retrieving of properties in bulk on nodes, using `set_node_attributes` `(G, name, attributes)` and `get_node_attributes(G, name)`, which return a dictionary mapping the nodes to the attribute requested (or saving the attribute to the group of nodes).

Exploring subgraphs within a heroic network

The graph in the previous recipe, *Importing networks*, is much too large for us to get a feel for what is happening at the individual level, although we'll soon look at analyses that tell us interesting things about populations and communities. However, in order for us to see something interesting immediately, let's extract a subgraph to play with. In particular, we'll collect a subgraph for a particular hero in our dataset. When a subgraph is generated with a single person or actor as a focal point, it is called an ego network, and, in fact, the degree of an ego network might be a measure of an individual's self-worth!

Getting ready

As long as you completed the previous recipe, you will be prepared for this one.

How to do it...

The following steps will lead you through extracting subgraphs from our large dataset and visualizing the ego networks:

1. Every social network has as many egos as nodes. The neighbors of an ego are called alters. The definition of the ego subgraph is bound by an n-step neighborhood, defining how many hops away from the ego to include in the subgraph. NetworkX provides a very simple mechanism to extract an ego graph, as shown in the following command:

   ```
   >>> ego = nx.ego_graph(graph, actor, 1)
   ```

   This function returns a subgraph of all the neighbors of the actor node, with a maximum path length as specified by the third argument.

2. To draw the graph of the ego network, we use the following function:

```python
def draw_ego_graph(graph, character, hops=1):
    """
    Expecting a graph_from_gdf
    """

    # Get the Ego Graph and Position
    ego = nx.ego_graph(graph, character, hops)
    pos = nx.spring_layout(ego)
    plt.figure(figsize=(12,12))
    plt.axis('off')

    # Coloration and Configuration
    ego.node[character]["TYPE"] = "center"
    valmap = { "comic": 0.25, "hero": 0.54, "center": 0.87 }
    types  = nx.get_node_attributes(ego, "TYPE")
    values = [valmap.get(types[node], 0.25) for node in
    ego.nodes()]

    # Draw
    nx.draw_networkx_edges(ego, pos, alpha=0.4)
    nx.draw_networkx_nodes(ego, pos,
                            node_size=80,
                            node_color=values,
                            cmap=plt.cm.hot, with_labels=False)

    plt.show()
```

3. Let's take a look at the ego networks for LONGBOW/AMELIA GREER, starting with a one-hop network:

```python
>>> graph = graph_from_gdf('comic-hero-network.gdf'))
>>> draw_ego_graph(graph, "LONGBOW/AMELIA GREER")
```

The preceding commands will give you the following graph:

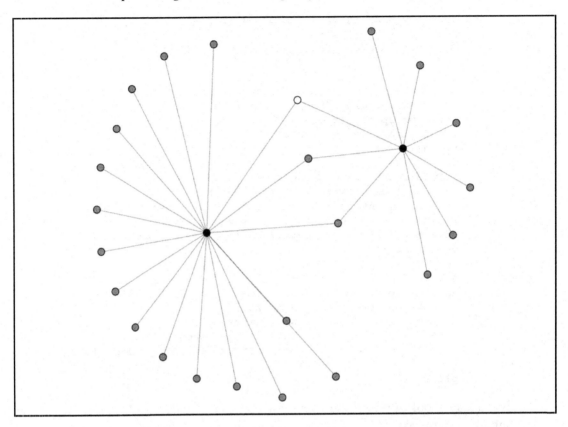

The preceding figure shows this one-hop ego network, which is derived from the expanded comic-to-hero social graph. Since there are two different types of nodes, we have visually colored them differently; orange nodes are characters and blue nodes are comic books. The ego node, LONGBOW/AMELIA GREER herself is white.

4. Let's create a two-hop ego network for the same character:

```
>>> draw_ego_graph(graph, "LONGBOW/AMELIA GREER", 2)
```

The preceding command will give you the following graph as output:

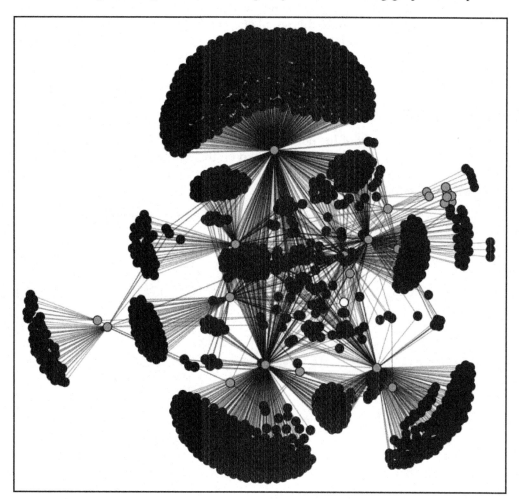

How it works...

Amelia Greer (also known as Longbow) is part of a mercenary special operations unit called the Harriers. She appears in two Marvel comics, particularly *The Uncanny X-Men Vol 1 #261* in May of 1990. Her ego network is very close knit (containing mostly members from the Harriers), as you can see in the preceding one-hop network figure.

The preceding two-hop network considerably expands the volume of the network. The black nodes represent the second hop to the next comic book community of characters. Clusters are readily apparent, even in this small ego network. Still, even one-hop network can say a lot about group membership and the importance of an actor. We will talk about how to build such graphs later on in this chapter.

There's more...

The ego can or cannot be a part of the network. In fact, membership testing on the ego is not important since the subgraph was generated based on the neighborhood of the ego! Instead, removal of the ego can show structural configurations of the network. Consider the social networks shown in the following figure:

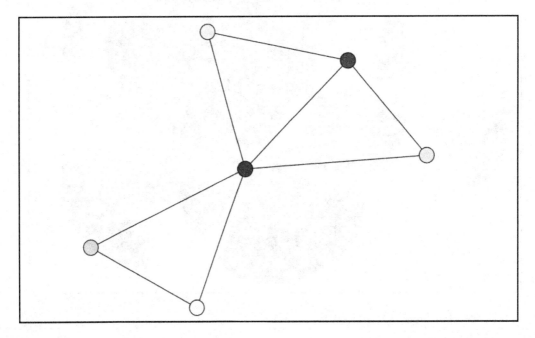

In the preceding figure, the ego is included as part of the graph; the structure of the network seems unified and cohesive.

As you can see, without the ego, isolations become important, as do obvious outliers. Aggregating these isolations across egos is how group membership and communities are discovered. We'll explore this more in the next sections.

Finding strong ties

Currently, our hero network simply measures whether two characters are connected. This computation is simple; do they appear in the same comic book together? We assume that in the small temporal space of a comic book, even cameos mean that the characters have interacted with each other. However, this does not tell us who the most important relations for a particular character are.

In order to determine the most important folks in an ego network (or to determine relative affinity between two actors), we need to determine edge weights. Since edges represent interaction, affiliation, or social relations, adding a weight determines the distance between two actors, relative to other actors with similar connections. Proxies for edge weights in social networks include:

- Frequency, for example, how often two actors communicate
- Reciprocity, for example, whether or not the relationship is reciprocal
- Type or attributes, for example, married actors have a stronger tie than college roommates
- Structure of the neighborhood, for example, the number of mutual friends

In our heroic social graph, we'll use the number of comic books in which a pair of characters appears together as a proxy for the strength of their tie. This seems to make sense; if one character is a villain that appears in the same comics as a hero, their relationship is that of a nemesis, it's not a simple protagonist/antagonist relationship! Another example is that of two heroes appearing together often. They might be part of a heroic team (for example, The Avengers) or share a sidekick relationship (for example, Bucky to Captain America).

Getting ready

If you completed the previous recipes, you should be ready to tackle this one.

How to do it...

The following steps will walk us through finding the strong ties in the network:

1. In order to compute the ties, we'll recreate the hero network graph from the comic hero network dataset. Since this represents an entire graph computation (for example, we will iterate through every node in the graph), we'll need to use a memory-safe iterator and save the intermediate data to disk. Here is the complete code; we'll go over it line by line, as follows:

```python
def transform_to_weighted_heros(comics):
    # Create new graph to fill in
    heros = nx.Graph(name="Weighted Heroic Social Network")
    # Iterate through all the nodes and their properties
    for node, data in graph.nodes(data=True):
        # We don't care about comics, only heros
        if data['TYPE'] == 'comic': continue
        # Add the hero and their properties (this will also update
data)
        heros.add_node(node, **data)

        # Find all the heros connected via the comic books
        for comic in graph[node]:
            for alter in graph[comic]:
                # Skip the hero that we're on
                if alter == node: continue

                # Setup the default edge
                if alter not in heros[node]:
                    heros.add_edge(node, alter, weight=0.0,
                    label="knows")

                # The weight of the hero is the fraction of
                connections / 2
                heros[node][alter]["weight"] += 1.0 /
                (graph.degree(comic) *2)
    return heros
```

2. Let's see Longbow's social weighted graph now:

```python
def draw_weighted_ego_graph(graph, character, hops=1):
    # Graph and Position
    ego = nx.ego_graph(graph, character, hops)
    pos = nx.spring_layout(ego)
    plt.figure(figsize=(12,12))
    plt.axis('off')
```

```
# Coloration and Configuration
ego.node[character]["TYPE"] = "center"
valmap = { "hero": 0.0, "center": 1.0 }
types  = nx.get_node_attributes(ego, "TYPE")
values = [valmap.get(types[node], 0.25) for node in
ego.nodes()]
char_edges = ego.edges(data=True, nbunch=[character,])
nonchar_edges = ego.edges(nbunch=[n for n in ego.nodes()
if n != character])
elarge=[(u,v) for (u,v,d) in char_edges if d['weight'] >=0.12]
esmall=[(u,v) for (u,v,d) in char_edges if d['weight'] < 0.12]
print set([d['weight'] for (u,v,d) in char_edges])

# Draw
nx.draw_networkx_nodes(ego, pos,
                       node_size=200,
                       node_color=values,
                       cmap=plt.cm.Paired,
                       with_labels=False)

nx.draw_networkx_edges(ego,pos,edgelist=elarge,
                       width=1.5, edge_color='b')
nx.draw_networkx_edges(ego,pos,edgelist=esmall,
                       width=1,alpha=0.5,
                    edge_color='b',style='dashed')
nx.draw_networkx_edges(ego,pos,edgelist=nonchar_edges,
                       width=0.5,alpha=0.2,style='dashed')
plt.show()
```

The preceding commands will give you the following graph as output:

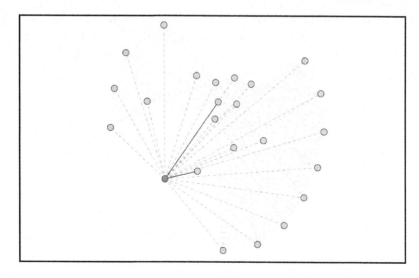

As you can see, Longbow shares two strong ties (represented by the heavy dark blue line), and this makes sense since she is in two comic books with only two other characters. The other characters she's directly related to have light blue dashed lines, representing her weaker ties to them.

Note that all characters are connected to the other characters with which they share ties in the ego network (represented by light grey dashed lines). Already, we can start to see clustering, as the characters from different comic books have moved to either side of Longbow's red node. Characters that have affinities with characters from both comics are in the middle.

How it works...

The `transform_to_weighted_heros` function is key to this recipe, and we explain it line by line here. First, we create an empty graph in which to add our transformation. Note that in NetworkX, there are functions such as `create_empty_graph` and `Graph.subgraph`; however, the former won't transfer the data that we need and the latter will transfer too much data. We'll go over each node in the original graph, skipping over comic books. Note that we'll add heroes twice using the `heros.add_node` method because every time we add an edge, it creates the node, if it doesn't exist already. However, to ensure that we get all the data over, we call `add_node` for each hero, and it will simply update the node's properties if it is already in the graph.

Next, we'll connect the heroes together through their comic-book relationships. We'll gather all the heroes connected to the same comic books our current hero is in (skipping the current hero to prevent self-loops). If there is no edge, we'll create a default edge, before adding our weight computation. The weight we'll assign is related to the number of characters in a comic book. It stands to reason that if a comic book has more characters in it, they are more loosely connected. Therefore, we compute our weight as the inverse of the degree of the comic book, divided by two. The division by two is required since this is an undirected graph, otherwise we will double all the weights!

There's more...

Weighted edges are essential to be able to make predictions on a graph, partially because they allow ranking of paths, but mostly because they reflect the underlying semantic associations of the social network. Making predictions relies on relationships that create **homophily** - this is the tendency of people with similar interests to gather together, and it leads to the formation of homogenous groups called clusters. Homophilous ties can be strong or weak; for instance, folks who go to the same school together represent a stronger tie than people who live in the same city.

Transitivity is the property of edges that allow us to make predictions. Simply stated, it offers the ability to perform triadic closures. If nodes A and B are connected, and A and C are also connected, then it is likely that B and C are connected too. Transitivity is evidence of the existence of strong ties, but it is not a necessary or sufficient condition, and it might not be applied equally to weak ties.

Bridges, on the other hand, are edges that connect nodes across groups. Bridges facilitate cluster communication, and are usually the product of weak ties or heterophilous relationships. Knowing and understanding these properties as they relate to your particular social graph essential for unlocking key insights and being able to make future predictions about how the graph might change.

Finding key players

In the previous recipe, *Finding strong ties*, we began exploring ego networks and strong ties between individuals in our social network. We started to see that actors with strong ties with other actors created clusters that centered on themselves. This leads to the obvious question: who are the key figures in the graph, and what kind of pull do they have? We'll look at a couple of measures to determine how important a node is or its centrality to try to discover the degree centrality, betweenness centrality, closeness centrality, and eigenvector centrality.

Getting ready

If you completed the previous recipes, you will be ready to start this one.

How to do it...

The following steps will identify key players in this network of comic book characters:

1. To find the top ten nodes in the heroes network, we compute the nodes' degree and sort them:

```
import operator

>>> degrees = sorted(graph.degree().items(),
key=operator.itemgetter(1), reverse=True)

>>> for node in degrees: print node
```

2. Additionally, we compute the percent of nodes in the graph that a node is connected to; NetworkX provides a helpful function, `degree_centrality`, to do this for us. While we're at it, we might as well also set this as a property for our nodes for easy lookup:

```
>>> centrality = nx.degree_centrality(graph)

>>> nx.set_node_attribues(graph, 'centrality', centrality)

>>> degrees = sorted(centrality.items(), key=itemgetter(1),
reverse=True)

>>> for item in degrees[0:10]: print "%s: %0.3f" % item
```

The preceding commands give us our top ten key players in the dataset, and I think it's obvious that they are the most influential characters in the Marvel universe:

```
1.  CAPTAIN AMERICA:        0.297 (1908)
2.  SPIDER-MAN/PETER PAR:   0.270 (1737)
3.  IRON MAN/TONY STARK :   0.237 (1522)
4.  THING/BENJAMIN J. GR:   0.220 (1416)
5.  MR. FANTASTIC/REED R:   0.215 (1379)
6.  WOLVERINE/LOGAN :       0.213 (1371)
7.  HUMAN TORCH/JOHNNY S:   0.212 (1361)
8.  SCARLET WITCH/WANDA :   0.206 (1325)
9.  THOR/DR. DONALD BLAK:   0.201 (1289)
10. BEAST/HENRY &HANK& P:   0.197 (1267)
```

These characters are hugely influential with a high number of connections, considering the average degree is *52.045*! While we're at it, we might as well create a histogram of the connectedness of the graph. A quick note before I show you the histogram: NetworkX does have a function, degree_histogram, which will return a list of the frequencies of degrees. However, in this case, the list's index is the degree value, and the bin width is 1; this means the length of the list can be very large (Order(len(edges))). Using graph.degree().values() is a bit more efficient, particularly for social network graphs, as we'll see next.

3. With the following little snippet, you should now be able to see just how far from normal our top characters are in terms of influence:

```
>>> import matplotlib.pyplot as plt
>>> plt.hist(graph.degree().values(), bins=500)
>>> plt.title("Connectedness of Marvel Characters")
>>> plt.xlabel("Degree")
>>> plt.ylabel("Frequency")
>>> plt.show()
```

The preceding snippet will give you the following graph as output:

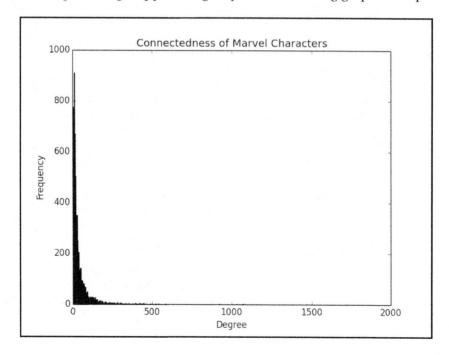

4. In fact, you can filter out the number of characters whose node degree is greater than 500, that is, the top one percent. This filter returns 98.8 percent of characters:

```
>>> filter(lambda v: v < 500, graph.degree().values())
```

If you do so, the curve becomes slightly more apparent:

```
>>> import matplotlib.pyplot as plt
>>> plt.hist(graph.degree().values(), bins=500)
>>> plt.title("Connectedness of Marvel Characters")
>>> plt.xlabel("Degree")
>>> plt.ylabel("Frequency")
```

The preceding commands will give you the following output:

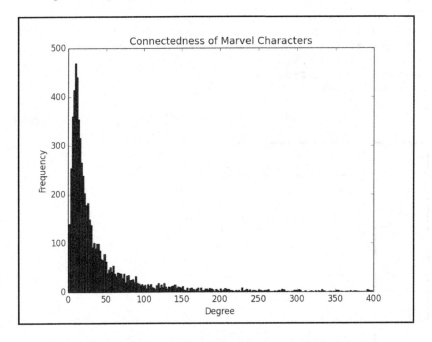

5. To compute other centrality metrics, we will use NetworkX built-in functions. To compute betweenness centrality, use the following functions:

```
>>> centrality = nx.betweenness_centrality(graph)
>>> normalied  = nx.betweenness_centrality(graph, normalized=True)
>>> weighted   = nx.betweenness_centrality(graph, weight="weight")
```

The preceding function allows you to compute betweenness centrality, which will be discussed later, and can be normalized or weighted.

6. To compute the closeness centrality, we can use the following functions, which are similar to the betweenness centrality:

```
>>> centrality = nx.closeness_centrality(graph)
>>> normalied  = nx.closeness_centrality(graph, normalized=True)
>>> weighted   = nx.closeness_centrality(graph, distance="weight")
```

7. Finally, to compute the eigenvector centrality, you have two choices with NetworkX:

```
>>> centrality = nx.eigenvector_centality(graph)
>>> centrality = nx.eigenvector_centrality_numpy(graph)
```

8. In order to easily explore these centrality metrics on our graph, let's create a function that generically prints the top 10 nodes based on the centrality metric:

```
def nbest_centrality(graph, metric, n=10, attribute="centrality",
**kwargs):
    centrality = metric(graph, **kwargs)
    nx.set_node_attributes(graph, attribute, centrality)
    degrees = sorted(centrality.items(), key=itemgetter(1),
reverse=True)
    for idx, item in enumerate(degrees[0:n]):
        item = (idx+1,) + item
        print "%i. %s: %0.3f" % item
```

9. Now, we can simply use this function with our centrality metric to find the nbest (by default top 10) nodes according to their centrality. The usage is as follows:

```
>>> nbest_centrality(graph, nx.degree_centrality)
>>> nbest_centrality(graph, nx.betweenness_centrality,
normalized=True)
>>> nbest_centrality(graph, nx.closeness_centrality)
>>> nbest_centrality(graph, nx.eigenvector_centrality_numpy)
```

How it works...

Clearly, there are far more minor characters in the **Marvel Universe**, and 100 or so major characters. Interestingly, this compares favorably with the real world! There are far more actors with few connections in real-world social graphs, and relatively few top echelon characters with a lot of ties. We know this intuitively, and we call the actors in the top one percent of connections celebrities.

In fact, celebrities are extreme outliers who exert such strong influence on their social graphs that we tend to call them *super nodes*. Super nodes have the property that to a far enough hop distance, all traversals of the graph will inevitably find their shortest path through a super node. This can be very bad for computation; even the earlier Longbow graph experienced a huge computational lag, and we had a tough time drawing the graph because of the two super nodes Longbow was connected to: Wolverine and Jean Grey. While it's not only proof of Kevin Bacon's six degrees of separation, dealing with super nodes is also an important part of graph computation.

On the other end of the scale, we can calculate Dunbar's number for our social network. Dunbar identified and measured the correlation between neocortical volume and social group size not only for human communities, but also for primates. In order to calculate this number, we cannot simply compute the average degree across all nodes due to the strong left-hand skew in this dataset. Let's compare the mean, mode, and median as our corollary to Dunbar's number. Later, we'll look at using weighted relationships to further induce strong ties:

```
>>> import numpy as np
>>> import scipy.stats as st
>>> data = np.array(graph.degree().values())
>>> np.mean(data)
52.0445066916
>>> st.mode(data)
(array([ 11.]), array([ 254.]))
>>> np.median(data)
20.0
```

Dunbar's number for comic book heroes appears to be much lower than a typical social graph, but proportional to natural scale graphs (consider that your social graph in high school was probably smaller than your adult social graph). It seems that the heroic Dunbar's number is somewhere between 11 and 20 connections. Could this be because alien or mutant neocortical volume is less than a human's? Or, is it because our heroes are naturally isolated given their abilities that set them apart?

There's more...

The most common, and perhaps simplest, technique to find the key actors of a graph is to measure the degree of each vertex. Degree is a signal that determines how connected a node is, which can be a metaphor for influence or popularity. At the very least, the most connected nodes are the ones that spread information the fastest, or have the greatest effect on their community. Measures of degree tend to suffer from dilution, and benefit from statistical techniques to normalize datasets.

The betweenness centrality

A path is a sequence of nodes between a start node and an end node, where no node appears twice on the path and is measured by the number of edges included (also called hops). The most interesting path to compute for two given nodes is the shortest path, for example, the minimum number of edges required to reach another node, which is also called the node distance.

Note that paths can be of length 0, the distance from a node to itself. Consider the following graph as an example:

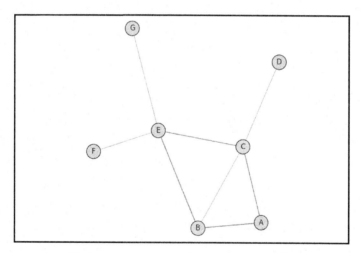

The shortest distance between **D** and **F** is the path {D, C, E, F}, which is a distance of three. On the other hand, the shortest paths from **A** to **E** are the two paths {A, C, E} and {A, B, E}, which share a path length of (highlighted in purple and red).

Finding the shortest paths between two nodes brings up a question from the last section. If key nodes are often traversed to find the shortest path, is there a shortest path-based measure of centrality? The answer is yes. The betweenness centrality identifies the nodes that are more likely to be in the shortest path than others. This is extremely useful at discovering not only strong points in the social graph, but also weak points that will be cut off if a central node is removed.

The computation for the betweenness centrality for a given node is as follows. For a node, **V**, the betweenness centrality is defined as the sum of the fraction of all the pairs of shortest paths that pass through v. The betweenness centrality can also be normalized for the number of nodes in the graph, or weighted to accept edge weights:

```
>>> centrality = nx.betweeenness_centrality(graph)
>>> normalied   = nx.betweenness_centrality(graph, normalized=True)
>>> weighted    = nx.betweenness_centrality(graph, weight="weight")
```

The preceding commands will give you the following output:

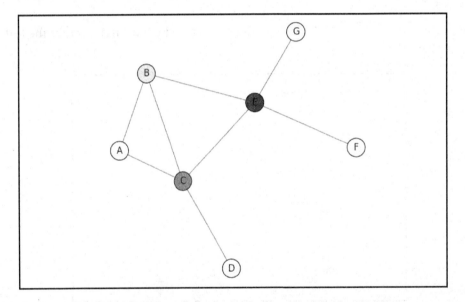

When the betweenness centrality is computed for our small example graph, **B** and **C** have good centrality scores (0.1 and 0.433, respectively). This is because they are in the middle of a large part of the network. **E**, however, has a centrality score of 0.6, which is because **E** connects two different sections of the network (there are no other paths to **G** and **F**).

As before, we can check the betweenness centrality for our heroic graph, and find the heroes that have the top betweenness centralities:

Note that this computation is extremely expensive and could take a long time on your computer!

```
>>> nbest_centrality(graph, nx.betweenness_centrality, normalized=True)
```

The following is the output:

```
1.  SPIDER-MAN/PETER PAR: 0.074
2.  CAPTAIN AMERICA:      0.057
3.  IRON MAN/TONY STARK:  0.037
4.  WOLVERINE/LOGAN:      0.036
5.  HAVOK/ALEX SUMMERS:   0.036
6.  DR. STRANGE/STEPHEN:  0.029
7.  THING/BENJAMIN J. GR: 0.025
8.  HAWK:                 0.025
9.  HULK/DR. ROBERT BRUC: 0.024
10. MR. FANTASTIC/REED R: 0.024
```

Compared to the degree centrality results, these numbers are very different. `Spider-Man` and `Captain America` have switched places at numbers one and two, but still share the top three spots with `Iron Man`. `Wolverine` has been promoted to number four, and `Mr. Fantastic` and The Thing have been demoted. Truly interesting, however, are the new appearances of `Hawk`, `Hulk`, `Dr. Strange`, and `Havok` to the list, replacing Beast, Thor, The Scarlet Witch, and The Human Torch, who, while popular, are not as able to link characters together!

The closeness centrality

Another centrality measure, closeness, takes a statistical look at the outgoing paths for a particular node, v. What is the average number of hops to reach any other node in the network from v? This is simply computed as the reciprocal of the mean distance to all other nodes in the graph, which can be normalized to *n-1 / size(G)-1*, where *n* is all nodes in the neighborhood, if all nodes in the graph are connected. The reciprocal ensures that nodes that are closer (for example, fewer hops) score better, for example closer to one as in other centrality scores:

```
>>> centrality = nx.closeness_centrality(graph)
>>> normalied  = nx.closeness_centrality(graph, normalized=True)
>>> weighted   = nx.closeness_centrality(graph, distance="weight")
```

Again, when we run this metric on our social network of heroes, you should find that it

takes a while to run; however, if you use the normalized method, the process can be accelerated drastically:

```
>>> nbest_centrality(graph, nx.closeness_centrality)
1.   CAPTAIN AMERICA:         0.584
2.   SPIDER-MAN/PETER PAR:    0.574
3.   IRON MAN/TONY STARK :    0.561
4.   THING/BENJAMIN J. GR:    0.558
5.   MR. FANTASTIC/REED R:    0.556
6.   WOLVERINE/LOGAN :        0.555
7.   HUMAN TORCH/JOHNNY S:    0.555
8.   SCARLET WITCH/WANDA :    0.552
9.   THOR/DR. DONALD BLAK:    0.551
10.  BEAST/HENRY &HANK& P:    0.549
```

Once again, we return to our original list, obtained via the degree centrality. In this case, Kevin Bacon's rule applies. These very popular super node celebrities are going to have the most reach, that is, they have the ability to get to all other nodes in the fastest amount of time. Things have changed for our smaller graph, however:

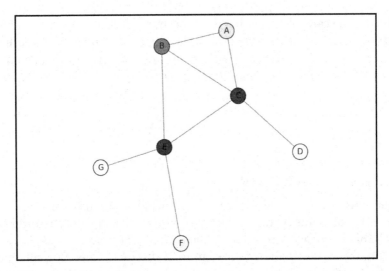

Here, we see that **C** and **E** are the most central nodes in terms of closeness; they can reach all other nodes equally. **B** is less close than **C** and **E**, but fares pretty well, and **A**, because it has two connections, does slightly better than **D**, **G**, or **F** at being able to reach all other nodes in the network.

The eigenvector centrality

The eigenvector centrality of a node, v, is proportional to the sum of the centrality scores of its neighbors. For example, the more important people you are connected to, the more important you are. This centrality measure is very interesting because an actor with a small number of hugely influential contacts might outrank ones with many more mediocre contacts. For our social network, it will hopefully allow us to get underneath the celebrity structure of heroic teams and see who actually is holding the social graph together.

To compute the eigenvector centrality, calculate the **argmax** of the eigendecomposition of the pairwise adjacency matrix of the graph. The *i*th element in the eigenvector gives the centrality of the *i*th node. If you're familiar with **Google's PageRank**, then this should sound familiar, and in fact, PageRank is a modified eigenvector centrality measure, where instead of computing against an adjacency matrix, Google uses probabilities and computes eigendecomposition across a stochastic matrix.

Adjacency matrices are two-dimensional matrices where each node's vector is a flag indicating if it and the other node share an edge. Undirected graphs always have symmetric adjacency matrices, while directed graphs can be more complex. For our simple graph example in this section, here is the adjacency matrix:

	A	B	C	D	E	F	G
A	–	1	1	0	0	0	0
B	1	–	1	0	1	0	0
C	1	1	–	1	1	0	0
D	0	0	1	–	0	0	0
E	0	1	1	0	–	1	1
F	0	0	0	0	1	–	0
G	0	0	0	0	1	0	–

However, we won't implement the algorithm to compute the eigenvector centrality, instead, we will rely on the many graph algorithms already built into NetworkX. In this case, we have two choices to compute the eigenvector centrality:

```
>>> centrality = nx.eigenvector_centrality(graph)
>>> centrality = nx.eigenvector_centrality_numpy(graph)
```

The first choice uses the power method to find the eigenvector, and will only run up to the preset maximum number of iterations, offering no guarantee of convergence. The second choice will use the NumPy eigenvalue solver. You should use the second algorithm whenever possible to ensure a complete result. Why should you, you might ask? The NumPy version will continue to run until convergence, which means it has the possibility of getting stuck depending on the input data. The NumPy version can also be made to overfit the solution. However, the number one reason for which you'd use the power method is speed; very typically, the power method will solve the eigenvalue faster than the NumPy method does because of the fixed number of iterations. These properties of the solver, however, are all completely dependent on the size of the graph (the input data). For larger graphs, you might be forced to use the power method because anything else will become intractable.

Note that there are also corresponding `pagerank` and `pagerank_numpy` module functions to compute these scores. Let's see how our heroes did:

```
>>> nbest_centrality(graph, nx.eigenvector_centrality_numpy)
1.   CAPTAIN AMERICA:       0.117
2.   IRON MAN/TONY STARK:   0.103
3.   SCARLET WITCH/WANDA:   0.101
4.   THING/BENJAMIN J. GR:  0.101
5.   SPIDER-MAN/PETER PAR:  0.100
6.   MR. FANTASTIC/REED R:  0.100
7.   VISION:                0.099
8.   HUMAN TORCH/JOHNNY S:  0.099
9.   WOLVERINE/LOGAN:       0.098
10.  BEAST/HENRY &HANK& P:  0.096
```

Once again, there is some upheaval in our top 10 list! `Captain America` takes the top spot again, but `Spider-Man` loses more than just a place, dropping half way down the list. The `Thing`, `Scarlet Witch`, and `Iron Man` move up the list, and, as a surprise, a new actor, `Vision`, moves onto the list.

Our smaller graph has now ranked our nodes a bit more strongly:

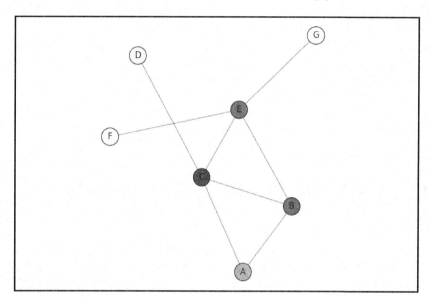

Now, **B** and **C** are the most strongly ranked nodes. **E** is also highly ranked, but it is not as central as before, and **A** is more central than it was. Additionally, **F**, **D**, and **G** have moved above zero for their centrality score, which can be important when determining thresholds.

Deciding on centrality algorithm

So, which measure of centrality should you use? Well, it depends on what you're looking for, as each centrality mechanism is designed to deal with different features of social networks. The following are a few measures of centrality:

- **Degree**: This is a measure of popularity, and it is useful in determining nodes that can quickly spread information to a localized area, for example, the neighborhood. Think celebrities; these are nodes that can reach many people directly.
- **Betweenness**: This shows which nodes are likely pathways of information, and can be used to determine where the graph will break apart if the node is removed. It is also used to show the direct path to other clusters or groups in the network.

- **Closeness**: This is a measure of reach, that is, how fast information will spread to all other nodes from this particular node. Nodes with the most central closeness enjoy short durations during broadcast communication.
- **Eigenvector**: This is a measure of related influence. Who is closest to the most important people in the graph? This can be used to show the power behind the scenes, or to show relative influence beyond popularity.

For many analyses, all measures of closeness can be used to achieve critical results for a single social network!

Exploring the characteristics of entire networks

In the next set of recipes, we will characterize our social network as a whole, rather than from the perspective of individual actors. This task is usually secondary to getting a feel of the most important nodes, but it is a chicken and an egg problem; determining the techniques to analyze and splitting the whole graph can be informed by key player analyses, and vice versa.

Getting ready

If you completed the previous recipes, you will be ready to proceed with this one.

How to do it...

The following steps will walk us through our first exploration of graph characteristics at the level of the whole graph:

1. Let's compute both the density of the entire network and that of the ego graphs:

```
>>> nx.density(graph)
0.00810031232554
>>> ego = nx.ego_graph(graph, "LONGBOW/AMELIA GREER")
>>> nx.density(ego)
0.721014492754
```

As you can see, our heroic social network is not very dense; it's not very cliquish as a whole. However, Longbow's social network is very dense and extremely cliquish. Typically speaking, density is used to compare subgraphs of the entire social network (like ego graphs), rather than as a model for how a particular graph will behave by itself.

2. Graphs can also be analyzed in terms of distance (the shortest path between two nodes). The longest distance in a graph is called the diameter of the social graph, and it represents the longest information flow along the graph. Typically, less dense (sparse) social networks will have a larger diameter than more dense networks. Additionally, the average distance is an interesting metric as it can give you information about how close nodes are to each other:

```
>>> for subgraph in nx.connected_component_subgraphs(graph):
...     print nx.diameter(subgraph)
...     print nx.average_shortest_path_length(subgraph)
diameter: 5
average distance: 2.638
```

Note that our heroic social graph is not completely connected, there are some isolated subgraphs, and therefore, we use the `nx.connected_component_subgraphs` generator to capture each subgraph. You can test if the social graph is connected with `nx.is_connected(G)` and determine the number of components via `nx.number_connected_components`. In the heroic social graph, there are four components, but only two have a significant number of nodes.

3. Finally, we can compute the reciprocity of the network, that is, the ratio of the number of relationships that are reciprocated (for example, if there is a bidirectional link) to the total number of relationships in the social network. Currently, there is no built-in NetworkX method to perform this computation. However, this methodology will work, using the `NetworkX.DiGraph` subclass of `Graph`:

```
>>> unigraph = digraph.to_undirected()
>>> return len(unigraph.edges()) / len(digraph.edges())
```

The reciprocal flag in the `to_undirected` method ensures that only edges that appear in both directions will be kept.

This method will only work for directed graphs. Unfortunately, our heroic network is completely reciprocal since we use the known relationship, and it has a reciprocity of 1.00, as a result.

How it works...

In this recipe, we examined three different graph characteristics. The density of a network is the ratio of the number of edges in the network to the total number of possible edges in the network. The possible number of edges for a graph of *n* vertices is $n(n-1)/2$ for an undirected graph (remove the division for a directed graph). Perfectly connected networks (every node shares an edge with every other node) have a density of 1, and are often called cliques.

Graphs can also be analyzed in terms of distance (the shortest path between two nodes). The longest distance in a graph is called the diameter of the social graph, and it represents the longest information flow along the graph. Typically, less dense (sparse) social networks will have a larger diameter than more dense networks. Additionally, the average distance is an interesting metric as it can give you information about how close nodes are to each other.

The last social network measure we'll discuss is reciprocity. This is the ratio of the number of relationships that are reciprocated (for example, there is a bidirectional link) to the total number of relationships in the social network. This only makes sense for directed graphs. For example, the Twitter social network is a directed graph; you can follow others, but this does not necessarily mean that they will also follow you. Since our social network of heroes is semantically undirected, we cannot perform this computation.

Clustering and community detection in social networks

Graphs exhibit clustering behavior, and identification of communities is an important task in social networks. A node's clustering coefficient is the number of triadic closures (closed triples) in the node's neighborhood. This is an expression of transitivity. Nodes with higher transitivity exhibit higher subdensity, and if completely closed, form cliques that can be identified as communities. In this recipe, we will look at clustering and community detection in social networks.

Getting ready

You will again need **NetworkX** and, for the first time in this chapter, the python-louvain library.

How to do it...

These steps will guide you through the detection of communities within social networks:

1. Let's actually get into some clustering. The `python-louvain` library uses NetworkX to perform community detection with the `louvain` method. Here is a simple example of cluster partitioning on a small, built-in social network:

```
G = nx.karate_club_graph()

#first compute the best partition
partition = community.best_partition(G)

#drawing
pos = nx.spring_layout(G)
plt.figure(figsize=(12,12))
plt.axis('off')

nx.draw_networkx_nodes(G, pos, node_size=200, cmap=plt.cm.RdYlBu,
node_color=partition.values())
nx.draw_networkx_edges(G,pos, alpha=0.5)
plt.savefig("figure/karate_communities.png")
```

The following is the resulting graph with shades of grey and/or colors representing different partitions:

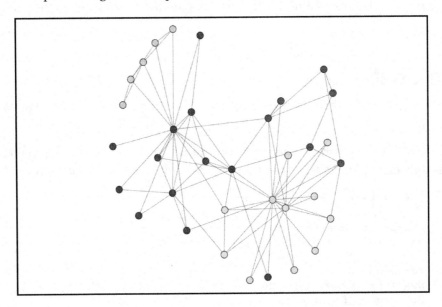

This is pretty neat! We can see there are yellow, light blue, and dark red cliques, but dark blue is pretty homogenous. We'll talk more about how to create graph visualizations with matplotlib later.

2. To partition our comic book characters, we'll add their partitions to each of their nodes; we'll then look at the relative sizes of each partition:

```
>>> graph = graph_from_csv(HERO_NETWORK)
>>> partition = community.best_partition(graph)
>>> print "%i partitions" % len(set(partition.values()))

25 partitions
>>> nx.set_node_attributes(graph, 'partition', partition)
```

As you can see, the `louvain` method has discovered 25 communities without our social graph.

3. To examine the relative size of each community, a histogram view may be helpful. To create the histogram, add the following function to your file:

```
import matplotlib.pyplot as plt

def communities_histogram(graph):
```

```
graph, partition = detect_communities(graph)
numbins = len(partition.values())

plt.hist(partition.values(), bins=numbins), color="#0f6dbc")
plt.title("Size of Marvel Communities")
plt.xlabel("Community")
plt.ylabel("Nodes")

plt.show()
```

This should produce the following figure:

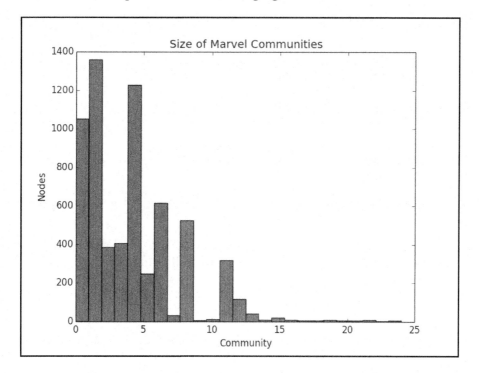

There are three major communities containing over a thousand nodes each. However, we also have eight medium-size communities around 400 actors strong. The other communities are much smaller, but it does appear that the Marvel social graph is indeed a real-world and small-world graph, much like the natural social networks observed in human culture!

4. An alternate, area-based approach to visualizing the size of the Marvel communities is to use a bubble chart. The area of each circle represents the size of each community. Graphs such as the following are often used to collapse large graphs into subgraphs based on community. To create this code, add the following function to your file:

```
def communities_bubblechart(graph):
graph, partition = detect_communities(graph)

parts = defaultdict(int)
for part in partition.values():
    parts[part] += 1

bubbles = nx.Graph()
for part in parts.items():
    bubbles.add_node(part[0], size=part[1])
pos = nx.random_layout(bubbles)
plt.figure(figsize=(12,12))
plt.axis('off')

nx.draw_networkx_nodes(bubbles, pos,
    alpha=0.6, node_size=map(lambda x: x*6, parts.
    values()),
    node_color=[random.random() for x in parts.values()],
    cmap=plt.cm.RdYlBu)

plt.show()
```

When run, this code should produce the following figure for our Hero network:

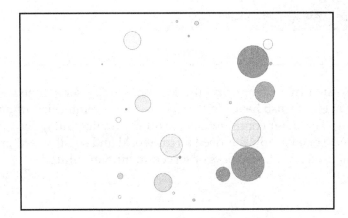

How it works...

NetworkX has several mechanisms to compute clusters:

```
>>> nx.transitivity(graph)
0.194539747093
>>> nx.average_clustering(graph)
0.774654121711
```

The nx.transitivity function uses the nx.triangles function to compute the ratio of the number of triangles to the number of possible triangles. The nx.clustering function computes the clustering coefficient for each node, and the nx_average_clustering function computes the average coefficient for the graph. Higher transitivity and clustering coefficients mean that the graph exhibits the small world effect.

The small world is a network that appears random, but it has a high transitivity and a short average path length. This is a very common structure for social networks because the semantics of modern networks have strong ties and, therefore, strong transitivity. This essentially means that there are a series of large clusters with few bridge nodes. The heroes' social network exhibits both the small-world effect as well as a preferential attachment; the majority of new edges are to nodes with an already high degree, thus creating a long-tail, left-skewed distribution as we've seen in our graph.

There's more...

The Louvian method is a greedy optimization method that partitions the network, and optimizes the modularity of each network partition. First, the method identifies small communities by attempting to optimize local modularity, and then it aggregates the nodes belonging to the same community and performs the process again. In this way, a hierarchical data structure of communities is returned. The method is simple, efficient, and works against large networks of millions of nodes with billions of links.

The original method was developed by Etienne Lefebvre at UCL (Louvain-la-Neuve); it was then co-authored and improved along with Vincent Blondel, Jean-Loup Guillaume, and Renaud Lambiotte. It is the "Louvain method" because the method is devised when all the members of the team were at the Université catholique de Louvain. Together, the authors have created a Python method to compute these hierarchical communities, a method that depends on NetworkX. The basic detection algorithm is as follows:

```
import community
import networkx as nx
def detect_communities(graph):
    partition = community.best_partition(graph)
```

```
nx.set_node_attributes(graph, 'partition', partition)
return graph, partition
```

This function expects an `nx.Graph` and uses the `community` module to compute the best root partition. The partition is hierarchical, so to get the subcommunities, we simply iterate over the parts in the partition and assign the nodes in our graph an attribute called `partition`, which identifies a node with their community. The function then returns both the modified graph and the partition to use in visualization.

Visualizing graphs

Throughout this chapter, we have been visualizing social networks to help develop our understanding and intuition around graphs. In this recipe, we dig a little bit deeper into

graph visualization.

Getting ready

Ensure that you have **NetworkX** and **matplotlib** installed.

How to do it...

Complete this list of steps to gain a better understanding of graph visualization in Python:

1. NetworkX wraps matplotlib or graphviz to draw simple graphs using the same charting library that we saw in the previous chapter. This is effective for smaller-size graphs, but with larger graphs, memory can quickly be consumed. To draw a small graph, simply use the `networkx.draw` function, and then use `pyplot.show` to display it:

```
>>> import networkx as nx
>>> import matplotlib.pyplot as plt
>>> nx.draw(graph)
>>> plt.show()
```

2. There is, however, a rich drawing library underneath that lets you customize how the graph looks and is laid out with many different layout algorithms. Let's take a look at an example using one of the social graphs that comes with the NetworkX library, the *Davis Southern Club Women* graph:

```
import networkx as nx
import matplotlib.pyplot as pl

# Generate the Graph
G=nx.davis_southern_women_graph()
# Create a Spring Layout
pos=nx.spring_layout(G)

# Find the center Node
dmin=1
ncenter=0
for n in pos:
    x,y=pos[n]
    d=(x-0.5)**2+(y-0.5)**2
    if d<dmin:
        ncenter=n
        dmin=d
```

3. Next, we'll colorize the graph. First, we have to determine the center node, as we'll color this the darkest. Then, all nodes that are farther away will be colored lighter, until they become white. The spring layout has already determined the (x, y) coordinates for each node, so it's simple to compute the Euclidean distance of each node to the center of the graph (the point (0.5, 0.5), in this case), and find the node that has the lowest distance. Once determined, we compute the number of hops (for example, the path length) of every node to the center node. The nx.single_source_shortest_path_length function returns a dictionary of nodes and their distance to the node supplied as an argument. We will then use these distances to determine colors:

```
p=nx.single_source_shortest_path_length(G,ncenter)
```

4. Up next, it's time to draw the graph. We create a matplotlib figure, and then draw the edges using the NetworkX draw function. Then, we draw the nodes. This function uses a colormap (the cmap argument) to determine the range of colors to use, determined by the hop distance:

```
plt.figure(figsize=(8,8))
nx.draw_networkx_edges(G,pos,nodelist=[ncenter],alpha=0.4)
nx.draw_networkx_nodes(G,pos,nodelist=p.keys(),
                       node_size=90,
```

```
        node_color=p.values(),
        cmap=plt.cm.Reds_r)
```

```
plt.show()
```

Calling this function will result in a graph as shown in the following figure:

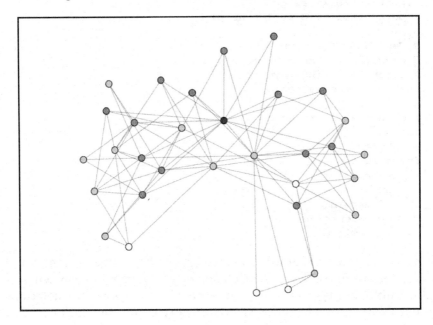

How it works...

In the preceding code, we create a graph, **G**, via the `davis_southern_women_graph`
function, one of the many built-in graph generation functions that is included with
NetworkX. We then find the position of every node in G using a layout. Layouts are
algorithms that are designed to determine where nodes are placed on the graph to create an
effective visualization. NetworkX comes with five positioning algorithms, by default.
Circular layouts position nodes in a circle, and shell layouts position nodes in concentric
circles. Random layouts uniformly distribute the nodes, and the spectral layout positions
using the eigenvectors of the Laplacian graph.

The spring layout is perhaps the most common. Spring layouts are a force-directed layout, which means each node repulses other nodes around it, while edges hold them together. All the nodes are dropped onto the graph, and the repulsion/attraction is computed in a recursive manner. For each iteration, nodes will repulse and attract each other into a stable layout. There are several force-directed algorithms, but NetworkX uses the Fruchterman-Reingold algorithm.

Social networks in R

The purpose of this brief section is to help the reader carry out the tasks done earlier in the chapter using the R statistical software. Luke (2015) is a comprehensive account of dealing with social networks in R. We will begin with a very simple and arbitrary social network and we will then consider the Bali terrorist network in detail.

Using a simple and arbitrary social network, we set the ball rolling related to R implementation. Simple and useful functions are taken up first. The next social network used is detailed in the following.

Bali Terrorist Network, *Stuart Koschade*'s, PhD thesis available at http://eprints.qut.edu.au/16591/ deals with the *Jemaah Islamiyah* 2002 Bali Terrorist Network. The ties here represent contacts among the Bali terrorist cell. The dataset consists of ordinal variable as an edge characteristic, IC, which measures the frequency and duration of the contact with one indicating a weak relationship, and progressively indicating better relationships, with five indicating the strongest relationship. Technically, the R network object Bali.rda is available at the Luke's GitHub link https://github.com/DougLuke/UserNetRas also his books *R package UserNetR*. However, we simply provide the reader with the required rda file.

The R packages that are generally useful in analysis of social networks are sna, statnet, network, and igraph. For more details, refer to Luke (2015).

Getting ready

The required R packages for carrying out the tasks in this recipe are sna, statnet, network, and igraph. The simple way to install these packages in R is running the command install.packages(c("sna","statnet","network","igraph")). The reader would also be required to have the Bali.rda file in the current working directory.

How to do it...

1. The first task is to load the required libraries:

```
library(statnet,quietly=TRUE)
library(network,quietly=TRUE)
```

The purpose of specifying the option `quietly=TRUE` is that a lot of comments are printed to the console and we can offset that with this option. Operationally, it makes no difference whether we use this option or not.

2. Next, we specify a matrix with four rows and columns, a square matrix as expected, which will be then used to set up a network:

```
netmat1 <- rbind(c(0,1,1,0),
                 c(1,0,1,0),
                 c(1,1,0,1),
                 c(0,0,1,0))
rownames(netmat1) <- c("A","B","C","D")
colnames(netmat1) <- c("A","B","C","D")
netmat1
```

3. A consequence is the following output in the R console:

```
> netmat1
  A B C D
A 0 1 1 0
B 1 0 1 0
C 1 1 0 1
D 0 0 1 0
```

4. The matrix will be used to set up the social network as the next step.

5. The matrix `netmat1` is transformed into a network using the same named function and package. The elementary functions are also applied on the network object to get the basic characteristics of the network:

```
net1 <- network(netmat1,matrix.type="adjacency")
class(net1)
summary(net1)
network.size(net1)
network.density(net1)
components(net1)
gplot(net1, vertex.col = 2, displaylabels = TRUE)
```

The R output in the console is as in the following:

```
> net1 <- network(netmat1,matrix.type="adjacency")
> class(net1)
[1] "network"
> summary(net1)
Network attributes:
vertices = 4
directed = TRUE
hyper = FALSE
loops = FALSE
multiple = FALSE
bipartite = FALSE
total edges = 8
missing edges = 0
non-missing edges = 8
density = 0.6666667
Vertex attributes:
vertex.names:
character valued attribute
4 valid vertex names
No edge attributes
Network adjacency matrix:
  A B C D
A 0 1 1 0
B 1 0 1 0
C 1 1 0 1
D 0 0 1 0
> network.size(net1)
[1] 4
> network.density(net1)
[1] 0.6666667
> components(net1)
Node 1, Reach 4, Total 4
Node 2, Reach 4, Total 8
Node 3, Reach 4, Total 12
Node 4, Reach 4, Total 16
[1] 1
> gplot(net1, vertex.col = 2, displaylabels = TRUE)
```

Executing the preceding R code chunk at the console, we can set up and inspect various facets of the network. The function `network` helps us to convert the matrix `netmat1` to a (social) network `net1` and this confirmation is provided by the line `class(net1)` whose output says that the class of the object is indeed a `network`. Next, the `summary` function tells us that the network tells us that we have `4vertices` in `net1`, the network is `directed` one, and that there are **8** total edges, also the number of 1's in the **netmat1** matrix. The network net1 size and density are respectively 4 and `0.6666667`. The `gplot` function from the `sna` package helps in visualizing the network:

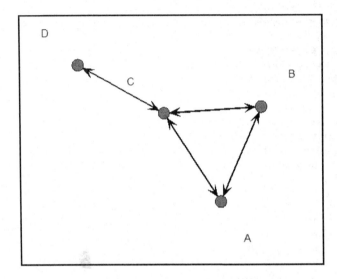

We will next look at a more complex and practical network and analyze it in R. The network is the Bali terrorist network and its explanation was given earlier. The **Bali.rda** file is taken from Luke's package, **UserNetR** . First, the network is imported in R and then we carry out the summary statistics as with the net1 network.

6. Load the `Bali` network and carry out the basic summary as follows:

```
load("Bali.rda")
class(Bali)
Bali
# Basic Properties
network.size(Bali)
network.density(Bali)
# VIsualization
windows(height=30,width=30)
gplot(Bali,vertex.col=2, displaylabels = TRUE)
```

For brevity purposes, we give only the graphical output as the rest of the interpretation is the same as with network `net1`:

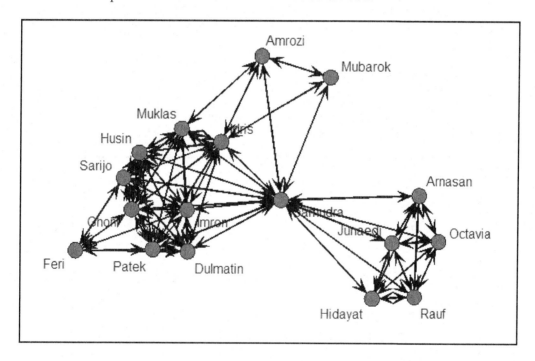

7. The matrix form of the **Bali** network can be obtained as follows:

```
Bali_Matrix <- as.matrix(Bali,matrix.type="adjacency")
Bali_Matrix[1:6,1:6]
```

The output would be as follows:

```
Muklas Amrozi Imron Samudra Dulmatin Idris
Muklas 0 1 1 1 1 1
Amrozi 1 0 0 1 0 1
Imron 1 0 0 1 1 1
Samudra 1 1 1 0 1 1
Dulmatin 1 0 1 1 0 1
Idris 1 1 1 1 1 0
```

Manipulations! It is very important to be able to do basic manipulations and we would restrain by addressing one simple task of deleting a single vertex.

8. The graph `net1` is first converted to the class `igraph` as `netg`, and then it is visualized with the `plot` function. The vertex D is then deleted and a new graph object, `netg_del_d`, is created and visualized. The output follows the following R program:

```
netg <- asIgraph(net1)
par(mfrow=c(1,2))
plot(netg,vertex.label=LETTERS[1:5])
netg_del_d <- delete.vertices(netg,v=5)
plot(netg_del_d,vertex.label=LETTERS[c(1:3,5)])
```

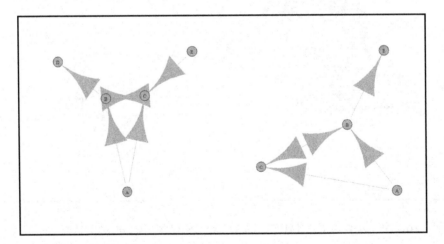

The identification of strong players and ties can be identified in R using the functions degree, closeness, and betweenness.

9. Applying the functions `degree`, `closeness`, and `betweenness`, we get an understanding of the Bali network through the next R program segment:

```
Bali %v% 'vertex.names'
sna::degree(Bali,gmode="graph")
closeness(Bali,gmode="graph")
betweenness(Bali,gmode="graph")
```

The output of the preceding program is as follows:

```
> Bali %v% 'vertex.names'
 [1] "Muklas"  "Amrozi"  "Imron"   "Samudra" "Dulmatin" "Idris"
 [7] "Mubarok" "Husin"   "Ghoni"   "Arnasan" "Rauf"     "Octavia"
[13] "Hidayat" "Junaedi" "Patek"   "Feri"    "Sarijo"

> degree(Bali,gmode="graph")
 [1]  9  4  9 15  9 10  3  9  9  5  5  5  5  5  9  6  9
> closeness(Bali,gmode="graph")
 [1] 0.6957 0.5517 0.6957 0.9412 0.6957 0.7273 0.5333 0.6957 0.6957
[10] 0.5714 0.5714 0.5714 0.5714 0.5714 0.6957 0.4848 0.6957
> betweenness(Bali,gmode="graph")
 [1]  2.3333  0.3333  1.6667 61.1667  1.6667  6.1667  0.0000  1.6667
 [9]  1.6667  0.0000  0.0000  0.0000  0.0000  0.0000  1.6667  0.0000
[17]  1.6667
```

Network cluster identification is an important task in network analysis. In the next step, we use appropriate functions to get the desired answers.

10. First convert the network to the `igraph` function. Apply the functions `clique.number`, `cliques`, and `largest.cliques` on the network to identify and separate the clusters:

```
Balig <- asIgraph(Bali)

clique.number(Balig)
 cliques(Balig,min=8)
 largest.cliques(Balig)
```

The desired output is the following:

```
> Balig <- asIgraph(Bali)
> clique.number(Balig)
[1] 9
> cliques(Balig,min=8)
[[1]]
+ 8/17 vertices:
```

```
[1] 1 3 4 5 6 8 9 15
[[2]]
+ 8/17 vertices:
[1] 1 3 4 5 6 8 9 17
[[3]]
+ 8/17 vertices:
[1] 1 3 4 5 6 8 15 17
[[4]]
+ 8/17 vertices:
[1] 1 3 4 5 6 9 15 17
[[5]]
+ 8/17 vertices:
[1] 1 3 4 5 8 9 15 17
[[6]]
+ 8/17 vertices:
[1] 1 3 4 6 8 9 15 17
[[7]]
+ 8/17 vertices:
[1] 1 3 5 6 8 9 15 17
[[8]]
+ 8/17 vertices:
[1] 1 4 5 6 8 9 15 17
[[9]]
+ 8/17 vertices:
[1] 3 4 5 6 8 9 15 17
[[10]]
+ 9/17 vertices:
[1] 1 3 4 5 6 8 9 15 17
> largest.cliques(Balig)
[[1]]
+ 9/17 vertices:
[1] 4 6 1 3 5 8 9 15 17
```

How it works...

The R network packages have simplified most of the tasks and they help in avoiding the need of writing complex codes. We saw how the R packages sna, igraph, intergraph, statnet, and network are useful in setting up and analyzingg social networks. We began with visualizing a simple network and then obtained the summaries. The task of subsetting a subnetwork and visualizing it gives nice early insights while we were also able to understand the interrelationships between vertex/edges and sub-networks within a network.

8
Recommending Movies at Scale (Python)

In this chapter, we will cover the following recipes:

- Modeling preference expressions
- Understanding the data
- Ingesting the movie review data
- Finding the highest-scoring movies
- Improving the movie-rating system
- Measuring the distance between users in the preference space
- Computing the correlation between users
- Finding the best critic for a user
- Predicting movie ratings for users
- Collaboratively filtering item by item
- Building a non-negative matrix factorization model
- Loading the entire dataset into the memory
- Dumping the SVD-based model to the disk
- Training the SVD-based model
- Testing the SVD-based model

Introduction

From books to movies to people to follow on Twitter, recommender systems carve the deluge of information on the internet into a more personalized flow, thus improving the performance of E-commerce, web, and social applications. It is no great surprise, given the success of Amazon-monetizing recommendations and the Netflix Prize, that any discussion of personalization or data-theoretic prediction would involve a recommender. What is surprising is how simple recommenders are to implement yet how susceptible they are to the vagaries of sparse data and over-fitting.

Consider a non-algorithmic approach to eliciting recommendations: one of the easiest ways to garner a recommendation is to look at the preferences of someone we trust. We are implicitly comparing our preferences to theirs, and the more similarities you share, the more likely you are to discover novel, shared preferences. However, everyone is unique, and our preferences exist across a variety of categories and domains. What if you could leverage the preferences of a great number of people and not just those you trust? In the aggregate, you would be able to see patterns, not just of people like you, but also *anti-recommendations* - things to stay away from, cautioned by the people not like you. You would, hopefully, also see subtle delineations across the shared preference space of groups of people who share parts of your own unique experience.

It is this basic premise that a group of techniques called *collaborative filtering* use to make recommendations. Simply stated, this premise can be boiled down to the assumption that those who have similar past preferences will share the same preferences in the future. This is from a human perspective, of course, and a typical corollary to this assumption is from the perspective of the things being preferred - sets of items that are preferred by the same people will be more likely to be preferred together in the future-and this is the basis for what is commonly described in literature as user-centric collaborative filtering versus item-centric collaborative filtering.

 The term **collaborative filtering** was coined by *David Goldberg* in a paper titled *Using collaborative filtering to weave an information tapestry*, *ACM*, where he proposed a system called Tapestry, which was designed at Xerox PARC in 1992, to annotate documents as interesting or uninteresting and to give document recommendations to people who are searching for good reads.

Collaborative filtering algorithms search large groupings of preference expressions to find similarities to some input preference or preferences. The output from these algorithms is a ranked list of suggestions that is a subset of all possible preferences, and hence, it's called *filtering*. The *collaborative* comes from the use of many other people's preferences in order to find suggestions for themselves. This can be seen either as a search of the space of preferences (for brute-force techniques), a clustering problem (grouping similarly preferred items), or even some other predictive model. Many algorithmic attempts have been created in order to optimize or solve this problem across sparse or large datasets, and we will discuss a few of them in this chapter.

The goals of this chapter are as follows:

- Understanding how to model preferences from a variety of sources
- Learning how to compute similarities using distance metrics
- Modeling recommendations using matrix factorization for star ratings

These two different models will be implemented in Python using readily available datasets on the web. To demonstrate the techniques in this chapter, we will use the oft-cited MovieLens database from the University of Minnesota that contains star ratings of moviegoers for their preferred movies.

Please note that this chapter is considered an advanced chapter and will most likely require significantly more time to complete than earlier chapters.

Modeling preference expressions

We have already pointed out that companies such as Amazon track purchases and page views to make recommendations, Goodreads and Yelp use five-star ratings and text reviews, and sites such as Reddit or Stack Overflow use simple up/down voting. You can see that preference can be expressed in the data in different ways, from Boolean flags, to voting, to ratings. However, these preferences are expressed by attempting to find groups of similarities in preference expressions in which you are leveraging the core assumption of collaborative filtering.

More formally, we understand that two people, Bob and Alice, share a preference for a specific item or widget. If Alice too has a preference for a different item, say, a sprocket, then Bob has a better than random chance of also sharing a preference for a sprocket. We believe that Bob and Alice's taste similarities can be expressed in an aggregate via a large number of preferences, and by leveraging the collaborative nature of groups, we can filter the world of products.

How to do it...

We will model preference expressions over the next few recipes, including the following:

- Understanding the data
- Ingesting the movie review data
- Finding the highest rated movies
- Improving the movie rating system

How it works...

A preference expression is an instance of a model of demonstrable relative selection. That is to say, preference expressions are data points that are used to show subjective ranking between a group of items for a person. Even more formally, we should say that preference expressions are not simply relative, but also temporal-for example, the statement of preference also has a fixed time relativity as well as item relativity.

> Preference expression is an instance of a model of demonstrable relative selection.

While it would be nice to think that we can subjectively and accurately express our preferences in a global context (for example, rate a movie as compared to all other movies), our tastes, in fact, change over time, and we can really only consider how we rank items relative to each other. Models of preference must take this into account and attempt to alleviate biases that are caused by it. The most common types of preference expression models simplify the problem of ranking by causing the expression to be numerically fuzzy, for example:

- Boolean expressions (yes or no)
- Up and down voting (such as abstain, dislike)

- Weighted signaling (the number of clicks or actions)
- Broad ranked classification (stars, hated or loved)

The idea is to create a preference model for an individual user a numerical model of the set of preference expressions for a particular individual. Models build the individual preference expressions into a useful user-specific context that can be computed against. Further reasoning can be performed on the models in order to alleviate time-based biases or to perform ontological reasoning or other categorizations.

As the relationships between entities get more complex, you can express their relative preferences by assigning behavioral weights to each type of semantic connection. However, choosing the weight is difficult and requires research to decide relative weights, which is why fuzzy generalizations are preferred. As an example, the following table shows you some well-known ranking preference systems:

Reddit Voting		Online Shopping		Star Reviews	
Up Vote	1	Bought	2	Love	5
No Vote	0	Viewed	1	Liked	4
Down Vote	-1	No purchase	0	Neutral	3
				Dislike	2
				Hate	1

For the rest of this chapter, we will only consider a single, very common preference expression: star ratings on a scale of 1 to 5.

Understanding the data

Understanding your data is critical to all data-related work. In this recipe, we will acquire and take a first look at the data that we will be using to build our recommendation engine.

Getting ready

To prepare for this recipe, and the rest of the chapter, download the **MovieLens** data from the **GroupLens** website of the University of Minnesota. You can find the data at `http://grouplens.org/datasets/movielens/`.

In this chapter, we will use the smaller MoveLens 100k dataset (4.7 MB in size) in order to load the entire model into the memory with ease.

How to do it...

Perform the following steps to better understand the data that we will be working with throughout this chapter:

1. Download the data from `http://grouplens.org/datasets/movielens/`. The 100K dataset is the one that you want (`ml-100k.zip`):

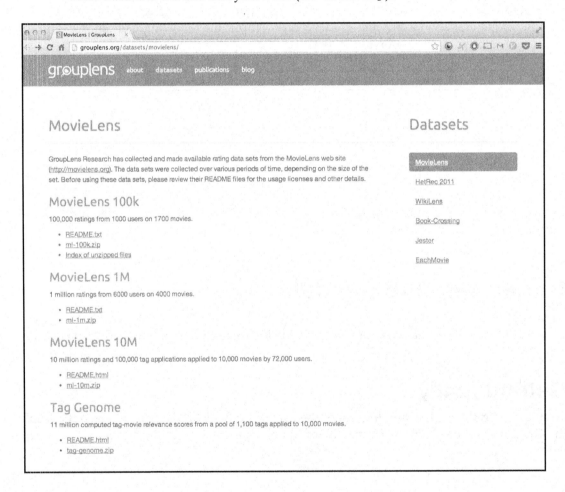

2. Unzip the downloaded data into the directory of your choice.

3. The two files that we are mainly concerned with are u.data, which contains the user movie ratings, and u.item, which contains movie information and details. To get a sense of each file, use the head command at the command prompt for Mac and Linux or the more command for Windows:

```
head -n 5 u.item
```

 Note that if you are working on a computer running the Microsoft Windows operating system and not using a virtual machine (not recommended), you do not have access to the head command; instead, use the following command: more u.item 2 n

4. The preceding command gives you the following output:

```
1|Toy Story (1995)|01-Jan-1995||http://us.imdb.com/M/title-
exact?Toy%20Story%20(1995)|0|0|0|0|1|1|1|0|0|0|0|0|0|0|0|0|0|0|0
2|GoldenEye (1995)|01-Jan-1995||http://us.imdb.com/M/title-
  exact?GoldenEye%20(1995)|0|1|1|0|0|0|0|0|0|0|0|0|0|0|0|0|0|1|0|0
3|Four Rooms (1995)|01-Jan-1995||http://us.imdb.com/M/title-
exact?Four%20Rooms%20(1995)|0|0|0|0|0|0|0|0|0|0|0|0|0|0|0|0|0|1|0|0
4|Get Shorty (1995)|01-Jan-1995||http://us.imdb.com/M/title-
exact?Get%20Shorty%20(1995)|0|1|0|0|0|1|1|0|0|1|0|0|0|0|0|0|0|0|0
5|Copycat (1995)|01-Jan-1995||http://us.imdb.com/M/title-
  exact?Copycat%20(1995)|0|0|0|0|0|0|1|0|1|0|0|0|0|0|0|0|1|0|0
```

The following command will produce the given output:

```
head -n 5 u.data
```

For Windows, you can use the following command:

```
more u.item 2 n
196    242    3    881250949
186    302    3    891717742
22    377    1    878887116
244    51    2    880606923
166    346    1    886397596
```

How it works...

The two main files that we will be using are as follows:

- `u.data`: This contains the user moving ratings
- `u.item`: This contains the movie information and other details

Both are character-delimited files; `u.data`, which is the main file, is tab delimited, and `u.item` is pipe delimited.

For `u.data`, the first column is the user ID, the second column is the movie ID, the third is the star rating, and the last is the timestamp. The `u.item` file contains much more information, including the ID, title, release date, and even a URL to IMDb. Interestingly, this file also has a Boolean array indicating the genre(s) of each movie, including (in order) action, adventure, animation, children, comedy, crime, documentary, drama, fantasy, film-noir, horror, musical, mystery, romance, sci-fi, thriller, war, and western.

There's more...

Free, web-scale datasets that are appropriate for building recommendation engines are few and far between. As a result, the movie lens dataset is a very popular choice for such a task, but there are others as well. The well-known Netflix Prize dataset has been pulled down by Netflix. However, there is a dump of all user-contributed content from the Stack Exchange network (including Stack Overflow) available via the internet Archive (`https://archive.org/details/stackexchange`). Additionally, there is a book-crossing dataset that contains over a million ratings of about a quarter of a million different books (`http://www2.informatik.uni-freiburg.de/~cziegler/BX/`).

Ingesting the movie review data

Recommendation engines require large amounts of training data in order to do a good job which is why they're often relegated to big data projects. However, to build a recommendation engine we must first get the required data into memory and due to the size of the data must do so in a memory-safe and efficient way. Luckily Python has all of the tools to get the job done and this recipe shows you how.

Getting ready

You will need to have the appropriate movie lens dataset downloaded, as specified in the preceding recipe. If you skipped the setup in Chapter 1, *Preparing Your Data Science Environment*, you will need to go back and ensure that you have NumPy correctly installed.

How to do it...

The following steps guide you through the creation of the functions that we will need in order to load the datasets into the memory:

1. Open your favorite Python editor or IDE. There is a lot of code, so it should be far simpler to enter it directly into a text file rather than a **Read-Eval-Print Loop (REPL)**.

2. We create a function to import the movie reviews:

```
In [1]: import csv
   ...: import datetime
In [2]: def load_reviews(path, **kwargs):
   ...: """
   ...: Loads MovieLens reviews
   ...: """
   ...: options = {
   ...: 'fieldnames': ('userid', 'movieid', 'rating', 'timestamp'),
   ...: 'delimiter': '\t',
   ...: }
   ...: options.update(kwargs)
   ...:
   ...: parse_date = lambda r,k: datetime.fromtimestamp(float(r[k]))
   ...: parse_int = lambda r,k: int(r[k])
   ...:
   ...: with open(path, 'rb') as reviews:
   ...: reader = csv.DictReader(reviews, **options)
   ...: for row in reader:
   ...: row['movieid'] = parse_int(row, 'movieid')
   ...: row['userid'] = parse_int(row, 'userid')
   ...: row['rating'] = parse_int(row, 'rating')
   ...: row['timestamp'] = parse_date(row, 'timestamp')
   ...: yield row
```

3. We create a helper function to help import the data:

```
In [3]: import os
...: def relative_path(path):
...: """
...: Returns a path relative from this code file
...: """
...: dirname = os.path.dirname(os.path.realpath('__file__'))
...: path = os.path.join(dirname, path)
...: return os.path.normpath(path)
```

4. We create another function to load the movie information:

```
In [4]: def load_movies(path, **kwargs):
...:
...: options = {
...: 'fieldnames': ('movieid', 'title', 'release', 'video', 'url'),
...: 'delimiter': '|',...: 'restkey': 'genre',
...: }
...: options.update(kwargs)
...:
...: parse_int = lambda r,k: int(r[k])
...: parse_date = lambda r,k: datetime.strptime(r[k], '%d-%b-%Y')
if r[k] else None
...:
...: with open(path, 'rb') as movies:
...: reader = csv.DictReader(movies, **options)
...: for row in reader:
...: row['movieid'] = parse_int(row, 'movieid')
...: row['release'] = parse_date(row, 'release')
...: row['video'] = parse_date(row, 'video')
...: yield row
```

5. Finally, we start creating a `MovieLens` class that will be augmented in later recipes:

```
In [5]: from collections import defaultdict
In [6]: class MovieLens(object):
...: """
...: Data structure to build our recommender model on.
...: """
...:
...: def __init__(self, udata, uitem):
...: """
...: Instantiate with a path to u.data and u.item
...: """
...: self.udata = udata
```

```
...: self.uitem = uitem
...: self.movies = {}
...: self.reviews = defaultdict(dict)
...: self.load_dataset()
...:
...: def load_dataset(self):
...: """
...: Loads the two datasets into memory, indexed on the ID.
...: """
...: for movie in load_movies(self.uitem):
...: self.movies[movie['movieid']] = movie
...:
...: for review in load_reviews(self.udata):...:
self.reviews[review['userid']][review['movieid']] = review
```

6. Ensure that the functions have been imported into your REPL or the Jupyter workspace, and type the following, making sure that the path to the data files is appropriate for your system:

```
In [7]: data = relative_path('../data/ml-100k/u.data')
...: item = relative_path('../data/ml-100k/u.item')
...: model = MovieLens(data, item)
```

How it works...

The methodology that we use for the two data-loading functions (load_reviews and load_movies) is simple, but it takes care of the details of parsing the data from the disk. We created a function that takes a path to our dataset and then any optional keywords. We know that we have specific ways in which we need to interact with the csv module, so we create default options, passing in the field names of the rows along with the delimiter, which is \t. The options.update(kwargs) line means that we'll accept whatever users pass to this function.

We then created internal parsing functions using a lambda function in Python. These simple parsers take a row and a key as input and return the converted input. This is an example of using lambda as internal, reusable code blocks and is a common technique in Python. Finally, we open our file and create a csv.DictReader function with our options. Iterating through the rows in the reader, we parse the fields that we want to be int and datetime, respectively, and then yield the row.

Note that as we are unsure about the actual size of the input file, we are doing this in a memory-safe manner using Python generators. Using `yield` instead of `return` ensures that Python creates a generator under the hood and does not load the entire dataset into the memory.

We'll use each of these methodologies to load the datasets at various times through our computation that uses this dataset. We'll need to know where these files are at all times, which can be a pain, especially in larger code bases; in the *There's more...* section, we'll discuss a Python pro-tip to alleviate this concern.

Finally, we created a data structure, which is the `MovieLens` class, with which we can hold our review's data. This structure takes the `udata` and `uitem` paths, and then it loads the movies and reviews into two Python dictionaries that are indexed by `movieid` and `userid`, respectively. To instantiate this object, you will execute something like the following:

```
data = relative_path('../data/ml-100k/u.data')
item = relative_path('../data/ml-100k/u.item')
model = MovieLens(data, item)
```

Note that the preceding commands assume that you have your data in a folder called `data`. We can now load the whole dataset into the memory, indexed on the various IDs specified in the dataset.

Did you notice the use of the `relative_path` function? When dealing with fixtures such as these to build models, the data is often included with the code. When you specify a path in Python, such as `data/ml-100k/u.data`, it looks it up relative to the current working directory where you ran the script. To help ease this trouble, you can specify the paths that are relative to the code itself:

```
import os
def relative_path(path):
    """
    Returns a path relative from this code file
    """
    dirname = os.path.dirname(os.path.realpath('__file__'))
    path = os.path.join(dirname, path)
    return os.path.normpath(path)
```

Keep in mind that this holds the entire data structure in memory; in the case of the 100k dataset, this will require 54.1 MB, which isn't too bad for modern machines. However, we should also keep in mind that we'll generally build recommenders using far more than just 100,000 reviews. This is why we have configured the data structure the way we have very similar to a database. To grow the system, you will replace the reviews and movies properties with database access functions or properties, which will yield data types expected by our methods.

Finding the highest-scoring movies

If you're looking for a good movie, you'll often want to see the most popular or best-rated movies overall. Initially, we'll take a naïve approach to compute a movie's aggregate rating by averaging the user reviews for each movie. This technique will also demonstrate how to access the data in our MovieLens class.

Getting ready

These recipes are sequential in nature. Thus, you should have completed the previous recipes in this chapter before starting with this one.

How to do it...

Follow these steps to output numeric scores for all movies in the dataset and compute a top-10 list:

1. Augment the MovieLens class with a new method to get all reviews for a particular movie:

```
In [8]: class MovieLens(object):
   ...:
   ...:
   ...: def reviews_for_movie(self, movieid):
   ...:     """
   ...:     Yields the reviews for a given movie
   ...:     """
   ...:     for review in self.reviews.values():
   ...:         if movieid in review:
   ...:             yield review[movieid]
   ...:
```

2. Then, add an additional method to compute the top 10 movies reviewed by users:

```
In [9]: import heapq
...: from operator import itemgetter
...: class MovieLens(object):
...:
...: def average_reviews(self):
...: """
...: Averages the star rating for all movies. Yields a tuple of
movieid,
...: the average rating, and the number of reviews.
...: """
...: for movieid in self.movies:
...: reviews = list(r['rating'] for r in
self.reviews_for_movie(movieid))
...: average = sum(reviews) / float(len(reviews))
...: yield (movieid, average, len(reviews))
...:
...: def top_rated(self, n=10):
...: """
...: Yields the n top rated movies
...: """
...: return heapq.nlargest(n, self.bayesian_average(),
key=itemgetter(1))
...:
```

Note that the ... notation just below `class MovieLens(object):` signifies that we will be appending the `average_reviews` method to the existing `MovieLens` class.

3. Now, let's print the top-rated results:

```
In [10]: for mid, avg, num in model.top_rated(10):
...: title = model.movies[mid]['title']
...: print "[%0.3f average rating (%i reviews)] %s" % (avg,
num,title)
```

4. Executing the preceding commands in your REPL should produce the following output:

```
Out [10]: [5.000 average rating (1 reviews)] Entertaining Angels:
The Dorothy Day Story (1996)
[5.000 average rating (2 reviews)] Santa with Muscles (1996)
[5.000 average rating (1 reviews)] Great Day in Harlem, A (1994)
[5.000 average rating (1 reviews)] They Made Me a Criminal (1939)
[5.000 average rating (1 reviews)] Aiqing wansui (1994)
```

```
[5.000 average rating (1 reviews)] Someone Else's America (1995)
[5.000 average rating (2 reviews)] Saint of Fort Washington, The
(1993)
[5.000 average rating (3 reviews)] Prefontaine (1997)
[5.000 average rating (3 reviews)] Star Kid (1997)
[5.000 average rating (1 reviews)] Marlene Dietrich: Shadow and
Light (1996)
```

How it works...

The new `reviews_for_movie()` method that is added to the `MovieLens` class iterates through our review dictionary values (which are indexed by the `userid` parameter), checks whether the `movieid` value has been reviewed by the user, and then presents that review dictionary. We will need such functionality for the next method.

With the `average_review()` method, we have created another generator function that goes through all of our movies and all of their reviews and presents the movie ID, the average rating, and the number of reviews. The `top_rated` function uses the `heapq` module to quickly sort the reviews based on the average.

The `heapq` data structure, also known as the priority queue algorithm, is the Python implementation of an abstract data structure with interesting and useful properties. Heaps are binary trees that are built so that every parent node has a value that is either less than or equal to any of its children nodes. Thus, the smallest element is the root of the tree, which can be accessed in constant time, which is a very desirable property. With `heapq`, Python developers have an efficient means to insert new values in an ordered data structure and also return sorted values.

There's more...

Here, we run into our first problem some of the top-rated movies only have one review (and conversely, so do the worst-rated movies). How do you compare *Casablanca*, which has a 4.457 average rating (243 reviews), with *Santa with Muscles*, which has a 5.000 average rating (2 reviews)? We are sure that those two reviewers really liked *Santa with Muscles*, but the high rating for *Casablanca* is probably more meaningful because more people liked it. Most recommenders with star ratings will simply output the average rating along with the number of reviewers, allowing the user to determine their quality; however, as data scientists, we can do better in the next recipe.

See also

The `heapq` documentation is available at
`https://docs.python.org/2/library/heapq.html`.

Improving the movie-rating system

We don't want to build a recommendation engine with a system that considers the likely straight-to-DVD *Santa with Muscles* as generally superior to *Casablanca*. Thus, the naïve scoring approach used previously must be improved upon and is the focus of this recipe.

Getting ready

Make sure that you have completed the previous recipes in this chapter first.

How to do it...

The following steps implement and test a new movie-scoring algorithm:

1. Let's implement a new Bayesian movie-scoring algorithm, as shown in the following function, adding it to the `MovieLens` class:

```
In [11]: def bayesian_average(self, c=59, m=3):
   ...:     """
   ...:     Reports the Bayesian average with parameters c and m.
   ...:     """
   ...:     for movieid in self.movies:
   ...:         reviews = list(r['rating'] for r in
self.reviews_for_movie(movieid))
   ...:         average = ((c * m) + sum(reviews)) / float(c +  len(reviews))
   ...:         yield (movieid, average, len(reviews))
```

2. Next, we will replace the `top_rated` method in the `MovieLens` class with the version in the following commands that uses the new `Bayesian_average` method from the preceding step:

```
In [12]: def top_rated(self, n=10):
...: """
...: Yields the n top rated movies
...: """
...: return heapq.nlargest(n, self.bayesian_average(),
key=itemgetter(1))
```

3. Printing our new top-10 list looks a bit more familiar to us and `Casablanca` is now happily rated number 4:

```
[4.234 average rating (583 reviews)] Star Wars (1977)
[4.224 average rating (298 reviews)] Schindler's List (1993)
[4.196 average rating (283 reviews)] Shawshank Redemption, The
(1994)
[4.172 average rating (243 reviews)] Casablanca (1942)
[4.135 average rating (267 reviews)] Usual Suspects, The (1995)
[4.123 average rating (413 reviews)] Godfather, The (1972)
[4.120 average rating (390 reviews)] Silence of the Lambs, The
(1991)
[4.098 average rating (420 reviews)] Raiders of the Lost Ark (1981)
[4.082 average rating (209 reviews)] Rear Window (1954)
[4.066 average rating (350 reviews)] Titanic (1997)
```

How it works...

Taking the average of movie reviews, as shown in the previous recipe, simply did not work because some movies did not have enough ratings to give a meaningful comparison to movies with more ratings. What we'd really like is to have every single movie critic rate every single movie. Given that this is impossible, we could derive an estimate for how the movie would be rated if an infinite number of people rated the movie; this is hard to infer from one data point, so we should say that we would like to estimate the movie rating if the same number of people gave it a rating on an average (for example, filtering our results based on the number of reviews).

This estimate can be computed with a Bayesian average, implemented in the `bayesian_average()` function, to infer these ratings based on the following equation:

$$rating = \frac{C \times m \times \sum stars}{C + n}$$

Here, m is our prior for the average of stars, and C is a confidence parameter that is equivalent to the number of observations in our posterior.

Determining priors can be a complicated and magical art. Rather than taking the complex path of fitting a Dirichlet distribution to our data, we can simply choose an m prior of 3 with our five-star rating system, which means that our prior assumes that star ratings tend to be reviewed around the median value. In choosing C, you are expressing how many reviews are needed to get away from the prior; we can compute this by looking at the average number of reviews per movie:

```
print float(sum(num for mid, avg, num in model.average_reviews()))
/
    len(model.movies)
```

This gives us an average number of 59.4, which we use as the default value in our function definition.

There's more...

Play around with the C parameter. You should find that if you change the parameter so that $C = 50$, the top-10 list subtly shifts; in this case, *Schindler's List* and *Star Wars* are swapped in rankings, as are *Raiders of the Lost Ark* and *Rear Window* - note that both the swapped movies have far more reviews than the former, which means that the higher C parameter was balancing the fewer ratings of the other movie.

See also

- See how Yelp deals with this challenge at
  `http://venturebeat.com/2009/10/12/how-yelp-deals-with-everybody-getting-four-stars-on-average/`.

Measuring the distance between users in the preference space

The two most recognizable types of collaborative filtering systems are user-based recommenders and item-based recommenders. If one were to imagine that the preference space is an *n*-dimensional feature space where either users or items are plotted, then we would say that similar users or items tend to cluster near each other in this preference space; hence, an alternative name for this type of collaborative filtering is nearest-neighbor recommenders.

A crucial step in this process is to come up with a similarity or distance metric with which we can compare critics to each other or mutually preferred items. This metric is then used to perform pairwise comparisons of a particular user to all other users, or conversely, for an item to be compared to all other items. Normalized comparisons are then used to determine recommendations. Although the computational space can become exceedingly large, distance metrics themselves are not difficult to compute, and in this recipe, we will explore a few as well as implement our first recommender system.

In this recipe, we will measure the distance between users; in the recipe after this one, we will look at another similarity distance indicator.

Getting ready

We will continue to build on the MovieLens class from the *Modeling preference expressions* section. If you have not had the opportunity to review this section, please have the code for that class ready. Importantly, we will want to access the data structures, MovieLens.movies and MovieLens.reviews, which have been loaded from the CSV files on the disk.

How to do it...

The following sets of steps provide instructions on how to compute the Euclidean distance between users:

1. Augment the `MovieLens` class with a new method, `shared_preferences`, to pull out movies that have been rated by two critics, A and B:

```
In [13]: class MovieLens(object):
   ...:
   ...:     def shared_preferences(self, criticA, criticB):
   ...:         """
   ...:         Returns the intersection of ratings for two critics, A and B.
   ...:         """
   ...:         if criticA not in self.reviews:
   ...:             raise KeyError("Couldn't find critic '%s' in data" % criticA)
   ...:         if criticB not in self.reviews:
   ...:             raise KeyError("Couldn't find critic '%s' in data" % criticB)
   ...:
   ...:         moviesA = set(self.reviews[criticA].keys())
   ...:         moviesB = set(self.reviews[criticB].keys())
   ...:         shared = moviesA & moviesB # Intersection operator
   ...:
   ...:         # Create a reviews dictionary to return
   ...:         reviews = {}
   ...:         for movieid in shared:
   ...:             reviews[movieid] = (
   ...:                 self.reviews[criticA][movieid]['rating'],
   ...:                 self.reviews[criticB][movieid]['rating'],
   ...:             )
   ...:         return reviews
   ...:
```

2. Then, implement a function that computes the Euclidean distance between two critics using their shared movie preferences as a vector for the computation. This method will also be part of the `MovieLens` class:

```
In [14]: from math import sqrt
   ...:
   ...:     def euclidean_distance(self, criticA, criticB, prefs='users'):
   ...:         """
   ...:         Reports the Euclidean distance of two critics, A and B by
   ...:         performing a J-dimensional Euclidean calculation of each of
their
   ...:         preference vectors for the intersection of books the critics
have
   ...:         rated.
```

```
...:  """
...:
...:  # Get the intersection of the rated titles in the data.
...:
...:  if prefs == 'users':
...:  preferences = self.shared_preferences(criticA, criticB)
...:  elif prefs == 'movies':
...:  preferences = self.shared_critics(criticA, criticB)
...:  else:
...:  raise Exception("No preferences of type '%s'." % prefs)
...:
...:  # If they have no rankings in common, return 0.
...:  if len(preferences) == 0: return 0
...:
...:  # Sum the squares of the differences
...:  sum_of_squares = sum([pow(a-b, 2) for a, b in
preferences.values()])
...:
...:  # Return the inverse of the distance to give a higher score to
...:  # folks who are more similar (e.g. less distance) add 1 to
prevent
...:  # division by zero errors and normalize ranks in [0, 1]
...:  return 1 / (1 + sqrt(sum_of_squares))
```

3. With the preceding code implemented, test it in the REPL:

```
>>> data = relative_path('data/ml-100k/u.data')
>>> item = relative_path('data/ml-100k/u.item')
>>> model = MovieLens(data, item)
>>> print model.euclidean_distance(232, 532)
0.1023021629920016
```

How it works...

The new `shared_preferences()` method of the `MovieLens` class determines the shared preference space of two users. Critically, we can only compare users (the `criticA` and `criticB` input parameters) based on the things that they have both rated. This function uses Python sets to determine the list of movies that both A and B reviewed (the intersection of the movies A has rated and the movies B has rated). The function then iterates over this set, returning a dictionary whose keys are the movie IDs and the values are a tuple of ratings, for example, (`ratingA`, `ratingB`) for each movie that both users have rated. We can now use this dataset to compute similarity scores, which is done by the second function.

The `euclidean_distance()` function takes two critics as the input, A and B, and computes the distance between users in preference space. Here, we have chosen to implement the Euclidean distance metric (the two-dimensional variation is well known to those who remember the Pythagorean theorem), but we could have implemented other metrics as well. This function will return a real number from 0 to 1, where 0 is less similar (farther apart) critics and 1 is more similar (closer together) critics.

There's more...

The Manhattan distance is another very popular metric and a very simple one to understand. It can simply sum the absolute values of the pairwise differences between elements of each vector. Or, in code, it can be executed in this manner:

```
manhattan = sum([abs(a-b) for a, b in preferences.values()])
```

This metric is also called the city-block distance because, conceptually, it is as if you were counting the number of blocks north/south and east/west one would have to walk between two points in the city. Before implementing it for this recipe, you would also want to invert and normalize the value in some fashion to return a value in the *[0, 1]* range.

See also

- The distance overview from Wikipedia is available at
  `http://en.wikipedia.org/wiki/Distance`.
- The Taxicab geometry from Wikipedia is available at
  `http://en.wikipedia.org/wiki/Taxicab_geometry`.

Computing the correlation between users

In the previous recipe, we used one out of many possible distance measures to capture the distance between the movie reviews of users. This distance between two specific users is not changed even if there are five or five million other users.

In this recipe, we will compute the correlation between users in the preference space. Like distance metrics, there are many correlation metrics. The most popular of these are Pearson or Spearman correlations or cosine distance. Unlike distance metrics, the correlation will change depending on the number of users and movies.

Getting ready

We will be continuing the efforts of the previous recipes again, so make sure you understand each one.

How to do it...

The following function implements the computation of the pearson_correlation function for two critics, which are criticA and criticB, and it is added to the MovieLens class:

```
In [15]: def pearson_correlation(self, criticA, criticB, prefs='users'):
    ...:     """
    ...:     Returns the Pearson Correlation of two critics, A and B by
    ...:     performing the PPMC calculation on the scatter plot of (a, b)
    ...:     ratings on the shared set of critiqued titles.
    ...:     """
    ...:
    ...:     # Get the set of mutually rated items
    ...:     if prefs == 'users':
    ...:         preferences = self.shared_preferences(criticA, criticB)
    ...:     elif prefs == 'movies':
    ...:         preferences = self.shared_critics(criticA, criticB)
    ...:     else:
    ...:         raise Exception("No preferences of type '%s'." % prefs)
    ...:
    ...:     # Store the length to save traversals of the len computation.
    ...:     # If they have no rankings in common, return 0.
    ...:     length = len(preferences)
    ...:     if length == 0: return 0
    ...:
    ...:     # Loop through the preferences of each critic once and compute the
    ...:     # various summations that are required for our final calculation.
    ...:     sumA = sumB = sumSquareA = sumSquareB = sumProducts = 0
    ...:     for a, b in preferences.values():
    ...:         sumA += a
    ...:         sumB += b
    ...:         sumSquareA += pow(a, 2)
```

```
...: sumSquareB += pow(b, 2)
...: sumProducts += a*b
...:
...: # Calculate Pearson Score
...: numerator = (sumProducts*length) - (sumA*sumB)
...: denominator = sqrt(((sumSquareA*length) - pow(sumA, 2))
...: * ((sumSquareB*length) - pow(sumB, 2)))
...:
...: # Prevent division by zero.
...: if denominator == 0: return 0
...:
...: return abs(numerator / denominator)
...:
```

How it works...

The Pearson correlation computes the product moment, which is the mean of the product of mean adjusted random variables and is defined as the covariance of two variables (a and b, in our case) divided by the product of the standard deviation of a and the standard deviation of b. As a formula, this looks like the following:

$$Pearson\ Correlation = \frac{cov(A, B)}{\sigma_A \sigma_B}$$

For a finite sample, which is what we have, the detailed formula, which was implemented in the preceding function, is as follows:

$$Pearson\ Correlation = \frac{\sum_{i=1}^{n}(A_i - mean(A)) \times \sum_{i=1}^{n}(B_i - mean(B))}{\sqrt{\sum_{i=1}^{n}(A_i - mean(A))^2} \times \sqrt{\sum_{i=1}^{n}(B_i - mean(B))^2}}$$

Another way to think about the Pearson correlation is as a measure of the linear dependence between two variables. It returns a score of -1 to 1, where negative scores closer to -1 indicate a stronger negative correlation, and positive scores closer to 1 indicate a stronger, positive correlation. A score of 0 means that the two variables are not correlated.

In order for us to perform comparisons, we want to normalize our similarity metrics in the space of [0, 1] so that *0* means less similar and *1* means more similar, so we return the absolute value:

```
>>> print model.pearson_correlation(232, 532)
0.06025793538385047
```

There's more...

We have explored two distance metrics: the Euclidean distance and the Pearson correlation. There are many more, including the Spearman correlation, Tantimoto scores, Jaccard distance, Cosine similarity, and Manhattan distance, to name a few. Choosing the right distance metric for the dataset of your recommender along with the type of preference expression used is crucial to ensuring success in this style of recommender. It's up to the reader to explore this space further based on their interest and particular dataset.

Finding the best critic for a user

Now that we have two different ways to compute a similarity distance between users, we can determine the best critics for a particular user and see how similar they are to an individual's preferences.

Getting ready

Make sure that you have completed the previous recipes before tackling this one.

How to do it...

Implement a new method for the MovieLens class, similar_critics(), which locates the best match for a user:

```
In [16]: import heapq
   ...:
   ...: def similar_critics(self, user, metric='euclidean', n=None):
   ...:     """
   ...:     Finds and ranks similar critics for the user according to the
   ...:     specified distance metric. Returns the top n similar critics.
   ...:     """
   ...:
```

```
...: # Metric jump table
...: metrics = {
...: 'euclidean': self.euclidean_distance,
...: 'pearson': self.pearson_correlation,
...: }
...:
...: distance = metrics.get(metric, None)
...:
...: # Handle problems that might occur
...: if user not in self.reviews:
...: raise KeyError("Unknown user, '%s'." % user)
...: if not distance or not callable(distance):
...: raise KeyError("Unknown or unprogrammed distance metric '%s'." %
metric)
...:
...: # Compute user to critic similarities for all critics
...: critics = {}
...: for critic in self.reviews:
...: # Don't compare against yourself!
...: if critic == user:
...: continue
...:
...: critics[critic] = distance(user, critic)
...:
...: if n:
...: return heapq.nlargest(n, critics.items(), key=itemgetter(1))
...: return critics
```

How it works...

The `similar_critics` method, added to the `MovieLens` class, serves as the heart of this recipe. It takes as parameters the targeted user and two optional parameters: the metric to be used, which defaults to `euclidean`, and the number of results to be returned, which defaults to `None`. As you can see, this flexible method uses a jump table to determine what algorithm is to be used (you can pass in `euclidean` or `pearson` to choose the distance metric). Every other critic is compared to the current user (except a comparison of the user against themselves). The results are then sorted using the flexible `heapq` module and the top n results are returned.

To test out our implementation, print out the results of the run for both similarity distances:

```
>>> for item in model.similar_critics(232, 'euclidean', n=10):
  print "%4i: %0.3f" % item
  688: 1.000
  914: 1.000
```

```
   47: 0.500
   78: 0.500
  170: 0.500
  335: 0.500
  341: 0.500
  101: 0.414
  155: 0.414
  309: 0.414
>>> for item in model.similar_critics(232, 'pearson', n=10):
    print "%4i: %0.3f" % item
   33: 1.000
   36: 1.000
  155: 1.000
  260: 1.000
  289: 1.000
  302: 1.000
  309: 1.000
  317: 1.000
  511: 1.000
  769: 1.000
```

These scores are clearly very different, and it appears that Pearson thinks that there are many more similar users than the Euclidean distance metric. The Euclidean distance metric tends to favor users who have rated fewer items exactly the same. Pearson correlation favors more scores that fit well linearly, and therefore, Pearson corrects grade inflation where two critics might rate movies very similarly, but one user rates them consistently one star higher than the other.

If you plot out how many shared rankings each critic has, you'll see that the data is very sparse. Here is the preceding data with the number of rankings appended:

```
Euclidean scores:
  688: 1.000 (1 shared rankings)
  914: 1.000 (2 shared rankings)
   47: 0.500 (5 shared rankings)
   78: 0.500 (3 shared rankings)
  170: 0.500 (1 shared rankings)
Pearson scores:
   33: 1.000 (2 shared rankings)
   36: 1.000 (3 shared rankings)
  155: 1.000 (2 shared rankings)
  260: 1.000 (3 shared rankings)
  289: 1.000 (3 shared rankings)
```

Therefore, it is not enough to find similar critics and use their ratings to predict our users' scores; instead, we will have to aggregate the scores of all of the critics, regardless of similarity, and predict ratings for the movies that we haven't rated.

Predicting movie ratings for users

To predict how we might rate a particular movie, we can compute a weighted average of critics who have also rated the same movies as the user. The weight will be the similarity of the critic to the user if a critic has not rated a movie, then their similarity will not contribute to the overall ranking of the movie.

Getting ready

Ensure that you have completed the previous recipes in this large, cumulative chapter.

How to do it...

The following steps walk you through the prediction of movie ratings for users:

1. First, add the `predict_ranking` function to the `MovieLens` class in order to predict the ranking that a user might give a particular movie with similar critics:

```
In [17]: def predict_ranking(self, user, movie, metric='euclidean',
critics=None):
...:     """
...:     Predicts the ranking a user might give a movie according to
the
...:     weighted average of the critics that are similar to the that
user.
...:     """
...:
...:     critics = critics or self.similar_critics(user, metric=metric)
...:     total = 0.0
...:     simsum = 0.0
...:
...:     for critic, similarity in critics.items():
...:         if movie in self.reviews[critic]:
...:             total += similarity * self.reviews[critic][movie]['rating']
...:             simsum += similarity
...:
...:     if simsum == 0.0: return 0.0
```

```
...: return total / simsum
```

2. Next, add the `predict_all_rankings` method to the `MovieLens` class:

```
In [18]: def predict_all_rankings(self, user, metric='euclidean',
n=None):
...: """
...: Predicts all rankings for all movies, if n is specified
returns
...: the top n movies and their predicted ranking.
...: """
...: critics = self.similar_critics(user, metric=metric)
...: movies = {
...: movie: self.predict_ranking(user, movie, metric, critics)
...: for movie in self.movies
...: }
...:
...: if n:
...: return heapq.nlargest(n, movies.items(), key=itemgetter(1))
...: return movies
```

How it works...

The `predict_ranking` method takes a user and a movie along with a string specifying the distance metric and returns the predicted rating for that movie for that particular user. A fourth argument, `critics`, is meant to be an optimization for the `predict_all_rankings` method, which we'll discuss shortly. The prediction gathers all critics who are similar to the user and computes the weighted total rating of the critics, filtered by those who actually did rate the movie in question. The weights are simply their similarity to the user, computed by the distance metric. This total is then normalized by the sum of the similarities to move the rating back into the space of 1 to 5 stars:

```
>>> print model.predict_ranking(422, 50, 'euclidean')
4.35413151722
>>> print model.predict_ranking(422, 50, 'pearson')
4.3566797826
```

Here, we can see the predictions for *Star Wars* (ID 50 in our MovieLens dataset) for the user 422. The Euclidean and Pearson computations are very close to each other (which isn't necessarily to be expected), but the prediction is also very close to the user's actual rating, which is 4.

The `predict_all_rankings` method computes the ranking predictions for all movies for a particular user according to the passed-in metric. It optionally takes a value, n, to return the top n best matches. This function optimizes the similar critics' lookup by only executing it once and then passing those discovered critics to the `predict_ranking` function in order to improve the performance. However, this method must be run on every single movie in the dataset:

```
>>> for mid, rating in model.predict_all_rankings(578, 'pearson', 10):
...         print "%0.3f: %s" % (rating, model.movies[mid]['title'])
5.000: Prefontaine (1997)
5.000: Santa with Muscles (1996)
5.000: Marlene Dietrich: Shadow and Light (1996)
5.000: Star Kid (1997)
5.000: Aiqing wansui (1994)
5.000: Someone Else's America (1995)
5.000: Great Day in Harlem, A (1994)
5.000: Saint of Fort Washington, The (1993)
4.954: Anna (1996)
4.817: Innocents, The (1961)
```

As you can see, we have now computed what our recommender thinks the top movies for this particular user are, along with what we think the user will rate the movie! The top-10 list of average movie ratings plays a huge rule here and a potential improvement could be to use the Bayesian averaging in addition to the similarity weighting, but that is left for the reader to implement.

Collaboratively filtering item by item

So far, we have compared users to other users in order to make our predictions. However, the similarity space can be partitioned in two ways. User-centric collaborative filtering plots users in the preference space and discovers how similar users are to each other. These similarities are then used to predict rankings, aligning the user with similar critics. Item-centric collaborative filtering does just the opposite; it plots the items together in the preference space and makes recommendations according to how similar a group of items are to another group.

Item-based collaborative filtering is a common optimization as the similarity of items changes slowly. Once enough data has been gathered, reviewers adding reviews does not necessarily change the fact that *Toy Story* is more similar to *Babe* than *The Terminator*, and users who prefer *Toy Story* might prefer the former to the latter. Therefore, you can simply compute item similarities once in a single offline process and use that as a static mapping for recommendations, updating the results on a semi-regular basis.

This recipe will walk you through item-by-item collaborative filtering.

Getting ready

This recipe requires the completion of the previous recipes in this chapter.

How to do it...

Construct the following function to perform item-by-item collaborative filtering:

```
In [19]: def shared_critics(self, movieA, movieB):
    ...:     """
    ...:     Returns the intersection of critics for two items, A and B
    ...:     """
    ...:
    ...:     if movieA not in self.movies:
    ...:         raise KeyError("Couldn't find movie '%s' in data" % movieA)
    ...:     if movieB not in self.movies:
    ...:         raise KeyError("Couldn't find movie '%s' in data" % movieB)
    ...:
    ...:     criticsA = set(critic for critic in self.reviews if movieA in self.reviews[critic])
    ...:     criticsB = set(critic for critic in self.reviews if movieB in self.reviews[critic])
    ...:     shared = criticsA & criticsB # Intersection operator
    ...:
    ...:     # Create the reviews dictionary to return
    ...:     reviews = {}
    ...:     for critic in shared:
    ...:         reviews[critic] = (
    ...:             self.reviews[critic][movieA]['rating'],
    ...:             self.reviews[critic][movieB]['rating'],
    ...:         )
    ...:     return reviews
In [20]: def similar_items(self, movie, metric='euclidean', n=None):
    ...:     # Metric jump table
```

```
...: metrics = {
...: 'euclidean': self.euclidean_distance,
...: 'pearson': self.pearson_correlation,
...: }
...:
...: distance = metrics.get(metric, None)
...:
...: # Handle problems that might occur
...: if movie not in self.reviews:
...: raise KeyError("Unknown movie, '%s'." % movie)
...: if not distance or not callable(distance):
...: raise KeyError("Unknown or unprogrammed distance metric '%s'."
% metric)
...:
...: items = {}
...: for item in self.movies:
...: if item == movie:
...: continue
...:
...: items[item] = distance(item, movie, prefs='movies')
...:
...: if n:
...: return heapq.nlargest(n, items.items(), key=itemgetter(1))
...: return items
...:
```

How it works...

To perform item-by-item collaborative filtering, the same distance metrics can be used, but they must be updated to use the preferences from `shared_critics` rather than `shared_preferences` (for example, item similarity versus user similarity). Update the functions to accept a `prefs` parameter that determines which preferences are to be used, but I'll leave that to the reader as it is only two lines of code (note that the answer is contained in the `sim.py` source file in the directory that contains the code for Chapter 7, *Working with Social Graphs (Python)*).

If you print out the list of similar items for a particular movie, you can see some interesting results. For example, review the similarity results for *The Crying Game* (1992), which has an ID of 631:

```
for movie, similarity in model.similar_items(631, 'pearson').items():
    print "%0.3f: %s" % (similarity, model.movies[movie]['title'])
    0.127: Toy Story (1995)
    0.209: GoldenEye (1995)
    0.069: Four Rooms (1995)
```

```
0.039: Get Shorty (1995)
0.340: Copycat (1995)
0.225: Shanghai Triad (Yao a yao yao dao waipo qiao) (1995)
0.232: Twelve Monkeys (1995)
...
```

This crime thriller is not very similar to *Toy Story*, which is a children's movie, but is more similar to *Copycat*, which is another crime thriller. Of course, critics who have rated many movies skew the results, and more movie reviews are needed before this normalizes into something more compelling.

It is presumed that the item similarity scores are run regularly, but they do not need to be computed in real time. Given a set of computed item similarities, computing recommendations are as follows:

```
In [21]: def predict_ranking(self, user, movie, metric='euclidean',
critics=None):
...:    """
...:    Predicts the ranking a user might give a movie according to the
...:    weighted average of the critics that are similar to the that user.
...:    """
...:
...:    critics = critics or self.similar_critics(user, metric=metric)
...:    total = 0.0
...:    simsum = 0.0
...:
...:    for critic, similarity in critics.items():
...:        if movie in self.reviews[critic]:
...:            total += similarity * self.reviews[critic][movie]['rating']
...:            simsum += similarity
...:
...:    if simsum == 0.0: return 0.0
...:    return total / simsum
```

This method simply uses the inverted item-to-item similarity scores rather than the user-to-user similarity scores. Since similar items can be computed offline, the lookup for movies via the `self.similar_items` method should be a database lookup rather than a real-time computation:

```
>>> print model.predict_ranking(232, 52, 'pearson')
3.980443976
```

You can then compute a ranked list of all possible recommendations in a similar way to the user-to-user recommendations.

Building a non-negative matrix factorization model

A general improvement on the basic cross-wise nearest-neighbor similarity scoring of collaborative filtering is a matrix factorization method, which is also known as **Singular Value Decomposition (SVD)**. Matrix factorization methods attempt to explain the ratings through the discovery of latent features that are not easily identifiable by analysts. For instance, this technique can expose possible features such as the amount of action, family friendliness, or fine-tuned genre discovery in our movies dataset.

What's especially interesting about these features is that they are continuous and not discrete values and they can represent an individual's preference along a continuum. In this sense, the model can explore shades of characteristics, for example, perhaps a critic in the movie reviews dataset, such as action flicks with a strong female lead that are set in European countries. A James Bond movie might represent a shade of that type of movie even though it only ticks the set in European countries and action genre boxes. Depending on how similarly reviewers rate the movie, the strength of the female counterpart to James Bond will determine how they might like the movie.

Also, extremely helpfully, the matrix factorization model does well on sparse data, that is data with few recommendation and movie pairs. Reviews data is particularly sparse because not everyone has rated the same movies and there is a massive set of available movies. SVD can also be performed in parallel, making it a good choice for much larger datasets.

How to do it...

In the remaining recipes in this chapter, we will build a non-negative matrix factorization model in order to improve our recommendation engine:

- Loading the entire dataset into the memory
- Dumping the SVD-based model to the disk
- Training the SVD-based model
- Testing the SVD-based model

How it works...

Matrix factorization, or SVD, works by finding two matrices such that when you take their dot product (also known as the inner product or scalar product), you will get a close approximation of the original matrix. We have expressed our training matrix as a sparse $N \times M$ matrix of users to movies where the values are the 5-star rating if it exists, otherwise the value is blank or 0. By factoring the model with the values that we have and then taking the dot product of the two matrices produced by the factorization, we hope to fill in the blank spots in our original matrix with a prediction of how the user would have rated the movie in that column.

The intuition is that there should be some latent features that determine how users rate an item, and these latent features are expressed through the semantics of their previous ratings. If we can discover the latent features, we will be able to predict new ratings. Additionally, there should be fewer features than there are users and movies (otherwise, each movie or user would be a unique feature). This is why we compose our factored matrices by some feature length before taking their dot product.

Mathematically, this task is expressed as follows. If we have a set of U users and M movies, let R of size $|U| \times |M|$ be the matrix that contains the ratings of users. Assuming that we have K latent features, find two matrices, P and Q, where P is $|U| \times K$ and Q is $|M| \times K$ such that the dot product of P and Q transpose approximates R. P, which therefore represent the strength of the associations between users and features and Q represents the association of movies with features:

$$ R \approx P \times Q^T = \hat{R} $$

There are a few ways to go about factorization, but the choice we made was to perform gradient descent. Gradient descent initializes two random P and Q matrices, computes their dot product, and then minimizes the error compared to the original matrix by traveling down a slope of an error function (the gradient). This way, the algorithm hopes to find a local minimum where the error is within an acceptable threshold.

Our function computed the error as the squared difference between the predicted value and the actual value:

$$e_{ij} = \left(r_{ij} - \hat{r}_{ij}\right)^2$$

To minimize the error, we modify the values p_{ik} and q_{kj} by descending along the gradient of the current error slope, differentiating our error equation with respect to p yields:

$$\frac{\partial}{\partial p_{ik}} e_{ij} = -2(r_{ij} - \hat{r}_{ij})(q_{kj}) = -2e_{ij}q_{kj}$$

We then differentiate our error equation with respect to the variable q yields in the following equation:

$$\frac{\partial}{\partial q_{ik}} e_{ij} = -2(r_{ij} - \hat{r}_{ij})(p_{ik}) = -2e_{ij}p_{ik}$$

We can then derive our learning rule, which updates the values in P and Q by a constant learning rate, which is α. This learning rate, α, should not be too large because it determines how big of a step we take toward the minimum, and it is possible to step across to the other side of the error curve. It should also not be too small; otherwise, it will take forever to converge:

$$p'_{ik} = p_{ik} + \alpha \frac{\partial}{\partial p_{ik}} e_{ij} = p_{ik} + 2\alpha e_{ij}q_{kj}$$

$$q'_{kj} = q_{kj} + \alpha \frac{\partial}{\partial q_{kj}} e_{ij} = q_{kj} + 2\alpha e_{ij}p_{ik}$$

We continue to update our P and Q matrices, minimizing the error until the sum of the error squared is below some threshold, 0.001 in our code, or until we have performed a maximum number of iterations.

Matrix factorization has become an important technique for recommended systems, particularly those that leverage Likert-scale-like preference expressions notably, star ratings. The Netflix Prize challenge has shown us that matrix-factored approaches perform with a high degree of accuracy for ratings prediction tasks. Additionally, matrix factorization is a compact, memory-efficient representation of the parameter space for a model and can be trained in parallel, can support multiple feature vectors, and can be improved with confidence levels. Generally, they are used to solve cold-start problems with sparse reviews and in an ensemble with more complex hybrid recommended that also compute content-based recommenders.

See also

- Wikipedia's overview of the dot product is available at
  `http://en.wikipedia.org/wiki/Dot_product`.

Loading the entire dataset into the memory

The first step in building a nonnegative factorization model is to load the entire dataset in the memory. For this task, we will be leveraging NumPy highly.

Getting ready

In order to complete this recipe, you'll have to download the MovieLens database from the **University of Minnesota's GroupLens** page at `http://grouplens.org/datasets/movielens/` and unzip it in a working directory where your code will be. We will also use NumPy in this code significantly, so please ensure that you have this numerical analysis package downloaded and ready. Additionally, we will use the `load_reviews` function from the previous recipes. If you have not had the opportunity to review the appropriate section, please have the code for that function ready.

How to do it...

To build our matrix factorization model, we'll need to create a wrapper for the predictor that loads the entire dataset into memory. We will perform the following steps:

1. We create the following `Recommender` class as shown. Please note that this class depends on the previously created and discussed `load_reviews` function:

```
In [22]: import numpy as np
...: import csv
...:
...: class Recommender(object):
...:
...: def __init__(self, udata):
...: self.udata = udata
...: self.users = None
...: self.movies = None
...: self.reviews = None
...: self.load_dataset()
...:
...: def load_dataset(self):
...: """
...: Loads an index of users and movies as a heap and a reviews
table
...: as a N x M array where N is the number of users and M is the
number
...: of movies. Note that order matters so that we can look up
values
...: outside of the matrix!
...: """
...: self.users = set([])
...: self.movies = set([])
...: for review in load_reviews(self.udata):
...: self.users.add(review['userid'])
...: self.movies.add(review['movieid'])
...:
...: self.users = sorted(self.users)
...: self.movies = sorted(self.movies)
...:
...: self.reviews = np.zeros(shape=(len(self.users),
len(self.movies)))
...: for review in load_reviews(self.udata):
...: uid = self.users.index(review['userid'])
...: mid = self.movies.index(review['movieid'])
...: self.reviews[uid, mid] = review['rating']
```

2. With this defined, we can instantiate a model by typing the following command:

```
data_path = '../data/ml-100k/u.data' model = Recommender(data_path)
```

How it works...

Let's go over this code line by line. The instantiation of our recommender requires a path to the u.data file; creates holders for our list of users, movies, and reviews; and then loads the dataset. We need to hold the entire dataset in memory for reasons that we will see later.

The basic data structure to perform our matrix factorization on is an *N x M* matrix where N is the number of users and M is the number of movies. To create this, we will first load all the movies and users into an ordered list so that we can look up the index of the user or movie by its ID. In the case of MovieLens, all of the IDs are contiguous from 1; however, this might not always be the case. It is good practice to have an index lookup table. Otherwise, you will be unable to fetch recommendations from our computation!

Once we have our index lookup lists, we create a NumPy array of all zeros in the size of the length of our users' list by the length of our movies list. Keep in mind that the rows are users and the columns are movies! We then go through the ratings data a second time and then add the value of the rating at the uid, mid index location of our matrix. Note that if a user hasn't rated a movie, their rating is 0. This is important! Print the array out by entering model.reviews, and you should see something like the following:

```
[[ 5.  3.  4.  ...,  0.  0.  0.]
 [ 4.  0.  0.  ...,  0.  0.  0.]
 [ 0.  0.  0.  ...,  0.  0.  0.]
 ...,
 [ 5.  0.  0.  ...,  0.  0.  0.]
 [ 0.  0.  0.  ...,  0.  0.  0.]
 [ 0.  5.  0.  ...,  0.  0.  0.]]
```

There's more...

Let's get a sense of how sparse or dense our dataset is by adding the following two methods to the Recommender class:

```
In [23]: def sparsity(self):
   ...:     """
   ...:     Report the percent of elements that are zero in the array
   ...:     """
   ...:     return 1 - self.density()
```

```
...:
In [24]: def density(self):
...:    """
...:    Return the percent of elements that are nonzero in the array
...:    """
...:    nonzero = float(np.count_nonzero(self.reviews))
...:    return nonzero / self.reviews.size
```

Adding these methods to our `Recommender` class will help us evaluate our recommender, and it will also help us identify recommenders in the future.

Print out the results:

```
print "%0.3f%% sparse" % model.sparsity()
print "%0.3f%% dense" % model.density()
```

You should see that the MovieLens 100k dataset is 0.937 percent sparse and 0.063 percent dense.

This is very important to keep note of along with the size of the reviews dataset. Sparsity, which is common to most recommender systems, means that we might be able to use sparse matrix algorithms and optimizations. Additionally, as we begin to save models, this will help us identify the models as we load them from serialized files on the disk.

Dumping the SVD-based model to the disk

Before we build our model, which will take a long time to train, we should create a mechanism for us to load and dump our model to the disk. If we have a way of saving the parameterization of the factored matrix, then we can reuse our model without having to train it every time we want to use it this is a very big deal since this model will take hours to train! Luckily, Python has a built-in tool for serializing and deserializing Python objects - the `pickle` module.

How to do it...

Update the `Recommender` class as follows:

```
In [26]: import pickle
...:    class Recommender(object):
...:    @classmethod
...:    def load(klass, pickle_path):
...:        """
...:        Instantiates the class by deserializing the pickle.
```

```
...:    Note that the object returned may not be an exact match
...:    to the code in this class (if it was saved
...:    before updates).
...:    """
...:    with open(pickle_path, 'rb') as pkl:
...:    return pickle.load(pkl)
...:
...:    def __init__(self, udata, description=None):
...:    self.udata = udata
...:    self.users = None
...:    self.movies = None
...:    self.reviews = None
...:
...:    # Descriptive properties
...:    self.build_start = None
...:    self.build_finish = None
...:    self.description = None
...:
...:    # Model properties
...:    self.model = None
...:    self.features = 2
...:    self.steps = 5000
...:    self.alpha = 0.0002
...:    self.beta = 0.02
...:    self.load_dataset()
...:
...:    def dump(self, pickle_path):
...:    """
...:    Dump the object into a serialized file using the pickle module.
...:    This will allow us to quickly reload our model in the future.
...:    """
...:    with open(pickle_path, 'wb') as pkl:
...:    pickle.dump(self, pkl)
```

How it works...

The @classmethod feature is a decorator in Python for declaring a class method instead of an instance method. The first argument that is passed in is the type instead of an instance (which we usually refer to as self). The load class method takes a path to a file on the disk that contains a serialized pickle object, which it then loads using the pickle module. Note that the class that is returned might not be an exact match with the Recommender class at the time you run the code this is because the pickle module saves the class, including methods and properties, exactly as it was when you dumped it.

Speaking of dumping, the `dump` method provides the opposite functionality, allowing you to serialize the methods, properties, and data to disk in order to be loaded again in the future. To help us identify the objects that we're dumping and loading from disk, we've also added some descriptive properties including a description, some build parameters, and some timestamps to our __init__ function.

Training the SVD-based model

We're now ready to write our functions that factor our training dataset and build our recommender model. You can see the required functions in this recipe.

How to do it...

We construct the following functions to train our model. Note that these functions are not part of the `Recommender` class:

```
In [27]: def initialize(R, K):
...:     """
...:     Returns initial matrices for an N X M matrix, R and K features.
...:
...:     :param R: the matrix to be factorized
...:     :param K: the number of latent features
...:
...:     :returns: P, Q initial matrices of N x K and M x K sizes
...:     """
...:     N, M = R.shape
...:     P = np.random.rand(N, K)
...:     Q = np.random.rand(M, K)
...:
...:     return P, Q
In [28]: def factor(R, P=None, Q=None, K=2, steps=5000, alpha=0.0002,
beta=0.02):
...:     """
...:     Performs matrix factorization on R with given parameters.
...:
...:     :param R: A matrix to be factorized, dimension N x M
...:     :param P: an initial matrix of dimension N x K
...:     :param Q: an initial matrix of dimension M x K
...:     :param K: the number of latent features
...:     :param steps: the maximum number of iterations to optimize in
...:     :param alpha: the learning rate for gradient descent
...:     :param beta: the regularization parameter
...:
```

```
...:     :returns: final matrices P and Q
...:     """
...:
...:     if not P or not Q:
...:     P, Q = initialize(R, K)
...:     Q = Q.T
...:
...:     rows, cols = R.shape
...:     for step in xrange(steps):
...:     for i in xrange(rows):
...:     for j in xrange(cols):
...:     if R[i,j] > 0:
...:     eij = R[i,j] - np.dot(P[i,:], Q[:,j])
...:     for k in xrange(K):
...:     P[i,k] = P[i,k] + alpha * (2 * eij * Q[k,j] - beta * P[i,k])
...:     Q[k,j] = Q[k,j] + alpha * (2 * eij * P[i,k] - beta * Q[k,j])
...:
...:     e = 0
...:     for i in xrange(rows):
...:     for j in xrange(cols):
...:     if R[i,j] > 0:
...:     e = e + pow(R[i,j] - np.dot(P[i,:], Q[:,j]), 2)
...:     for k in xrange(K):
...:     e = e + (beta/2) * (pow(P[i,k], 2) + pow(Q[k,j], 2))
...:     if e < 0.001:
...:     break
...:
...:     return P, Q.T
```

How it works...

We discussed the theory and the mathematics of what we are doing in the previous recipe, *Building a nonnegative matrix factorization model*, so let's talk about the code. The initialize function creates two matrices, P and Q, which have a size related to the reviews matrix and the number of features, namely N x K and M x K, where N is the number of users and M is the number of movies. Their values are initialized to random numbers that are between 0.0 and 1.0. The factor function computes P and Q using gradient descent such that the dot product of P and Q is within a mean squared error of less than 0.001 or 5000 steps that have gone by, whichever comes first. Especially note that only values that are greater than 0 are computed. These are the values that we're trying to predict; therefore, we do not want to attempt to match them in our code (otherwise, the model will be trained on zero ratings)! This is also the reason that you can't use NumPy's built-in **Singular Value Decomposition (SVD)** function, which is np.linalg.svd or np.linalg.solve.

There's more...

Let's use these factorization functions to build our model and to save the model to disk once it has been built-this way, we can load the model at our convenience using the `dump` and `load` methods in the class. Add the following method to the `Recommender` class:

```
In [29]: def build(self, output=None, alternate=False):
    ...: """
    ...: Trains the model by employing matrix factorization on our training
    ...: data set, the sparse reviews matrix. The model is the dot product
    ...: of the P and Q decomposed matrices from the factorization.
    ...: """
    ...: options = {
    ...: 'K': self.features,
    ...: 'steps': self.steps,
    ...: 'alpha': self.alpha,
    ...: 'beta': self.beta,
    ...: }
    ...:
    ...: self.build_start = time.time()
    ...: nnmf = factor2 if alternate else factor
    ...: self.P, self.Q = nnmf(self.reviews, **options)
    ...: self.model = np.dot(self.P, self.Q.T)
    ...: self.build_finish = time.time()
    ...:
    ...: if output:
    ...: self.dump(output)
```

This helper function will allow us to quickly build our model. Note that we're also saving P and Q - the parameters of our latent features. This isn't necessary, as our predictive model is the dot product of the two factored matrices. Deciding whether or not to save this information in your model is a trade-off between retraining time (you can potentially start from the current P and Q parameters although you must beware of the overfit) and disk space, as `pickle` will be larger on the disk with these matrices saved. To build this model and dump the data to the disk, run the following code:

```
model = Recommender(relative_path('../data/ml-100k/u.data'))
model.build('reccod.pickle')
```

Warning! This will take a long time to build! On a 2013 MacBook Pro with a 2.8 GHz processor, this process took roughly 9 hours 15 minutes and required 23.1 MB of memory; this is not insignificant for most of the Python scripts that you might be used to writing! It is not a bad idea to continue through the rest of the recipe before building your model. It is also probably not a bad idea to test your code on a smaller test set of 100 records before moving on to the entire process! Additionally, if you don't have the time to train the model, you can find the `pickle` module of our model in the errata of this book.

Testing the SVD-based model

This recipe brings this chapter on recommendation engines to a close. We will now use our new *non-negative matrix factorization based* model and take a look at some of the predicted reviews.

How to do it...

The final step in leveraging our model is to access the predicted reviews for a movie based on our model:

```
In [30]: def predict_ranking(self, user, movie):
...: uidx = self.users.index(user)
...: midx = self.movies.index(movie)
...: if self.reviews[uidx, midx] > 0:
...: return None
...: return self.model[uidx, midx]
```

How it works...

Computing the ranking is relatively easy; we simply need to look up the index of the user and the index of the movie and look up the predicted rating in our model. This is why it is so essential to save an ordered list of the users and movies in our `pickle` module; this way, if the data changes (we add users or movies), but the change isn't reflected in our model, an exception is raised. Because models are historical predictions and not sensitive to changes in time, we need to ensure that we continually retrain our model with new data. This method also returns `None` if we know the ranking of the user (for example, it's not a prediction); we'll leverage this in the next step.

There's more...

To predict the highest-ranked movies, we can leverage the previous function to order the highest predicted rankings for our user:

```
In [31]: import heapq
...: from operator import itemgetter
...:
...: def top_rated(self, user, n=12):
...: movies = [(mid, self.predict_ranking(user, mid)) for mid in
self.movies]
...: return heapq.nlargest(n, movies, key=itemgetter(1))
```

We can now print out the top-predicted movies that have not been rated by the user:

```
>>> rec = Recommender.load('reccod.pickle')
>>> for item in rec.top_rated(234):
...      print "%i: %0.3f" % item
 814: 4.437
1642: 4.362
1491: 4.361
1599: 4.343
1536: 4.324
1500: 4.323
1449: 4.281
1650: 4.147
1645: 4.135
1467: 4.133
1636: 4.133
1651: 4.132
```

It's then simply a matter of using the movie ID to look up the movie in our movies database.

9
Harvesting and Geolocating Twitter Data (Python)

In this chapter, we will cover the following recipes:

- Creating a Twitter application
- Understanding the Twitter API v1.1
- Determining your Twitter followers and friends
- Pulling Twitter user profiles
- Making requests without running afoul of Twitter's rate limits
- Storing JSON data to the disk
- Setting up MongoDB for storing Twitter data
- Storing user profiles in MongoDB using PyMongo
- Exploring the geographic information available in profiles
- Plotting geospatial data in Python

Introduction

In this chapter, we are going to dive into the world of social media analysis through the use of RESTful web service APIs. Twitter is a microblogging social network whose stream is invaluable for data mining, particularly text mining, and they have an excellent API that we will learn how to interact with via Python. We will use the API to fetch Twitter social connections and collect and store JSON data using both traditional file storage and the popular NoSQL database, MongoDB. Our analysis will attempt to ascertain the geographic location of connections and produce visualization from the data.

Throughout the chapter, you should begin to notice patterns about how APIs are designed and their intended use. Interaction with APIs is an extremely important data science topic, and having a solid understanding of them will unlock a whole new world of data upon which you can perform a myriad of analyses.

API stands for Application Programming Interface, and in traditional computer science, it refers to methods that allow software applications to interact with each other. These days, most references to APIs refer to a web API the use of the internet to share data between your software application and a web application (such as Twitter). Data acquisition and management is an important part of the data science pipeline, and knowing how to use APIs is essential for getting actionable datasets off the internet.

A special subset of APIs, called **RESTful APIs**, are actually the backbone of most web applications, and they are everywhere. Although we can avoid most of the technical jargon, we should point out that **REST** stands for **Representational State Transfer**, which is a fancy way of saying that documents or objects exist as representations, and modifications to their state should be transferred via the API. RESTful APIs are a direct extension of the **Hypertext Transfer Protocol** (HTTP) that the World Wide Web was built upon, which is why they are so popular as web APIs. HTTP allows for clients to connect to servers by making requests in the form of verbs: GET, POST, DELETE, and PUT. Traditionally, the response is an HTML document. Similarly, a RESTful API uses these verbs to make requests whose response is a JSON document. The former is for human consumption (such as when you visit a website such as http://www.google.com) and the latter is for application consumption.

For this chapter, we will only use HTTP GET requests and the occasional POST request. A GET request is just like it sounds; it asks the server to give you a particular resource. A POST request, on the other hand, means that a client is trying to provide data to the server (as in, submitting a form or uploading a file). An API provider, such as Twitter, allows us to make HTTP GET requests to a particular resource URL, which is often called an endpoint. For example, the endpoint to GET all the most recent tweets for a particular user is https://api.twitter.com/1.1/statuses/user_timeline.json. If we make the correctly authenticated HTTP GET request to this endpoint, Twitter will supply the data that composes the current user's timeline in the JSON format.

Creating a Twitter application

Twitter is the ubiquitous microblogging social media platform with 253 million active members as of 2014. Fortunately for us, Twitter makes the service's data more open and available to third parties than just about any other social media site of similar size and standing in the tech community. Additionally, Twitter offers a rich and user-friendly RESTful API that we will make use of extensively. This recipe will show you how to create a new Twitter application, which is a required step to access Twitter data programmatically.

Getting ready

Make sure that you have a web browser installed, and open up a new browser tab or window.

How to do it...

The following steps will walk you through the creation of a new Twitter application:

Note that Twitter does like to update its **user interface** (**UI**) frequently and these steps, or the web-based forms, might change accordingly

1. First, make sure that you have created a Twitter account. If you have not created one, go to `http://twitter.com` and sign up. If you have an account, simply log in to your Twitter account with your web browser.

2. Next, go to `https://dev.twitter.com/apps` and select the light blue button labeled **Create New App** on the right-hand side of the screen:

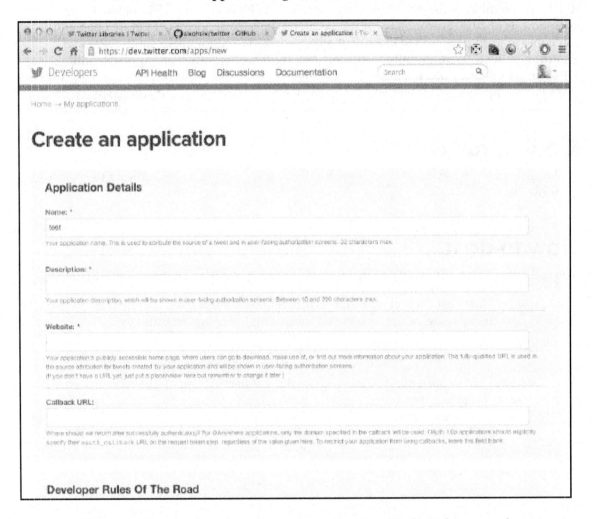

3. Here, it will prompt you to enter your application details in three mandatory fields and one optional one. Choose a name for your application that is no more than 32 characters.

4. Next, supply a brief description of your application between 10 and 200 characters.

5. You must supply a website for your application, although it is not applicable for our use case. Also, there is a specific format that is required for the form to be submitted successfully. Enter `http://127.0.0.1`.

6. Finally, you can ignore the **Callback URL** field, which is the last field on the form.

7. Go ahead and take some time to read the **Developer Rules of the Road** section, as this document details in plain and simple text what you should and should not do using your application.

8. Click on **Create your Twitter Application**. After a few moments, you should be on the main settings page of your new application with a tabbed menu at the top of the screen. The current tab should be labeled **Details**.

9. Click on the **Keys and Access Tokens** tab and you should see the following screenshot:

10. Now, click on **Create my access token** in the **Token** actions gray box at the bottom to authorize your application for your own account (you might have to click the button more than once). The result should look like the following screenshot:

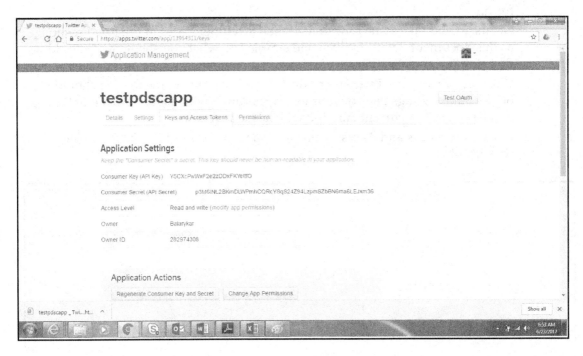

11. Record the **API key**, **API secret**, **Access token**, and **Access token secret** in a text file. These are important, but they must be protected like you would protect your E-mail password or ATM pin. You can take a screenshot to save the information, but it would be easier to copy and paste these values into a text file for now.

Now that you have **MinGW** and **MSYS**, there's no need to be jealous of those with a Linux installation anymore, since they implement in your system the most important parts of a Linux development environment.

How it works...

You might be asking yourself why we needed to create an application if all we want to do is pull some simple data from Twitter. Early versions (1.0 and before) of the Twitter API allowed applications to make anonymous API requests, retrieving data from Twitter without Twitter knowing who was actually making the request. Since the deprecated Version 1.0 of the company's API was retired on *June 11, 2013*, all API requests to Twitter require authentication. This allows Twitter to keep track of who requests what information and how much information was requested.

In general, there are several signs in the industry that the halcyon days of social media data harvesting might be waning. Facebook's newest set of APIs, specifically Version 2.0 of Facebook Login, has strongly locked down what data can be obtained from the social graph. Furthermore, Twitter acquired Gnip in April, 2014; Gnip is a reseller of Twitter data, and it allows its customers to buy large portions of Twitter data. This move suggests that Version 2.0 of the Twitter API might limit further access to Twitter verse.

See also

The following articles can be referred to:

- The *Obtaining access tokens* article at
  https://dev.twitter.com/docs/auth/obtaining-access-tokens
- The *Tokens from dev.twitter.com* article at
  https://dev.twitter.com/docs/auth/tokens-devtwittercom

Understanding the Twitter API v1.1

APIs are both a blessing and a curse. Application Programming Interfaces make it much easier to gather data from services such as Twitter, Facebook, or LinkedIn and define exactly what data the company wants, and does not want, you to have. Unfortunately, companies set rate limits on accessing their APIs in order to control the frequency (and therefore, the amount) of data that can be harvested. They have also been known to radically alter their APIs from one version to the next, thus resulting in a great deal of code rewrites for all efforts dependent on the original API. Twitter's large API change from Version 1.0 to Version 1.1 offers a cautionary tale.

Twitter offers three main APIs: the **Search API**, the **REST API**, and the **Streaming API**. The search API gives us a programmatic method that makes queries to Twitter in order to retrieve historical content, namely tweets. The REST API offers access to Twitter's core features, including timelines, status updates, and user information. Finally, the streaming API is the real-time API designed for low latency access to Twitter's global stream of Tweet data.

With the streaming API, one must keep a persistent HTTP connection open to Twitter. For our data mining and analysis purposes, this is overkill as we will only be periodically requesting data from Twitter. Thus, we will be focusing on the first two APIs and don't have to concern ourselves with the streaming API.

Getting ready

Once you have created your application in the preceding recipe and copied your keys, you are ready to proceed.

How to do it...

Perform the following steps in order to access the Twitter API programmatically using Python:

1. First, install the `twython` library. Open a new Command Prompt and type the following:

   ```
   (sudo) pip install twython
   ```

   The `sudo` command is needed if your current user account does not have sufficient privileges.

2. Next, open a new Terminal and start the default Python REPL or IPython. If you want to go the extra mile, you can also use IPython Notebook.

3. Enter and execute the following Python code, filling in the needed application keys:

   ```
   In [1]: '''
      ...: Understanding the Twitter API v1.1
      ...: '''
      ...: from twython import Twython
   In [2]: API_KEY = 'INSERT HERE'
      ...: API_SECRET = 'INSERT HERE'
   ```

```
    . . . :
    ...: ACCESS_TOKEN = 'INSERT HERE'
    ...: ACCESS_TOKEN_SECRET = 'INSERT HERE'
In [3]: twitter = Twython(API_KEY, API_SECRET, ACCESS_TOKEN,
ACCESS_TOKEN_SECRET)
```

 Note that Twitter updates its developer interface frequently and the API_KEY used to be called CONSUMER_KEY. Also, note that the keys given in the code snippet need to be replaced with the values collected during the previous recipe.

4. If you are using IPython, type the following at the REPL and then hit the Tab key:

```
In [4]:twitter
```

This will bring up an impressive list of API calls that are now available to you.

5. As a test, we can enter the following at the Python prompt:

```
In [4]: temp = twitter.get_user_timeline()
```

This command will fetch the last 20 status updates from your timeline as a 20-element list of Python dictionaries.

6. Furthermore, Twython gives us access to the response headers received from Twitter:

```
In [5]: twitter.get_lastfunction_header('x-rate-limit-remaining')
   ...:

Out[5]: '899'
```

How it works...

With the preceding code, we are setting up our API keys and access tokens that we pass in order to instantiate an instance of the `Twython` class. This new object serves as our main interface to the Twitter API and defaults to using `OAuth v1` for authentication purposes. As this is a pretty common requirement, we can wrap this functionality in its own function, as shown in the following snippet. Before using the following function code, make sure that you enter the needed application keys:

```
In [6]: def twitter_oauth_login():
   ...: API_KEY = 'INSERT HERE'
   ...: API_SECRET = 'INSERT HERE'
   ...: ACCESS_TOKEN = 'INSERT HERE'
   ...: ACCESS_TOKEN_SECRET = 'INSERT HERE'
   ...:
   ...: twitter = Twython(API_KEY, API_SECRET, ACCESS_TOKEN,
ACCESS_TOKEN_SECRET)
   ...: return(twitter)

   return(twitter)
```

If you are checking your code into GitHub or another cloud-based version control solution (such as Bitbucket), please check whether that repository is public or private. All free repositories on GitHub are public. If your repository is public, the world will have access to your *secret* Twitter API keys. We strongly advise that you only use private repositories for such matters and note that `bitbucket.org` provides private repositories for free.

OAuth, which stands for the **Open Authentication protocol**, allows a user to give permission to a third-party application to access an aspect of the user's account (in this case, their Twitter account) without giving up the user's login and password. Diving into the details of how OAuth works is outside the scope of this recipe. However, it is important to discuss the two different types of resource authentication for Twitter applications. The most common authentication is the application-user authentication, which we will not use. In this mode, your application makes a request on behalf of a user who has granted the needed permissions to your application. For our project, we care about the application-only authentication, where our application makes API requests not for a user, but for itself. Note that some API calls do not support application-only requests and that the rate limits for such requests are typically different.

There's more...

The `Twython` library is not the only Python library available to simplify access to Twitter's API. The following are three popular choices, including the popular **Python Twitter Tools**, and you are free to explore or choose whichever you see fit:

- **Python Twitter Tools** (`https://github.com/sixohsix/twitter`): This is a minimalist Python API for Twitter that includes a command-line tool in order to get friends' tweets and send your own announcements.
- **Twython 3.1.2** (`https://github.com/ryanmcgrath/twython`): This is a pure Python wrapper that supports both search and streaming APIs, which are actively maintained. This is the library that we will be using.
- **python-twitter** (`https://github.com/bear/python-twitter`): This is a pure Python interface for the current v1.1 Twitter API.

Twitter maintains a list of alternatives across programming languages at `https://dev.twitter.com/docs/twitter-libraries`. Please note that the code from this chapter uses Twython exclusively, but it could be a useful exercise for the reader to rewrite examples using the other Python libraries.

See also

You can also refer to:

- The Twython documentation at `http://twython.readthedocs.org/en/latest/`
- *Detailed OAuth 1.0 Guide* at `http://hueniverse.com/oauth/guide/`
- The Twitter's OAuth implementation at

```
https://dev.twitter.com/docs/auth/oauth
```
- Twitter's *OAuth FAQ* web page
  ```
  https://dev.twitter.com/docs/auth/oauth/faq
  ```
- The OAuth home page at `http://oauth.net/`
- *Additional Twitter libraries* at `https://dev.twitter.com/docs/twitter-libraries`

Determining your Twitter followers and friends

In the Twitter social network, users are labeled either as followers or friends relative to a particular user. Your friends are the people that you follow and your followers are the people that follow you. In this recipe, we determine who your friends are, who your followers are, and how much overlap there is in each group.

Getting ready

For this recipe, we will be using the results of the previous two recipes and the `twitter_oauth_login()` function. Also, we will be working in IPython or the default Python REPL, if you prefer that instead. Feel free to use an editor in order to start capturing and modifying the code as it grows in complexity.

How to do it...

The following steps will allow you to determine all of your Twitter friends and followers:

1. In IPython or your favorite REPL, enter the following:

   ```
   In [8]: twitter = twitter_oauth_login()
      ...: friends_ids = twitter.get_friends_ids(count=5000)
      ...: friends_ids = friends_ids['ids']

   In [9]: followers_ids = twitter.get_followers_ids(count=5000)
      ...: followers_ids = followers_ids['ids']
   ```

2. With all of your followers' and friends' Twitter IDs collected, let's see how many you have:

```
In [10]: len(friends_ids), len(followers_ids)
   ...:
Out[10]: (22, 40)
```

3. We will use Python sets, which are based on the sets that you might have encountered in math class, to examine some properties of our friends and followers:

```
In [11]: friends_set = set(friends_ids)
   ...: followers_set = set(followers_ids)
   ...:
In [12]: print('Number of Twitter users who either are our friend
or follow you (union):')
   ...: print(len(friends_set.union(followers_set)))
   ...:
Number of Twitter users who either are our friend or follow you
(union):
56
In [13]: len(friends_set | followers_set)
   ...: len(set(friends_ids+followers_ids))
   ...:
Out[13]: 56

In [14]: print('Number of Twitter users who follow you and are your
friend (intersection):')
   ...: print(len(friends_set & followers_set))
   ...:
Number of Twitter users who follow you and are your friend
(intersection):
6

In [15]: print("Number of Twitter users you follow that don't
follow you (set difference):")
   ...: print(len(friends_set - followers_set))
   ...:

In [16]: Number of Twitter users you follow that don't follow you
(set difference):
16
print("Number of Twitter users who follow you that you don't follow
(set difference):")
   ...: print(len(followers_set - friends_set))
   ...:
Number of Twitter users who follow you that you don't follow (set
```

```
difference):
34
```

The preceding snippet should result in the following output:

```
Number of Twitter users who either are our friend or follow you (union):
980
Number of Twitter users who follow you and are your friend (intersection):
205
Number of Twitter users you follow that don't follow you (set difference):
354
Number of Twitter users who follow you that you don't follow (set difference):
421
```

 The numbers shown in the preceding screenshot will most likely be different based on the number of friends and followers you have.

How it works...

This recipe demonstrates just how useful the `twython` package is and how easy it makes certain tasks. After we logged in using the `twitter_oauth_login` function, we make two basic calls using the `twitter` object, one to get friends' IDs and one to get followers' IDs. Note that we set the count parameter to 5000, which is the maximum value allowed by the Twitter API. The `twitter` object returned a dictionary from which we extracted the actual IDs.

One of the nice things about the Twython interface is how closely it mirrors the Twitter API. If you ever have a question about a particular function, just check the Twitter documents.

Once we have collected our list of friends' and followers' IDs, we turn to the Python set type for some quick navel gazing. The Python `set` type, which has been built into Python since Version 2.4, is an unordered collection of unique objects. The key word for us is the word unique. If we create a set from a list with duplicates, we will get a set with only unique elements; `set([1, 2, 2, 3, 3, 3])` will return `{1, 2, 3}`.

We unite the set of friends' IDs with the followers' IDs to determine the total set of unique IDs of Twitter users that either follow or are followed by us. In the preceding code, we use the union method of the `set` type, but there are several other ways in which we could have done this:

```
(friends_set | followers_set)
(set(friends_ids + followers_ids))
```

There's more...

While Twython's beautiful abstraction hides some of the complexity of using the API, this simplicity or magic can be problematic if we don't have an understanding of what is actually happening behind the scenes. When we call the `twitter.get_friends_ids(count=5000)` method, we are sending an HTTP GET request to a particular URL. In the case of `twitter.get_friends_ids()`, the URL is `https://api.twitter.com/1.1/friends/ids.json`.

The `count=5000` input parameter to the function call shows up as field-value pairs in the URL and as such, the URL becomes `https://api.twitter.com/1.1/friends/ids.json?count=5000`.

Now, the actual API endpoint requires some default parameter values that Twython fills in for us, as shown in the following URL for clarity:

```
https://api.twitter.com/1.1/friends/ids.json?cursor=-
1&screen_name=sayhitosean&count=5000
```

The Twitter v1.1 API requires all requests to be authenticated using OAuth. The required information is actually embedded in the header of the GET request, and the process of constructing the appropriate header is extensive (for more information, go to `https://dev.twitter.com/docs/auth/authorizing-request`). Thus, Twython not only forms the proper URL for making the request, but also handles the relatively painful Open Authorization so that we don't have to. If you are interested, you can go down a level lower and construct your own GET requests using the excellent request library or an alternative of your choosing. We leave this for the reader to explore.

 Note that different Twitter API endpoints have different rate limits. In the case of GET friends/IDs, we are only allowed 15 calls over a 15 minute period for Version 1.1 of the API as of May 2014. Other endpoints are less stingy with their data.

See also

You can also refer to the following:

- The *GET friends/ids* article at
  `https://dev.twitter.com/docs/api/1.1/get/friends/ids`
- The *GET followers/ids* article at
  `https://dev.twitter.com/docs/api/1.1/get/followers/ids`
- The *Requests: HTTP for Humans* article at
  `http://docs.python-requests.org/en/latest/`

Pulling Twitter user profiles

For this recipe, we are going to use the Twitter API to pull JSON data about Twitter users. Each Twitter user, identified by either a screen name (such as SayHiToSean) or a unique integer, has a profile containing a rich set of information about someone.

Getting ready

You will need the list of followers' and friends' IDs from the previous recipe, *Determining your Twitter followers and friends*.

How to do it...

The following steps guide you through retrieving a set of Twitter users' profiles:

1. First, we create a function that will manage pulling Twitter profiles:

```
In [18]: def pull_users_profiles(ids):
    ...: users = []
    ...: for i in range(0, len(ids), 100):
    ...: batch = ids[i:i + 100]
    ...: users += twitter.lookup_user(user_id=batch)
    ...: print(twitter.get_lastfunction_header('x-rate-limit-
remaining'))
    ...: return (users)
```

2. We put this function to use, pulling profiles of both friends and followers:

```
In [19]: friends_profiles = pull_users_profiles(friends_ids)
    ...: followers_profiles = pull_users_profiles(followers_ids)
899
898
```

3. To check whether everything works, we use a list comprehension to extract all of the friends' screen names from the profiles:

```
In [20]: friends_screen_names = [p['screen_name'] for p in
friends_profiles]
```

4. Using the following command, you should be greeted by a list of your friends' screen names:

```
In [21]: friends_screen_names
    ...:
Out[21]:
['nammamechanik',
'Ruchir78',
'nspothnis',

'jdelaney666',
'zakaas4u',
'arunkumar_n_t']
```

How it works...

The first step in this recipe was the creation of a function that manages the `twitter.lookup_user` method call. The Twitter users/lookup endpoint accepts 100 user IDs at a time. Thus, we need to loop over our list of friends' or followers' IDs and batch them into groups of 100 for the requests. Twitter returns a JSON object that Twython converts into a list of Python dictionaries, ready for use.

There is an alternative way of retrieving profiles. Instead of pulling friends' and followers' IDs and then using those to request user profiles, we could have queried the friends/list endpoint with simply the current user's screen name (in this case, mine, which is @SayHiToSean) or user ID. Twitter would then return up to 200 user profiles per request. If you work out the API limits, either path works out to the same number of user profiles pulled in the 15 minute default time window that Twitter uses for rate-limiting purposes.

There's more...

The `pull_users_profiles` function that we created has an extra feature in the last line of the loop:

```
print(twitter.get_lastfunction_header('x-rate-limit-remaining'))
```

We retrieve the header of the response from the last API call and check the `x-rate-limit-remaining` value. This value tells us exactly how many API calls we have left in a given 15 minute window. Although we print this value out with each loop, we do absolutely nothing to prevent us from slamming up against Twitter's rate limit, which varies by the endpoint.

Furthermore, the list comprehension that we used in step 3 can fail if, for some reason, one of the Twitter user profiles that were received did not have a `screen_name` key. Thus, it would be better to add a condition to the comprehension:

```
In [22]: friends_screen_names = [p['screen_name'] for p in friends_profiles
if 'screen_name' in p]
```

Or, as an alternative and potentially a more Pythonic way, we could use the GET method of the dictionary:

```
In [23]: friends_screen_names = [p.get('screen_name',{}) for p in
friends_profiles]
```

In this case, profiles that do not have a `screen_name` key are not skipped, but are replaced with `None`, instead.

See also

You can also refer to the following:

- The description of the Twitter user profile JSON at
  https://dev.twitter.com/docs/platform-objects/users
- The *GET users/lookup* documentation at
  https://dev.twitter.com/docs/api/1.1/get/users/lookup
- The *GET friends/list* documentation at
  https://dev.twitter.com/docs/api/1.1/get/friends/list

Making requests without running afoul of Twitter's rate limits

For this recipe, we are going to modify the function created in the previous recipe, *Pulling Twitter user profiles,* in order to avoid hitting the dreaded Twitter API rate limits.

Getting ready

You will again need the list of followers' and friends' IDs from the previous recipe, *Pulling Twitter user profiles,* as well as the authenticated Twython object.

How to do it...

The following function demonstrates how you can retrieve a set of Twitter users' profiles in a rate-limit-aware fashion:

```
In [25]: import time
    ...: import math

In [26]: rate_limit_window = 15 * 60 #900 seconds

In [27]: def pull_users_profiles_limit_aware(ids):
    ...: users = []
    ...: start_time = time.time()
    ...: # Must look up users in
    ...: for i in range(0, len(ids), 10):
    ...: batch = ids[i:i + 10]
    ...: users += twitter.lookup_user(user_id=batch)
    ...: calls_left = float(twitter.get_lastfunction_header('x-rate-limit-
remaining'))
    ...: time_remaining_in_window = rate_limit_window - (time.time()-
start_time)
    ...: sleep_duration = math.ceil(time_remaining_in_window/calls_left)
    ...: print('Sleeping for: ' + str(sleep_duration) + ' seconds; ' +
str(calls_left) + ' API calls remaining')
    ...: time.sleep(sleep_duration)
    ...: return (users)
```

How it works...

This function is a modified version of the previous recipe's function that pulls users' profiles so that we do not run afoul of Twitter's ubiquitous rate limit. We insert a dynamic pause into each iteration of the loop with the length determined by the number of API calls remaining in the time window. Before the loop starts, we capture the current system time in the `start_time` variable. After each API call made by the `twitter` object, we grab the header of the response and check the number of API calls remaining in the 15-minute time window. We compute the time that has elapsed since `start_time` and subtract this from 900 seconds, yielding the time left in the 15-minute window. Finally, we compute the number of seconds needed per remaining API calls and sleep for the required period. We use the `math.ceil` function to round up and make sure that we always give just a little bit of extra time so as to not hit the rate limit.

You might ask why one would care about hitting the Twitter API rate limit. Why not just keep hitting the API even after the limit has been reached? The simple answer is that Twitter can and will block applications that abuse the prescribed rate limits too often. Thus, it is in your best interest to play by the rules. Furthermore, you can't pull any additional information if you try once the rate limit has been exceeded, so why bother?

Storing JSON data to disk

Calls to the API can be expensive in terms of bandwidth and the rate limits that service providers place on their API. While Twitter is quite generous about these limits, other services are not. Regardless, it is good practice to save the retrieved JSON structures to disk for later use.

Getting ready

For this recipe, you will need previously retrieved data, preferably from the previous recipes.

How to do it...

The following steps walk us through saving the JSON data to disk and then loading it back into the Python interpreter's memory:

1. First, we must import the `json` package and create two helper functions:

```
In [31]: import json
    ...: def save_json(filename, data):
    ...: with open(filename, 'wb') as outfile:
    ...: json.dump(data, outfile)

In [32]: def load_json(filename):
    ...: with open(filename) as infile:
    ...: data = json.load(infile)
    ...: return data
```

2. At the Python prompt, let's test our functions by saving our friends' JSON-based Twitter profiles to disk:

```
In [33]: fname = 'test_friends_profiles.json'
    ...: save_json(fname, friends_profiles)
```

3. Check to make sure that the file was created. If you are using IPython, simply type `ls` or open up a Terminal shell, change to the current directory, and type `ls`. You should see `test_friends_profiles.json` in the current directory.

4. Now, let's load the file back into our Python workspace:

```
In [34]: test_reload = load_json(fname)
    ...: print(test_reload[0])
```

How it works...

The `json` library, which is part of the Python standard library, provides a simple but effective JSON encoder and decoder. When writing a file via the `save_json` function, we use the `json.dump` method to serialize the data object (in this case, a Python dictionary) as a JSON-formatted stream with a default UTF-8 encoding and send it to the outfile. Conversely, the `load_json` function uses `json.load`, which deserializes the infile to a Python object.

Setting up MongoDB for storing Twitter data

The default response format for the REST API is JSON, and thus, it is easiest to store this data as JSON in order to avoid extra data wrangling. While there are a number of different databases and data stores that can handle JSON data, we want to choose one that is relatively easy to set up, handles JSON data natively, is free to use, and is relatively popular. Thus, we will go with MongoDB.

Getting ready

For this recipe, you will need to download MongoDB on your local machine, so make sure that you have a broadband connection to the internet.

How to do it...

The following steps will walk you through setting up MongoDB and using it through the command shell:

1. The first step for this stage is to install MongoDB. The easiest way to do this is to download the latest binary distribution (currently, 3.4) from the `http://www.mongodb.org/downloads`. 64-bit binary distributions that is available for Windows, Linux, macOS X, and Solaris.

2. Once downloaded, follow the pertinent installation guide at `http://docs.mongodb.org/manual/installation/`.

3. Next, we need to start MongoDB by typing in `mongod` at the Command Prompt.

4. With the DB running, we need to connect to it via the included mongo shell. For this, open another terminal window or command line and type the following:

   ```
   mongo
   ```

5. This command assumes that MongoDB is running on port *27017* and at localhost. If this is not the case, start the mongo shell as shown, with the correct address of host and port number specified:

   ```
   mongo address_of_host:port_number
   ```

6. Now that we are running the mongo shell, we can get to work. Let's create a database named `test`, so type in the following:

   ```
   use test
   ```

7. Once the `test` database has been created, we need to create the tweets collection that will actually store all of the tweets that we are going to harvest. For this, use the following:

   ```
   db.createCollection('user_profiles')
   ```

8. We want to check whether the collection was created, so we must first switch to the current database by using the following command:

   ```
   use test
   ```

9. Ask the `mongo` shell to show all collections in this database, and you will receive a simple list of collections in the local database:

   ```
   show collections
   ```

How it works...

In this straightforward recipe, we have laid the foundations for how to use the popular MongoDB. We have installed and run MongoDB and have connected to it using the mongo shell. Furthermore, we have named a new database, which is `test` , and created a document collection called `user_profiles`. Collections in MongoDB are groupings of MongoDB documents that are somewhat similar to a table in a relational database, such as `Postgres`. These documents are usually similar in structure and purpose, but unlike relational databases, do not have to be completely uniform and can evolve easily over time. For our purposes, the group of Twitter users' profiles make a great collection.

Personally, we don't like to run the `mongod` process either in the background or upon login, so we start MongoDB from the command line. This way, when we're not using MongoDB, it is not running in the background, consuming CPU cycles or draining the battery.

There's more...

MongoDB is not the only NOSQL document store that is well suited for JSON data and many alternatives exist, including **CouchDB** (http://couchdb.apache.org/). Most key/value stores such as **Amazon's Dynamo** or **Riak** from Basho are great for storing JSON data with relatively minimal setup and configuration as well. With Amazon's Dynamo, you also get the added benefit of it being a fully cloud-based, pay-as-you-go solution that can scale almost infinitely. Finally, some relational databases, including **Postgres**, natively support a JSON datatype and perform error checking on the data in order to make sure that the stored data is valid JSON. However, the setup and configuration of Postgres tends to be a bit more challenging than MongoDB.

An additional advantage with MongoDB, although not an exclusive advantage, is that free, hosted platform-as-a-service options exist. In other words, you can provision a completely configured MongoDB database running in the cloud without doing anything more than walking through a fairly straightforward, web-based interface to log in and create your database. The best part is that both MongoLab and MongoHQ offer a free service tier, which means that you set up and use your own MongoDB database in the cloud without paying any money!

 Since this section was written, the authors have had the opportunity to test and use **RethinkDB** (http://rethinkdb.com/), which is a relatively new open-sourced distributed database that easily handles JSON datatypes yet offers joins across tables of documents much like a relational database. If we were to rewrite this chapter, we would do so using RethinkDB.

See also

You can also refer to the following:

- *The MongoDB v2.4 Manual* at http://docs.mongodb.org/v2.4/
- The *Getting Started with MongoDB* guide at http://docs.mongodb.org/manual/tutorial/getting-started/
- CRUD in MongoDB at http://docs.mongodb.org/manual/crud/
- The **CouchDB** home page at http://couchdb.apache.org/
- The **MongoLab** home page https://mongolab.com/welcome/
- The **MongoHQ** home page at http://www.mongohq.com/

Storing user profiles in MongoDB using PyMongo

With user profile data retrieved and MongoDB installed and ready for action, we need to store the user profile JSON into the appropriate collection, and we want to do so from within our Python scripts and not using the mongo shell. For this, we are going to use PyMongo, which is the recommended way to work with MongoDB from Python, as per the MongoDB people themselves. As of January 2014, **PyMongo** was sitting at Version 2.6.3 (`http://api.mongodb.org/python/current/`).

Getting ready

You must already have MongoDB installed and have some sample user profile data to be ready pulled for this recipe.

How to do it...

The following steps will guide you through saving Python dictionaries as JSON documents within MongoDB:

1. To get started, we must install **PyMongo** on our systems. On a Command-line Prompt, type the following:

   ```
   pip install pymongo
   ```

2. Depending on your current user privileges, you might have to use sudo with these commands:

   ```
   sudo pip install pymongo
   ```

3. If the preceding installations do not work and report errors, please see the more detailed instructions online at `http://api.mongodb.org/python/current/installation.html`, as there are some potential C dependencies that might have to be compiled separately, depending on your system.

4. With PyMongo installed, drop in to a Python, IPython, or IPython Notebook session and enter the following:

```
In [36]: import pymongo

In [37]: host_string = "mongodb://localhost"
    ...: port = 27017
    ...: mongo_client = pymongo.MongoClient(host_string, port)

In [38]: mongo_db = mongo_client['test']

In [39]: user_profiles_collection = mongo_db['user_profiles']

In [40]: user_profiles_collection.insert(friends_profiles)
    ...: user_profiles_collection.insert(followers_profiles)
```

How it works...

After we installed pymongo, there weren't many steps required to get us connected to and then storing JSON, in our local MongoDB database.

We first created a **MongoClient** that is connected to the mongod specified in the host string and port. We then use dictionary-style access to access the needed mongo_db database (in this case, test) and the particular collection (in this case, user_profiles). We call the insert method of the collection and pass it the JSON data to save. For this effort, we receive either one ObjectID or a list of ObjectIDs for the newly stored objects.

There are a number of things to be noted here. We choose to use the dictionary-style access (mongo_client['test']) just in case the database name contains characters such as – that would prevent the attribute style access to the database (client.test). Also, please note that MongoDB does nothing until a document is actually stored in the collection.

Alternatively, we can wrap the preceding commands in a function for easier reuse later. In the following command, save_json_data_to_mongo takes either a single JSON document or an iterable list of JSON documents and the specifications required in order to access the particular database and collection in MongoDB. The host_string parameter defaults to localhost and the port defaults to 27017:

```
In [41]: def save_json_data_to_mongo(data, mongo_db,
    ...: mongo_db_collection,
    ...: host_string = "localhost",
    ...: port = 27017):
    ...: mongo_client = pymongo.MongoClient(host_string, port)
```

```
...: mongo_db = mongo_client[mongo_db]
...: collection = mongo_db[mongo_db_collection]
...: inserted_object_ids = collection.insert(data)
...: return(inserted_object_ids)
```

We can improve this function by performing a check to see whether the number of JSON documents matches the number of ObjectIDs returned, but we will leave this exercise to the reader.

Exploring the geographic information available in profiles

The Twitter users' profiles contain two different, potential sources of geographic information: the profile itself and the most recently tweeted status update. We will utilize both options in this recipe with an eye towards usability in constructing a geographic visualization of our friends.

Getting ready

You will need the harvested friends' and/or followers' profiles from Twitter, as directed in the previous recipes.

How to do it...

Perform the following steps to extract the geographic data that we need to visualize the approximate locations of our connections:

1. We start this exercise in IPython or your favorite Python REPL. Load your friends' profiles from the file:

   ```
   In[1]: fname = 'test_friends_profiles.json'
   In[2]: load_json(fname)
   ```

2. Next, we build lists from all of the values of the geo_enabled field in the user profiles' data structures for our friends. Then, we use the count method to find the number of user profiles that have the geo_enabled flag set to true:

```
In[3]: geo_enabled = [p['geo_enabled'] for p in friends_profiles]
In[4]: geo_enabled.count(1)
Out[4]: 127
```

3. We repeat a very similar process to the one used in the second step to count how many friends' user profiles have a blank location field:

```
In[5]: location = [p['location'] for p in friends_profiles]
In [6]: location.count('')
Out[6]: 79
```

4. To get a quick ID of the data contained in the location field of user profiles, we print out a unique list and note the messiness of the data. It would appear that location is a free text field, which is very disappointing:

```
In[7]: print(set(location))

Out[7]:
. . .
u'Washington D.C.',
u'Washington DC',
u'iPhone: 50.122643,8.670158',
u'london',
u'new world of work',
u'san francisco',
u'seattle, wa',
u'usually in Connecticut',
u'washington, dc',
. . .
```

5. Now, we turn our attention to the time_zone field:

```
In[8]: time_zone = [p['time_zone'] for p in friends_profiles]
In[9]: time_zone.count(None)
Out[9]: 62
In[10]: print(set(time_zone))
Out[10]: {None, u'Alaska', u'Amsterdam', u'Arizona', u'Atlantic
Time (Canada)', u'Berlin',
. . .
```

6. Finally, as each user profile contains that user's most recent status update (or tweet), we want to check how many of these tweets were geo-tagged by the user. Note the logical and conditional portion of the list comprehension. We only want `p['status']['geo']` if these keys are present in the data structure:

```
In[11]: status_geo = [p['status']['geo'] for p in friends_profiles
if ('status' in p and p['status']['geo'] is not None)]
In [12]: if status_geo: print status_geo[0]
Out[12]: {u'coordinates': [38.91431189, -77.0211878], u'type':
u'Point'}
In[13]: len(status_geo)
Out[13]: 13
```

How it works...

In this recipe, we are using list comprehensions to extract potentially useful geographic information contained in the user profiles of friends. With each data element, we are asking two questions:

- What percentage of profiles contain this information, as coverage is important?
- What form and, therefore, how useful is the information that is available in the profiles?

We find that about 80 percent of profiles have a location set in their profile (very promising) and an even higher percentage have a time zone set (an even coarser grained geographic indicator). Of the last status update that is captured in the user profile data, more than 90 percent is not geocoded even though a third of user profiles (127/352) have `geo_enabled` set to `True`, which means that users might sometimes opt to **geocode** a tweet. Thus, if we harvested historical tweets for our friends, we should be able to get locations for about a third of them, at best.

With the coverage established, we look back at the actual data available, which paints a more complicated picture of the problem. The location characteristic of the user profile is available in most profiles, but it is a jumble of content. Some locations are a latitude and longitude value (highly useful), some are a recognizable address as a text string, some are a city and state, and some are not quite a traditional address format or even a location. The time zone data appears to be less obviously problematic, but we would still have to ensure that the time zone names captured by Twitter cleanly and unambiguously map to *real* time zones.

There's more...

If we want to plot our friends on Twitter, we can do so using a few approaches, listed as follows:

- If we use the coordinates of geo-tagged tweets, we can immediately jump to plotting. The only concern here is the sparsity of the data. To ameliorate this situation, we should pull tweets for each friend in an attempt to uncover more geo-tagged tweets. Doing this, we would expect to uncover geographic data for as much as a third of our friends.

- Although the location characteristic is quite messy, we can run the results through a geocoding service such as Google Maps or Bing and see what happens. Given the creativity of some of the locations in user profiles, this might not be the most productive path possible. Alternatively, we could attempt to pull out state abbreviations or ZIP codes using regular expressions, but this too would be a bit messy and time consuming.

- Graphing the count of friends in different time zones can be really interesting, and it would appear that this data might be easy to extract. The one question that becomes relevant is how hard will it be to graph time zones?

See also

You can also refer to the *Users* Twitter documentation at
`https://dev.twitter.com/docs/platform-objects/users`

Plotting geospatial data in Python

One of Python's greatest strengths is the number and diversity of available packages that make many complex tasks simple, as someone else has already written most of the code. As a result, we sometimes encounter the paradox of choice where too many options confuse the issue and we just want one good option. In this recipe, we will plot a set of latitude and longitude coordinates using an excellent Python package: `folium` - that wraps a JavaScript library, which is `leaflet.js`. You will learn more about folium further along in the recipe.

Getting ready

You will need the geographic data extracted in the previous recipes (a set of longitude and latitude coordinates). Also, we need to install the `folium` package, which is shown in the following section, so you will need an internet connection.

How to do it...

The following steps will help you convert the latitude and longitude data you have to plot on a map:

1. Open your terminal. We need to install the Python package folium:

   ```
   (sudo) pip install folium
   ```

2. Change to your source directory and start up IPython or your favorite Python REPL. We first need to create two lists that will contain the geographic data and the associated screen names that we will use for labels. The following code is very similar to the last list comprehension in the previous recipe, *Exploring the geographic information available in profiles*, but is represented as a loop:

   ```
   status_geo = []
   status_geo_screen_names = []
   for fp in friends_profiles:
       if ('status' in fp and fp['status']['geo'] is not None and
         'screen_name' in fp):
           status_geo.append(fp['status']['geo'])
           status_geo_screen_names.append(fp['screen_name'])
   ```

3. We now import the two libraries that we will need:

   ```
   In [44]: import folium
       ...: from itertools import izip
   ```

4. We instantiate the `Map` object, setting the desired initial view location and level of zoom, add markers and labels to the map in a loop, and finally, render the map to HTML:

   ```
   In [44]: map = folium.Map(location=[48, -102], zoom_start=3)
       ...: for sg, sn in izip(status_geo, status_geo_screen_names):
       ...: map.simple_marker(sg['coordinates'], popup=str(sn))
       ...: map.create_map(path='us_states.html')
   ```

5. Now, there should be an HTML file in your working directory. Double-click on it and you should see something similar to what is shown in the following screenshot:

```
Number of Twitter users who either are our friend or follow you (union):
980
Number of Twitter users who follow you and are your friend (intersection):
205
Number of Twitter users you follow that don't follow you (set difference):
354
Number of Twitter users who follow you that you don't follow (set difference):
421
```

How it works...

It is impressive that we went from less than a dozen lines of code to a fully interactive map, complete with geographic markers denoting the location of some of the users that follow us on Twitter. For this, we leveraged the power of the folium Python package, which in turn, is a Pythonic wrapper for the `leaflet.js` JavaScript library. Folium allows us to bind data from Python to a map for choropleth visualizations or render markers at specific map locations, as we did in the fourth step.

Folium uses the Jinja2 template package to create an HTML file containing a very simple HTML page with a single `div` container that holds the map and the customized JavaScript code in order to use the `leaflet.js` library. It is the `leaflet.js` library that handles the actual map generation:

```html
<!DOCTYPE html>
<head>
    <link rel="stylesheet" href="http://cdn.leafletjs.com/leaflet-
    0.5/leaflet.css" />
    <script src="http://cdn.leafletjs.com/leaflet-
    0.5/leaflet.js"></script>

<style>
#map {
  position:absolute;
  top:0;
  bottom:0;
  right:0;
  left:0;
}
</style>
</head>
<body>
```

```
    <div id="map" style="width: 960px; height: 500px"></div>
<script>
var map = L.map('map').setView([48, -102], 4);

L.tileLayer('http://{s}.tile.openstreetmap.org/{z}/{x}/{y}.png', {
    maxZoom: 18,
    attribution: 'Map data (c) <a
     href="http://openstreetmap.org">OpenStreetMap</a>
     contributors'
}).addTo(map);

var marker_1 = L.marker([38.56127809, -76.04610616]);
marker_1.bindPopup("Pop Text");
map.addLayer(marker_1)

</script>
</body>
```

We highly recommend that you take a closer look at both the additional features of folium (and `leaflet.js`) and the underlying source code of this library.

There's more...

Visualizing geographic data is complex. Not only do you need the ability to render one or more complex coordinate systems, but you also need the original map data that defines countries, roads, rivers, and anything else you might want on display, in addition to your own data. We are fortunate that Python provides so many options when tackling this problem.

These packages tend to fall into two broad categories. The first class of geospatial visualization packages arose out of scientific and research needs that have existed for decades. For this software, the renderer and the required geographic data reside on the user's local machine. This typically necessitates the compilation and installation of several additional layers of the software in order to get the Python package working.

The very powerful **Matplotlib Basemap** Toolkit is an excellent example of this. Browsing the instructions, we see numerous dependencies. While we have already handled matplotlib and NumPy, two additional requirements - `GEOS` and `Proj4 map` library-stand out as potentially problematic. The C++ source code for the **Geometry Engine - Open Source (GEOS)** is actually included with the basemap, but it must be compiled and built separately. This need to compile software in another language is a giant red flag. For Python packages, this often leads one down a rabbit hole of compile errors and technical issues (missing header files, slightly nonstandard directory structures, wrong compiler, and so on) that can take hours or days to resolve. If you are on mac OS X, especially Mavericks, you are in for even more fun, as Apple has a tendency to make slight alterations with each release, which break previously functional make files. As a result, we chose a mapping library from category two, which is described as follows.

The second class of the package provides a Pythonic way of interacting with a JavaScript library that actually handles the rendering of maps and data. This often requires us to output our results as HTML, which is more often than not fine. These JavaScript libraries themselves fall into two categories. First, there are more pure mapping libraries such as Google Maps and `Leaflet.js` that were built to render maps online but can be repurposed for more specialized geospatial data visualization needs. Second, there is `D3.js`, the all-purpose library for manipulating documents based on data that is capable of some beautiful geographic visualization. We chose folium due to its simplicity and elegance; when software works, it makes our lives and analyses easier.

See also

You can also refer to the following:

- The **GEOS** home page at `http://trac.osgeo.org/geos/`
- The **Cartopy** home page at `http://scitools.org.uk/cartopy/`
- The **Shapely** home page at `http://toblerity.org/shapely/`
- The **Kartograph** home page at `http://kartograph.org/`
- The **Leaflet.js** home page at `http://leafletjs.com/`

10
Forecasting New Zealand Overseas Visitors

In this chapter, we will cover the following recipes:

- Creating time series objects
- Visualizing time series data
- Exploratory methods and insights
- Trend and season analysis
- ARIMA modeling
- Accuracy assessment
- Fitting Seasonal ARIMA modeling

Introduction

Weather prediction, Sensex prediction, sales prediction, and so on, are some of the common problems that are of interest to most who look up to Statistics or Machine Learning methods. The purpose is, of course, to get the prediction for the next few periods using models with reasonable accuracy. Weather prediction helps in planning for the vocational trip, Sensex prediction helps in investment planning, and sales prediction in an optimum inventory planning. The common structure among each of the three problems is that the observations are available, in general, at equally spaced time/epoch. The observations may have been obtained on a daily, weekly, or monthly basis and we will refer to such data as *time series data*. The observations are collected over a long time in the past and we believe that we have captured enough characteristics/traits of the series so that analytical models built on such historic data will have predictable power and we can obtain fairly accurate forecasts.

The structure of time series data possesses new challenges and it can't be analyzed with methods as discussed earlier in the book. The major challenge arises from the fact that the observations obtained at regular intervals can't be treated as independent observations. For example, the rain on successive days depends on the recent past as we have a logical belief, and complemented with our empirical experience too, the rain intensity for tomorrow depends on today's rain and that it is not the same if today had rain or it was very sunny. If one accepts conceptually that the observations are not independent of each other, how does one specify the dependency? First, we consider the New Zealand overseas visitor's data.

A trip to a foreign locale is always fascinating, and especially if they are holiday trips. For the tourism department of any country, it is important to know the trend of the overseas travelers to their country so that the logistics can be worked out. A lot of other work is also related with the overseas visitors, for instance, the ministries may be interested to know if the visitors for the next quarter would increase or decrease. The tourism department needs to factor in various facets of the industry, for example, is there a yearly growth? Is there seasonal factor, such as summer time during which the travel is maximum?

The `osvisit.dat`, available at multiple web links
`https://www.stat.auckland.ac.nz/~ihaka/courses/726-/osvisit.dat` and
`https://github.com/AtefOuni/ts/blob/master/Data/osvisit.dat`, consists of the overseas visitors to New Zealand. The data is collected at monthly level and it begins at *January 1977* and continues up to *December 1995*. Thus, we have 228 monthly numbers of the visitors. The following questions arise, which will be addressed through the recipes in this chapter:

- How does one visualize time series data?
- How do you identify if the data has trend and seasonal components?
- What are the measures of relationships that capture the dependent nature of time series data?
- How do you build the appropriate model for the data?
- Which tests need to be applied for validating the assumptions of the model?

In the next recipe, we will show what **ts** objects are and how does one set up such objects from raw data.

The ts object

The core R package `datasets` contains lot of datasets that are essentially time series data: AirPassengers, BJsales, EuStockMarkets, JohnsonJohnson, LakeHuron, Nile, UKgas, UKDriverDeaths, UKLungDeaths, USAccDeaths, WWWusage, airmiles, austres, co2, discoveries, lynx, nhtemp, nottem, presidents, treering, gas, uspop, and sunspots. The AirPassengers data is one of the most popular datasets and it is used as a benchmark dataset. The data can be loaded in an R session with `data(mydata)` and its class can be verified as time series as follows:

```
data (JohnsonJohnson)
 class (JohnsonJohnson)

## [1] "ts"
JohnsonJohnson
## Qtr1 Qtr2 Qtr3 Qtr4
## 1960 0.71 0.63 0.85 0.44
## 1961 0.61 0.69 0.92 0.55
## 1962 0.72 0.77 0.92 0.60
## 1978 11.88 12.06 12.15 8.91
## 1979 14.04 12.96 14.85 9.99
## 1980 16.20 14.67 16.02 11.61

frequency (JohnsonJohnson)
## [1] 4
```

The JohnsonJohnson dataset is a time series dataset and it is verified by applying the class function. Details about the dataset can be obtained by running `?JohnsonJohnson` at the R terminal. This time series contains the quarterly earnings of the company Johnson & Johnson for the period 1960-80. Since we are having quarterly earnings, the frequency of the time series is four per year and this is verified by using the function frequency on the **ts** object. The reader may carry out similar exercise for the rest of the datasets given at the beginning of the section.

A few questions are in order now. If we have raw datasets, how do we import them in R? As the imported dataset would be either a `numeric` vector or a `data.frame`, how do we change them into **ts** objects? As we see that the JohnsonJohnson time series begins at 1960 and ends at 1980, and it is a quarterly data, how does one specify such characteristics for a new **ts** data object? The next recipe will address all these questions.

Getting ready

We assume that the reader has the osvisit.dat file in the R working directory. This file has been obtained from https://github.com/AtefOuni/ts/blob/master/Data/osvisit. datand the reader can use the same source too.

How to do it

The raw data is converted to a desired ts object through the following steps:

1. Import the data into R using the **read.csv utils** function:

   ```
   osvisit <- read.csv ( "osvisit.dat" , header= FALSE)
   ```

2. Convert the preceding data.frame to a **ts** object with:

   ```
   osv <- ts (osvisit$V1, start = 1977 , frequency = 12 )
   class (osv)
   ## [1] "ts"
   ```

3. Display the first four years' data using the window function:

   ```
   window (osv, start= c ( 1977 , 1 ), end= c ( 1980 , 12 ))

   ## Jan Feb Mar Apr May Jun Jul Aug Sep Oct Nov
   ## 1977 48176 35792 36376 29784 21296 17032 22804 27476 21168 29928
   37516
   ## 1978 44672 40500 36608 28524 23060 15760 20892 28992 23048 35052
   40564
   ## 1979 49968 42068 41512 29272 25868 18216 23166 29808 25232 33780
   43916
   ## 1980 48224 51353 46784 31284 26681 22817 26944 32902 25567 37113
   44788
   ## Dec
   ## 1977 62156
   ## 1978 69304
   ## 1979 69576
   ## 1980 70706
   ```

How it works...

The `read.csv` function helps in importing the data from external files to an R `data.frame` object, here `osvisit`. We knew that the data observations in this study is in the period January, 1977 to December, 1995, and that for each year we have 12 monthly observations of the visitors count to New Zealand. Thus, we first used the `ts` function to convert the `data.frame` object into a time series **ts** object as `osv`. The beginning of the study period is specified with the `start =` option and the time series periodicity is defined through `frequency = 12`. The `class` function is then applied over the `osv` object to verify that we have successfully converted the `data.frame` into a **ts** object and that the frequency is also correct. In the last step, we intend to view the data for the period 1977-80 and using the `window` function, we subset the time series and display the data at the console with the arguments `start` and `end`.

It can be thus seen that the numeric vectors/data frames can be converted into time series object using the **ts** function. The frequency argument helps us to define the cycle of the time series such as weekly, monthly, or quarterly. As required, the time stamp can also be specified. We will now look at methods of visualizing the time series data in the next recipe.

Visualizing time series data

Visual depiction of time series is important to get early insights into the nature of the data. Visualization of time series is very simple in the sense that simply plotting the time series variable against the time itself gives insight about the behavior of the data. The R function **plot.ts** can be applied on the **ts** objects and the time series can be visualized. For the overseas visitors problem, we plot the number of visitors for the month against that time instance.

Getting ready

The reader needs to have the `osv` object from the previous session in the current environment.

How to do it...

1. We will now apply the `plot.ts` function to obtain the visual depiction of the overseas data.

2. Run the following line in the R session:

```
plot.ts (osv, main="New Zealand Overseas
Visitors",ylab="Frequency")
```

The output given by running the R line is shown in the following diagram:

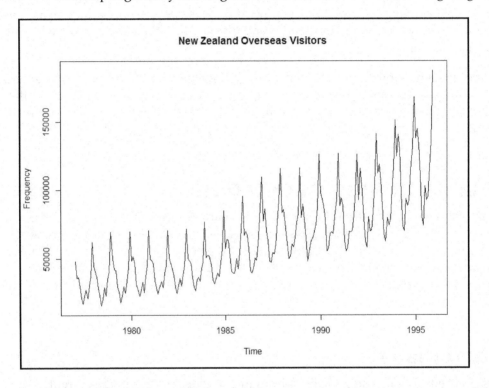

It may be seen from the diagram that a certain pattern is recurrent and that cycle appears as 12 data points or a year. Also, it appears from the data that year-on-year, the visitors count is increasing. However, we would like to find which month sees the highest number of visitors, and other such patterns. In this direction, we would plot the visitors count against the month and then repeat the exercise for all the years.

3. Define the month frame and for each year plot the visitors count against the month number:

```
mt <- 1 : 12
names (mt) <- month.name
windows ( height= 20 , width= 30 )
plot (mt,osv[ 1 : 12 ], "l" , col= 1 , ylim= range (osv), ylab=
"Overseas Visitors" , xlim= c ( 0 , 13 ))
for(i in 2 : 19 ) points (mt,osv[mt+(i -1 )* 12 ], "l" , col= i)
legend ( x= 4, y= 190000 , legend= c ( 1977 : 1982 ), lty= 1 : 6,
col= 1 : 6 )
legend ( x= 6, y= 190000 , legend= c ( 1983 : 1988 ), lty= 7 : 12,
col= 7 : 12 )
legend ( x= 8, y= 190000 , legend= c ( 1989 : 1995 ), lty= 13 :
19,
col= 13 : 19 )
points (mt,osv[mt+(i -1 )* 12 ], pch= month.abb)
```

The resulting diagram is given as follows:

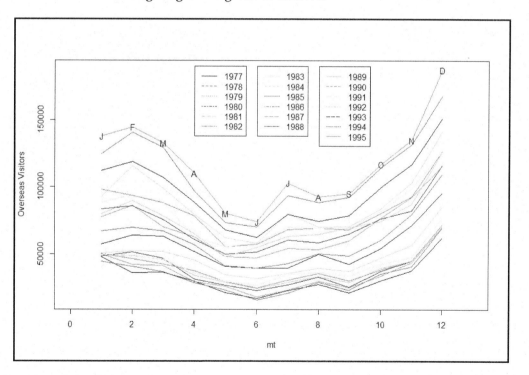

The working of the R program is given in the *How it works ...* section. We can see that we have a peak in the month of July and then during the December-February period. Though the default `plot.ts` gives good insight, we can also better understand the time series by plotting the year-on-year monthly sales too. A unified insight from the two diagrams is that we are having a trend as well as seasonal impact on the overseas visitor. It is possible in R to alienate the seasonal and trend impact from the time series data. Such an analysis is provided by the `stl` function.

4. Decompose the time series into trend, seasonal, and irregular parts as follows:

```
osv_stl <- stl (osv, s.window= 12 )
plot.ts (osv_stl$time.series)
```

The decomposed time series plot looks as follows:

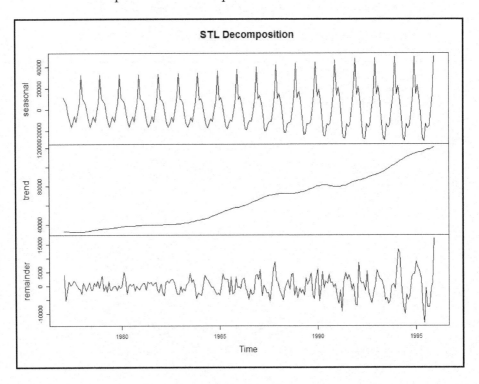

The STL decomposition shows how the trend and seasonal terms vary over the years.

How it works...

For the first diagram, the time series plot is enhanced with the right title and y-axis name through the options `main` and `ylab`. Default settings almost always produce bland output. After ascertaining the trend effect over the years, we plot the year-wise month-on-month plot. To obtain the second diagram, we first created an **mt** variable, which takes the values 1, 2, ..., 12. The `windows` option produces a good framework on the computer screen though the R markdown Microsoft Word is not equally impressive. At the beginning, we plot only 1977 years' visitors count against the month and then using the `for` loop, the yearly visitors count is imposed on the scatter plot. The `ylim` option ensures that we have enough range in the y-axis to visualize all the time points. The `legend` option gives nice indication of the color-year combination. Finally, using `month.abb` we can check which month of the year has the peak visitors.

In the `stl` decomposition, we get three components, seasonal, trend, and irregular components. It may be seen that the original time series would be the sum of these three components, run `round(rowSums(osv_stl$time.series),1)==osv`. It can be seen from the STL decomposition diagram that the variance in each of the components is increasing in time. We will now consider a simple linear regression model approach for understanding the trend and seasonal impact on the visitors count.

Simple linear regression models

Linear regression models can be built to obtain preliminary insight about the trend and seasonal impact on the time series variable. The trend and seasonal components are specified as independent variables while the time series, visitors count here, is the dependent variable. We make the following assumptions while building the linear regression model:

1. The time series is linear in the trend and seasonal variables.
2. The trend and seasonal components are independent of each other.
3. The observations, time series values, are independent of each other.
4. The error associated with the observation follows normal distribution.

Let Y, $1 \leq t \leq T$, denote the time series which observations at the time points $1, 2, ..., T$. For example, in our overseas visitors data, we have $T = 228$. In the simplistic regression model, the trend variable is the vector $1, 2, ..., T$, that is, $X^{Tr} = (1, 2, ..., T)$. We know that for monthly data, we have the month name as the seasonal indicator, that is, if we have monthly data with 24 observations starting from January of one year and ending on December the next year, the values of seasonal variable would be January, February, ..., November, December, January, February, ..., November, December. Thus, seasonal variables would be a categorical variable. Similarly, if we have quarterly data, the seasonal variables would have observations as Quarter 1, Quarter 2, Quarter 3, and Quarter 4. We indicate the seasonal variable by X^{se}, and some examples of the seasonal variable are $X^{se} = (Jan, Feb, ..., Nov, Dec, Jan, Feb, ..., Nov, Dec)$ and $X^{se} = (Q_1, Q_2, Q_3, Q_4, Q_1, Q_2, Q_3, Q_4)$. The linear regression model incorporating the trend and seasonal variables would be then given by

$$Y_t = \beta_0 + \beta^{Tr} X_t^{Tr} + \beta^{Se} X_t^{Se} + \epsilon_t, 1 \leq t \leq T.$$

We will next build the trend and seasonal linear regression model for the overseas visitors dataset. The core function would be the `lm` function.

Getting ready

The `osvts` object needs to be there in the current R environment.

How to do it...

Defining the trend and seasonal variables, we would be able to build the linear models. We would build three linear models here:

- with the trend variable,
- with the seasonable variable, and
- with both variables:

1. Create R objects `osv_time` and `osv_mths` for the trend and seasonal variables:

```
osv_time <- 1 : length (osv)
osv_mths <- as.factor ( rep (month.abb, times= 19 ))
```

Using the `length` function, we now have a numeric vector with values starting from 1 and ending at 228. The seasonal variable is created with the rep function, which repeats the month name 19 times successively. The `month.abb` is a standard character vector in R that has the month abbreviations as its content.

2. Create the linear model using the trend variable only and produce its summary:

```
osv_trend <- lm (osv~osv_time)
 summary (osv_trend)

##
## Call:
## lm(formula = osv ~ osv_time)
##
## Residuals:
## Min 1Q Median 3Q Max
## -33968 -13919 -3066 10497 79326
##
## Coefficients:
## Estimate Std. Error t value Pr(>|t|)
## (Intercept) 20028.62 2585.63 7.746 3.17e-13 ***
## osv_time 385.36 19.58 19.683 < 2e-16 ***
## ---
## Signif. codes: 0 '***' 0.001 '**' 0.01 '*' 0.05 '.' 0.1 ' ' 1
##
## Residual standard error: 19460 on 226 degrees of freedom
## Multiple R-squared: 0.6316, Adjusted R-squared: 0.6299
## F-statistic: 387.4 on 1 and 226 DF, p-value: < 2.2e-16
```

3. The p-value, in the last line of preceding R output, associated with the **F-statistic** is significant, which indicates the overall model is significant. The p-value associated with `osv_time` is also small, which implies that the trend impact is significantly different from 0. The R^2 is about 63%, which is the percent of variation in visitors count as explained by the trend variable. We will now look at the seasonable variable.

4. Create the linear model with the seasonal variable and produce its summary:

```
osv_season <- lm(osv~osv_mths)
summary(osv_season)

##
## Call:
## lm(formula = osv ~ osv_mths)
##
## Residuals:
## Min 1Q Median 3Q Max
## -45099 -23919 -2738 17161 79961
##
## Coefficients:
## Estimate Std. Error t value Pr(>|t|)
## (Intercept) 57116 6277 9.100 < 2e-16 ***
## osv_mthsAug -4226 8877 -0.476 0.6345
## osv_mthsDec 50139 8877 5.648 5.07e-08 ***
## osv_mthsFeb 20143 8877 2.269 0.0242 *
## osv_mthsJan 17166 8877 1.934 0.0544 .
## osv_mthsJul -5670 8877 -0.639 0.5236
## osv_mthsJun -15351 8877 -1.729 0.0852 .
## osv_mthsMar 13799 8877 1.555 0.1215
## osv_mthsMay -12883 8877 -1.451 0.1481
## osv_mthsNov 19286 8877 2.173 0.0309 *
## osv_mthsOct 7190 8877 0.810 0.4188
## osv_mthsSep -5162 8877 -0.582 0.5615
## ---
## Signif. codes: 0 '***' 0.001 '**' 0.01 '*' 0.05 '.' 0.1 ' ' 1
##
## Residual standard error: 27360 on 216 degrees of freedom
## Multiple R-squared: 0.3038, Adjusted R-squared: 0.2683
## F-statistic: 8.567 on 11 and 216 DF, p-value: 1.63e-12
```

5. The seasonal variable is a factor variable and hence we have the variable summary at 11 levels of the factor variable. Since some of the factor levels are significant, the overall variable is significant though the R^2 is very poor at 30%. We will now include both the variables in the next step.

6. Create the linear model with trend and seasonal variables and produce its summary:

```
osv_trend_season <- lm(osv~osv_time+osv_mths)
 summary(osv_trend_season)
 ##
 ## Call:
 ## lm(formula = osv ~ osv_time + osv_mths)
 ##
 ## Residuals:
 ## Min 1Q Median 3Q Max
 ## -17472 -5482 -1120 3805 38559
 ##
 ## Coefficients:
 ## Estimate Std. Error t value Pr(>|t|)
 ## (Intercept) 14181.157 2269.500 6.249 2.19e-09 ***
 ## osv_time 383.346 8.944 42.860 < 2e-16 ***
 ## osv_mthsAug -5759.017 2880.198 -2.000 0.0468 *
 ## osv_mthsDec 47072.650 2880.864 16.340 < 2e-16 ***
 ## osv_mthsOct 4890.027 2880.475 1.698 0.0910 .
 ## osv_mthsSep -7078.837 2880.323 -2.458 0.0148 *
 ## ---
 ## Signif. codes: 0 '***' 0.001 '**' 0.01 '*' 0.05 '.' 0.1 ' ' 1
 ##
 ## Residual standard error: 8877 on 215 degrees of freedom
 ## Multiple R-squared: 0.927, Adjusted R-squared: 0.923
 ## F-statistic: 227.7 on 12 and 215 DF, p-value: < 2.2e-16
```

7. Note that here the model and both variables are significant. Also, the R^2, as well as the Adj R^2, increases to 93%. Thus, both the variables are useful for understanding the visitors count.

8. However, there are some hurdles with the linear model approach. The first problem is a conceptual one and that the assumption of independence looks very unrealistic. Also, if we look at the empirical residual distribution, which are estimates of the error term, the normality assumption looks out of place here.

9. Use the `residuals` function on the fitted models and the `hist` graphical function for depicting the error distributions:

```
windows ( height = 24 , width= 20 )
 par ( mfrow= c ( 3 , 1 ))
 hist ( residuals (osv_trend), main = "Trend Error" )
 hist ( residuals (osv_season), main= "Season Error" )
 hist ( residuals (osv_trend_season), main= "Trend+Season Error" )
```

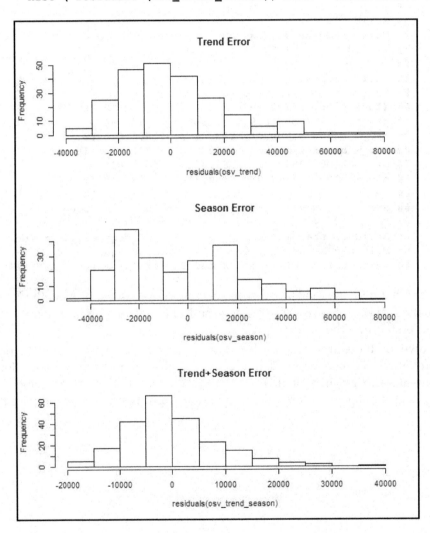

It is seen from the preceding histograms that the normality assumption for error is not appropriate for the time series data.

How it works...

The `lm` function in R is useful to fit linear models. A formula is central to build the linear model and its generic form is `lhs ~ rhs`. The term on the left side of tilde `~` is taken as the dependent variable and the right as independent variable(s) or covariates. The details of `lm` can be fetched with `?lm`. The function summary gets more details of the fitted models and we have used it three times here to see how each of the models perform on the data. To validate the normality assumption for the error distribution, we obtain the histogram by `hist(residuals(lm),...)`.

See also

The dependence among the observations is the main complexity of time series data and overlooking it would lead to erroneous conclusions. We will next consider methods and measures that help us construct models that incorporate the dependent nature of time series.

ACF and PACF

We have the time series Y, $1 \leq t \leq T$ which may be conceptualized as a stochastic process Y observed at times $1 \leq t \leq T$. If a process is observed at successive times, it is also plausible that the process value at time t depends on the process values at time $t-1$, $t-2$, ... The specification of the dependency is the crux of time series modeling. As in the regression models, we have the error process in ε, $1 \leq t \leq T$ which is generally assumed to be white-noise process. Now, the process/time series Y, $1 \leq t \leq T$ may depend on its own past values, or on the past error terms. The two measures/metrics useful in understanding the nature of dependency are the **Autocorrelation function (ACF)** and **Partial-autocorrelation function (PACF)**. We need the lag concept first though. For the process Y, $2 \leq t \leq T$ the lag 1 process is Y_{t-1}, $1 \leq t \leq T - 1$. In general, for the variable Y_t the *k-th* lag variable is Y_{t-k}. The *lag k* ACF is defined as the correlation between the random variable Y_t and the *k-th* lagged variable Y_{t-k}:

$$\rho_k = \frac{E(Y_t - \mu)(Y_{t-k} - \mu)}{\sigma^2}$$

where σ^2 is the variance of the time series. The partial autocorrelation function PACF between Y_t and its' *k-th lag* Y_{t-k} is the partial correlation of the time series while controlling the values at shorter *lags* $Y_{t-1}, Y_{t-2}, ..., Y_{t-k+1}$. It is not possible to go into the mathematical details of the PACF concept and the reader may refer to *Box, et al. (2015)*. The ACF and PACF values help in determining the terms of the error variables or the time series. We consider the simple random walk as an example of time series to understand these concepts.

Let the sequence of white noise (error) be ε_t, $1 \le t \le T$ and the observed time series/random walk be

$Y_i = \varepsilon_1 + \varepsilon_2 + ... + \varepsilon_i$, $1 \le i \le T$

Note that the series can also be (re)written as

$Y_i = Y_{i-1} + \varepsilon_i$, $1 \le i \le T$.

Thus, the Y_i value is seen to be dependent on the previous i errors, or the Y_{i-1} value and current error. We will next simulate a random walk and obtain the ACF and PACF plots in R.

Getting ready

An open R session is all that is required.

How to do it...

First we simulate 500 (pseudo-) observations of a random walk and then visualize it. Applying `acf` and `pacf` functions, we then examine the nature of the plot.

1. First set the seed to the number `12345`:

   ```
   set.seed ( 12345 )
   ```

2. Simulate 500 observations from standard normal distribution and compute the random walk at each epoch by taking the cumulative sum:

   ```
   y <- rnorm ( 500 )
   rwy <- cumsum (y)
   ```

3. Visualize the time series and then apply the `acf` and `pacf` function on the random walk created in the previous step:

```
windows ( height= 24 , width= 8 )
par ( mfrow= c ( 3 , 1 ))
plot.ts (rwy, main= "Random Walk" )
acf (rwy, lag.max= 100 , main= "ACF of Random Walk" )
pacf (rwy, main= "PACF of Random Walk" )
```

4. The resulting diagram is given as follows:

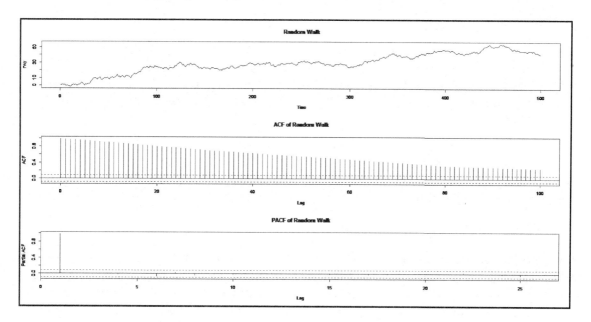

The ACF and PACF are effective tools in suggesting the type of model that may be generating the time series. For example, we can find here that the influence of the past observations Y_{t-1}'s is on a decline, whereas if we look at the partial correlation, only the previous one observation is important and the rest are all zero. The observations here are in lieu with the theoretical ACF and PACF, see http://stats.stackexchange.com/quest ions/87000/sample-acf-and-pacf-of-a-random-walk for example.

How it works...

The `set.seed` function is used to ensure reproducibility of the program and `rnorm` and `cumsum` together give us the necessary random walk. The functions `acf` and `pacf` are essential time series functions that would be required in almost all the time series analysis. The `lag.max=100` option has been used to show that the `acf` is indeed on a decline, which is not very apparent if we take the default settings.

ARIMA models

In the previous section, we saw the random walk and the role of ACF and PACF functions. The random walk may be seen as a series that depends on past observations as well as past errors. It is thus possible to visualize time series as functions of past observations, errors, or both. In general, given the time series Y_t, $1 \leq t \leq T$ and the error process ε_t, $1 \leq t \leq T$ a *linear process* is defined as:

$$Y_t = \epsilon_t + \psi_1 \epsilon_{t-1} + \psi_2 \epsilon_{t-2} + \psi_3 \epsilon_{t-3} + \cdots.$$

The terms $\psi_1, \psi_2, \psi_3, \cdots$ are the coefficients of linear processes. Now, suppose that we are interested in a model where Y_t depends on the past p observations:

$$Y_t = \phi_1 Y_{t-1} + \phi_2 Y_{t-2} + \cdots + \phi_p Y_{t-p} + \epsilon_t.$$

The preceding model is well known as the *autoregressive model of order p* and it is denoted by **AR(p)**. It is important to note here that the AR coefficients $\phi_1, \phi_2, \cdots, \phi_p$ are not unrestricted and we simply note that their absolute values need to be less than 1 if the time series is assumed to be stationary. Next, we define the *moving average model of order q*, abbreviated as **MA(q)**, as:

$$Y_t = \epsilon_t - \theta_1 \epsilon_{t-1} - \theta_2 \epsilon_{t-2} - \cdots - \theta_q \epsilon_{t-q}.$$

The parameters of the MA(q) model are $\theta_1, \theta_2, \cdots, \theta_q$. It is indeed possible that a time series may depend on past observations as well as errors and such models can be captured through *autoregressive moving average model*, denoted by **ARMA(p,q)**, and given by:

$$Y_t = \phi_1 Y_{t-1} + \phi_2 Y_{t-2} + \cdots + \phi_p Y_{t-p} + \epsilon_t - \theta_1 \epsilon_{t-1} - \theta_2 \epsilon_{t-2} - \cdots - \theta_q \epsilon_{t-q}.$$

The theoretical ACF and PACF can be obtained for the ARMA models. The following table shows the expected behavior of ACF and PACF for such models:

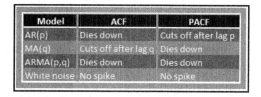

Model	ACF	PACF
AR(p)	Dies down	Cuts off after lag p
MA(q)	Cuts off after lag q	Dies down
ARMA(p,q)	Dies down	Dies down
White noise	No spike	No spike

To understand the nature of ACF and PACF in the context of ARMA models, we simulate observations using the `arima.sim` function and plot the corresponding ACF and PACF and check for the behavior suggested in the preceding table.

Getting ready

The reader will need the R session and the `osv` object that was created earlier.

How to do it...

`AR(1)`, `MA(1)`, and `ARMA(1,1)` models are simulated first and the ACF and PACF plots are obtained:

1. First set the seed to the number `123`. Produce three time series `AR(1)`, `MA(1)`, and `ARMA(1,1)`:

```
set.seed ( 123 )
 t1 <- arima.sim ( list ( order = c ( 1 , 0 , 0 ), ar = 0.6 ), n =
100 )
 t2 <- arima.sim ( list ( order = c ( 0 , 0 , 1 ), ma = - 0.2 ), n
= 100 )
 t3 <- arima.sim ( list ( order = c ( 1 , 0 , 1 ), ar = 0.6, ma= -
0.2 ), n = 100 )
 tail (t1); tail (t2); tail (t3) #output suppressed
```

The underlying `AR(1)` model for `t1` is

$$Y_t = 0.6 \, Y_{t-1} + \epsilon_t$$

and similarly for t2 and t3, the associated underlying models are:

$$Y_t = \epsilon_t - (-0.2)\epsilon_{t-1}$$

$$Y_t = 0.6\,Y_{t-1} + \epsilon_t + 0.2\,\epsilon_{t-1}$$

2. Obtain the ACF and PACF plots of t1, t2, and t3:

```
windows ( height= 30 , width= 20 )
  par ( mfrow= c ( 3 , 2 ))
  acf (t1); pacf (t1)
  acf (t2); pacf (t2)
  acf (t3); pacf (t3)
```

3. The resulting diagram is as follows:

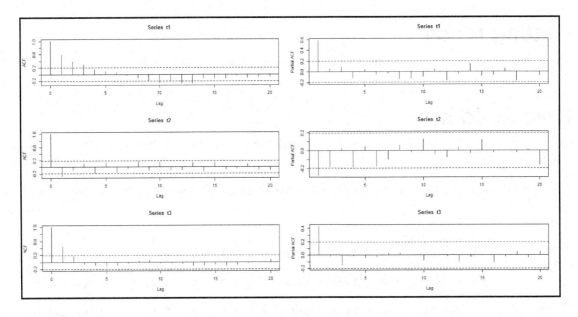

The t1 object is simulated as an AR(1) process and the theoretical ACF is expected to die down or tail off while the theoretical PACF must have a cut off after one lag. We see this behavior in the empirical ACF and PACF of **t1**. Similarly, the ACF and PACF of t2 is seen to respectively have a cut off after lag 1 and gradual decline, which suggests that MA(1) is an appropriate model. Also, the ACF and PACF plots of series t3 shows expected behavior in the theoretical quantities and thus suggesting that an ARMA model might be appropriate. Note that the order of the ARMA model is not reflected by the correlation plots.

4. The reader should ask the questions about what happens if the absolute value of the autoregressive coefficients value is more than 1. Run the next two lines in R and draw an appropriate conclusion:

```
arima.sim ( list ( order = c ( 1 , 0 , 0 ), ar = 1.6 ), n = 100 )
arima.sim ( list ( order = c ( 0 , 0 , 1 ), ma = 10.2 ), n = 100 )
```

We will next look at the ACF and PACF plot of osv.

5. Apply the `acf` and `pacf` functions on `osv`:

```
windows ( height= 10 , width= 20 )
  par ( mfrow= c ( 1 , 2 ))
  acf (osv)
  pacf (osv)
```

6. The resulting diagram is as follows:

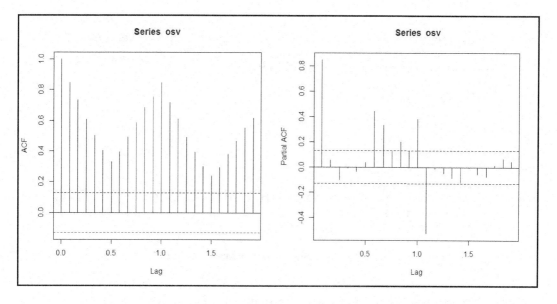

Note the change in the scale of the x-axis in the preceding diagram. In the earlier ACF and PACF diagrams, we had the range of the x-axis varying from 0 to 20 or more as `lag.max` specified. Here, though we are still having the ACF's and PACF's calculated from 20 lags, the range is from 0 to 2 with fractional values 0.5 and 1.5 too. This is because we are having the `frequency=12` for the `osv` time series object.

Here, the ACF and PACF plot is anything but the description of ARMA models as detailed in the earlier table. The ACF is having a cyclic behavior and the PACF does not conclusively say if there is a decline after certain lag. Recall from the time series plot of the `osv` that we had an increasing average mean (as well as variance). In simple terms, the behavior of the time series is changing over time and thus we have non-stationary data. In many practical scenarios, stationary can be obtained by differencing the series Y_t, that is, instead of modeling for Y_t, we consider the difference $Y_t - Y_{t-1}$. The difference $Y_t - Y_{t-1}$ is *first* order difference and sometimes one may require higher order difference, and in most practical scenarios, differencing up to order 4 has been noted to bring stationary. The order of difference is generally denoted by letter *d* and applying ARMA models on the difference is referred as autoregressive integrated moving average model, or ARIMA model. A succinct abbreviation is ARIMA(*p*,*d*,*q*). In the next steps, we will build AR, MA, and the ARIMA model for the overseas visitor data.

The `ar` function when applied on a time series object automatically selects the order *p* and the models are fit by using the **Yule-Walker** method.

7. Apply the `ar` function on the `osv` object:

```
osv_ar <- ar (osv)
 osv_ar
 ## Call:
 ## ar(x = osv)
 ##
 ## Coefficients:
 ## 1 2 3 4 5 6 7 8
 ## 0.6976 0.1015 -0.0238 0.0315 0.0106 -0.1569 0.0183 0.1238
 ## 9 10 11 12 13
 ## 0.0223 0.0279 -0.0039 0.6398 -0.5227
 ##
 ## Order selected 13 sigma^2 estimated as 123787045
```

The AR order p is selected as 13. Next, we look at the residuals of the fitted model and check whether the normality assumption holds good.

8. Obtain the histogram of the residuals and look at the ACF plot of the residuals:

```
windows ( height= 10 , width= 20 )
par ( mfrow= c ( 1 , 2 ))
hist ( na.omit (osv_ar$resid), main= "Histogram of AR Residuals" )
acf ( na.omit (osv_ar$resid), main= "ACF of AR Residuals" )
```

The histogram and ACF plots look as follows:

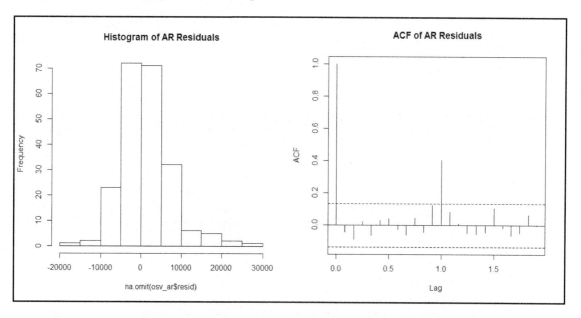

The histogram looks skewed and the ACF suggests that there is dependency among the residuals, which violates the assumption of the AR model.

Unlike the `ar` function, we don't have one for fitting moving average models that would automatically select the order q. Thus, we first define a new function that would try to find the best model for a given maximum error lag among the moving average models by the **aic** criteria.

9. Define the `auto_ma_order` function and find the best moving average model for `osv` data as follows:

```
auto_ma_order <- function (x, q) {
aicc <- NULL
for (i in 1 :q) {
tmodel <- arima (x, order= c ( 0 , 0 ,i))
aicc [i] <- as.numeric (tmodel$aic)
```

```
}
return ( which.min (aicc))
}
auto_ma_order (osv, 15 )
```

```
## [1] 14
```

There might be a technical reason for which an auto moving-average model fitting function is not defined. It generally happens that the `auto_ma_order` function finds the best moving average lag at the maximum lag as is seen next.

10. For the `osv` time series data, find the best moving average model for various maximum lags:

```
sapply ( 1 : 20 ,auto_ma_order, x= osv)
```

```
## [1] 1 2 3 4 5 6 6 8 9 9 9 9 13 14 14 16 17 18 18 20
```

Since the `auto_ma_order` function generally finds the best order at the maximum lag, it is not a useful function. For the mathematical reason behind this behavior, the reader should consult a good time series book like Box, et al. (2015). Now, we fit ARIMA models of various orders.

11. Fit three ARMA models and three ARIMA models for the `osv` data:

```
# ARIMA Model Fitting
osv_arima_1 <- arima (osv, order= c ( 1 , 0 , 1 ))
osv_arima_2 <- arima (osv, order= c ( 2 , 0 , 1 ))
osv_arima_3 <- arima (osv, order= c ( 1 , 0 , 2 ))
osv_arima_4 <- arima (osv, order= c ( 1 , 1 , 1 ))
osv_arima_5 <- arima (osv, order= c ( 2 , 1 , 1 ))
osv_arima_6 <- arima (osv, order= c ( 1 , 1 , 2 ))
osv_arima_1; osv_arima_2; osv_arima_3

##
## Call:
## arima(x = osv, order = c(1, 0, 1))
##
## Coefficients:
## ar1 ma1 intercept
## 0.9030 0.0008 68427.30
## s.e. 0.0348 0.0659 10168.16
##
## sigma^2 estimated as 233640077: log likelihood = -2521.06, aic
= 5050.13
```

```
##
## Call:
## arima(x = osv, order = c(2, 0, 1))
##
## Coefficients:
## ar1 ar2 ma1 intercept
## -0.0871 0.9123 0.9931 68374.33
## s.e. 0.0306 0.0306 0.0091 10714.84
##
## sigma^2 estimated as 216211876: log likelihood = -2513.14, aic
= 5036.27

##
## Call:
## arima(x = osv, order = c(1, 0, 2))
##
## Coefficients:
## ar1 ma1 ma2 intercept
## 0.8755 0.0253 0.1315 67650.666
## s.e. 0.0428 0.0792 0.0607 9106.606
##
## sigma^2 estimated as 229397770: log likelihood = -2518.99, aic
= 5047.98
```

osv_arima_4; osv_arima_5; osv_arima_6

```
##
## Call:
## arima(x = osv, order = c(1, 1, 1))
##
## Coefficients:
## ar1 ma1
## -0.602 0.5313
## s.e. 0.356 0.3761
##
## sigma^2 estimated as 2.41e+08: log likelihood = -2512.67, aic =
5031.35

##
## Call:
## arima(x = osv, order = c(2, 1, 1))
##
## Coefficients:
## ar1 ar2 ma1
## -0.2669 0.0912 0.2256
## s.e. 0.4129 0.0743 0.4103
##
## sigma^2 estimated as 239665946: log likelihood = -2512.07, aic
```

```
= 5032.13

##
## Call:
## arima(x = osv, order = c(1, 1, 2))
##
## Coefficients:
## ar1 ma1 ma2
## -0.4164 0.3784 0.0901
## s.e. 0.2893 0.2920 0.0703
##
## sigma^2 estimated as 239508475: log likelihood = -2511.99, aic
= 5031.99
```

The AIC values for the six different models are 5050.13, 5036.27, 5047.98, 5031.35, 5032.13, and 5031.99. An `auto.arima` function is available in Hyndman's `forecast` package, which within maximum p, d, and q values, finds the best ARIMA model. However, there are other metrics for time series modeling and AIC might not be the best evaluation method. Some of the measures are defined in the next section.

How it works...

In this section, for simulation purposes the `arima.sim` function is useful and the options `list`, `order`, `ar`, `ma`, and `n` are useful as required. The `acf` and `pacf` function can be used to obtain the necessary correlation plots. We used the `ar` function to find the best auto-regressive model. Moving average models can be fit using the `arima` function and specifying the model order through the **order** option. Residuals of the fitted `ar` object can be extracted with `ar_fit$resid`.

Accuracy measurements

Model selection in regression models is addressed through the use metrics such as `aic`, `bic`, and so on. Though we have earlier used such models for selecting the models, it is important to note that the general purpose of time series is forecasting. Thus, time series modeling has some customized metrics, which are useful for forecasting purpose. Here, a comparison is made between the actual values and the fitted values.

To get the perspective, we have the time series in Y_t, $1 \le t \le T$ and suppose that the forecast values by virtue of using a certain model, say AR(p), MA(q), or ARIMA(p,d,q), for the time series is $\hat{Y}_t$, $1 \le t \le T$. We can then capture the fit of the model by comparing $\hat{Y}_t$ with Y_t. The residuals due to the model is defined by $r_t = Y_t - \hat{Y}_t$, $1 \le t \le T$. The accuracy measurements are then defined as follows:

$$\text{Mean Error: } ME = \frac{1}{T}\sum_{t=1}^{T} r_t = \frac{1}{T}\sum_{t=1}^{T}(Y_t - \hat{Y}_t)$$

$$\text{Root Mean Square Error: } RMSE = \left(\frac{1}{T}\sum_{t=1}^{T} r_t^2\right)^{1/2} = \left(\frac{1}{T}\sum_{t=1}^{T}(Y_t - \hat{Y}_t)^2\right)^{1/2}$$

$$\text{Mean Absolute Error: } MAE = \frac{1}{T}\sum_{t=1}^{T} |r_t| = \frac{1}{T}\sum_{t=1}^{T}|Y_t - \hat{Y}_t|$$

$$\text{Mean Percentage Error: } MPE = 100\times\frac{1}{T}\sum_{t=1}^{T} \frac{r_t}{Y_t} = 100\times\frac{1}{T}\sum_{t=1}^{T} \frac{Y_t - \hat{Y}_t}{Y_t}$$

$$\text{Mean Absolute Percentage Error: } MAPE = 100\times\frac{1}{T}\sum_{t=1}^{T} \left|\frac{r_t}{Y_t}\right| = 100\times\frac{1}{T}\sum_{t=1}^{T} \left|\frac{Y_t - \hat{Y}_t}{Y_t}\right|$$

The computations would be performed using *raw* codes.

Getting ready

The R object `osv` would be required in the current R environment. The reader will require the ARIMA objects `osv_arima_1`, `osv_arima_2`, `osv_arima_3`, and `osv_arima_4`. The R package `forecast` will also be required.

How to do it...

The accuracy measurement formulas are straightforward to calculate and we use the residuals function to simplify our program.

1. The functions mean, sqrt, abs, residuals, and accuracy from the forecast package are used to obtain the accuracy measurements:

```
mean ( residuals (osv_arima_1)) # Mean Error
## [1] 106.6978
sqrt ( mean ( residuals (osv_arima_1)^ 2 )) # Root Mean Square
Error
## [1] 15285.29
mean ( abs ( residuals (osv_arima_1))) # Mean Absolute Error
## [1] 11672.7
mean ( residuals (osv_arima_1)/osv)* 100 # Mean Percentage Error
## [1] -5.35765
mean ( abs ( residuals (osv_arima_1)/osv))* 100 # Mean Absolute
Percentage Error
## [1] 19.04502
accuracy (osv_arima_1)
## ME RMSE MAE MPE MAPE MASE
## Training set 106.6978 15285.29 11672.7 -5.35765 19.04502
0.9717733
 ## ACF1
 ## Training set 0.004153521
mean ( abs ( residuals (osv_arima_2)/osv))* 100
## [1] 19.01274
mean ( abs ( residuals (osv_arima_3)/osv))* 100
## [1] 18.75919
mean ( abs ( residuals (osv_arima_4)/osv))* 100
## [1] 19.01341
```

Using the MAPE criteria, one would use osv_arima_3 as it has the least value among the four models. We can also see that the calculations from the raw codes matches with the accuracy function from the forecast package.

How it works...

The accuracy measurements formulas have been straightforward to implement. It is important that one uses such metrics when analyzing time series data. The raw codes show the formula implementation though the simple accuracy function also provides the solution.

In general, the MAPE metric is more effective and widely used. However, the MAPE for the four models varies in the range *18.76%* to *19.05%*. Seasonality is a huge factor and we would like to build ARIMA models that account for such factors and this forms the topic of discussion in the next section.

Fitting seasonal ARIMA models

The meaning of ARIMA models for the monthly overseas visitors is that past observations and errors have impact on the current observation. The order of 13 as suggested by the `ar` function applied on the `osv` data indicates that the monthly visitor count of the previous year also influences the visitors this month. However, it looks intriguing that the visitor count for each of the past 13 months should have an influence. Also, this increases the model complexity and we would prefer meaningful models based on as less past observations as possible. Note that the variance of the fitted models has been very large and we would like to reduce the variance too.

A good and appealing approach to integrate the seasonal impact is to use the **seasonal-ARIMA** model, see *Chapter 10 of Cryer and Chan* (2008). To understand how seasonal-ARIMA models work, we will consider the simple seasonal AR models first. Here, we allow the past few Y_t's to influence the current Y_t and then the past few corresponding seasonal Y_t's. For example, let $p = 3$ and the frequency of the time series is say 12 months and we want to consider the impact of the past two seasonal terms. It means that Y_t is now influenced by $Y_{t-1}, Y_{t-2}, Y_{t-3}, Y_{t-12}, Y_{t-24}$. It is customary to denote the seasonal Y_t lags by capital letter P. Similarly, the seasonal moving average model with two moving average lags and three seasonal moving average lags consists of $\varepsilon_{t-1}, \varepsilon_{t-2}, \varepsilon_{t-12}, \varepsilon_{t-24}, \varepsilon_{t-36}$. The seasonal moving average lags is denoted by the capical letter Q, and similarly the difference by D. The seasonal ARIMA models are generally denoted by $(p, d, q)x(P, D, Q)_{(freq)}$. The `arima` function can fit seasonal ARIMA models too and we will see the action next.

Getting ready

If the reader has the **osv** object in the R environment, it will be sufficient.

How to do it...

Using the **seasonal** option in the **arima** function, we will build the seasonal ARIMA models.

1. We build the seasonal models as follows: $(1, 1, 0) \times (0, 1, 0)_{12}$, $(1, 1, 0)x(1, 1, 0)_{12}$, $(0, 1, 1)x(0, 1, 1)_{12}$, $(1, 1, 0)x(0, 1, 1)_{12}$, $(0, 1, 1)x(1, 1, 0)_{12}$, $(1, 1, 1)x(1, 1, 1)_{12}$, $(1, 1, 1)x(1, 1, 0)_{12}$, $(1, 1, 1)x(0, 1, 1)_{12}$.

```
osv_seasonal_arima2 <- arima (osv, order= c ( 1 , 1 , 0 ),
seasonal= c ( 0 , 1 , 0 ))
 osv_seasonal_arima3 <- arima (osv, order= c ( 1 , 1 , 0 ),
seasonal= c ( 1 , 1 , 0 ))
 osv_seasonal_arima4 <- arima (osv, order= c ( 0 , 1 , 1 ),
seasonal= c ( 0 , 1 , 1 ))
 osv_seasonal_arima5 <- arima (osv, order= c ( 1 , 1 , 0 ),
seasonal= c ( 0 , 1 , 1 ))
 osv_seasonal_arima6 <- arima (osv, order= c ( 0 , 1 , 1 ),
seasonal= c ( 1 , 1 , 0 ))
 osv_seasonal_arima7 <- arima (osv, order= c ( 1 , 1 , 1 ),
seasonal= c ( 1 , 1 , 1 ))
 osv_seasonal_arima8 <- arima (osv, order= c ( 1 , 1 , 1 ),
seasonal= c ( 1 , 1 , 0 ))
 osv_seasonal_arima9 <- arima (osv, order= c ( 1 , 1 , 1 ),
seasonal= c ( 0 , 1 , 1 ))
```

2. Obtain the MAPE of all the models built in the previous step:

```
accuracy (osv_seasonal_arima2) [ 5 ]
# [1] 5.525674
accuracy (osv_seasonal_arima3) [ 5 ]
## [1] 5.206777
accuracy (osv_seasonal_arima4) [ 5 ]
## [1] 4.903352
accuracy (osv_seasonal_arima5) [ 5 ]
## [1] 5.113835
accuracy (osv_seasonal_arima6) [ 5 ]
## [1] 4.946375
accuracy (osv_seasonal_arima7) [ 5 ]
## [1] 4.603231
accuracy (osv_seasonal_arima8) [ 5 ]
## [1] 4.631682
accuracy (osv_seasonal_arima9) [ 5 ]
## [1] 4.5997
```

3. Among the models specified here, the order $(1, 1, 1)x(0, 1, 1)_{12}$ leads to the lease MAPE. Since it is often difficult to search for the best model among different possible combinations of $(p, d, q)x(P, D, Q)_f$, we use the `auto.arima` function from the `forecast` package.

4. Use the `auto.arima` function to obtain the best model:

```
opt_model <- auto.arima (osv, max.p= 6 , max.q= 6 , max.d= 4 ,
max.P= 3 , max.Q= 3 , max.D= 3 )
opt_model

## Series: osv
## ARIMA(5,1,3)(0,1,1)[12]
##
## Coefficients:
## ar1 ar2 ar3 ar4 ar5 ma1 ma2 ma3
## 0.3732 0.5802 -0.2931 -0.3063 -0.2003 -0.8537 -0.6079 0.7898
## s.e. 0.1172 0.1172 0.0931 0.0760 0.0853 0.0946 0.1348 0.0802
## sma1
## -0.4880
## s.e. 0.0636
##
## sigma^2 estimated as 17089028: log likelihood=-2093.09
## AIC=4206.17 AICc=4207.25 BIC=4239.88


accuracy (opt_model)
## ME RMSE MAE MPE MAPE MASE
## Training set 236.9483 3929.388 2820.913 0.07114353 4.592125
0.5239947
## ACF1
## Training set -0.02654602
```

The preceding result suggests that the best seasonal ARIMA model is `ARIMA(5,1,3)(0,1,1)[12]`.

How it works...

The option of `seasonal` helps set up the desired seasonal order in the ARIMA model. The `auto.arima` function helps in finding the best ARIMA model within the specified lags for (p,d,q) and (P,D,Q).

There's more...

The scope of time series modeling is much beyond this short chapter. *Box, et al. (2015)*, *Cryer and Chan (2008)*, and *Chatfield (2003)* are examples of some of the excellent exposure to time series methods.

11
German Credit Data Analysis

In this chapter, we will cover the following recipes:

- Transforming the data
- Visualizing categorical data
- Discriminant analysis for identifying defaults
- Fitting logistic regression model
- A decision tree for the German Data
- Finer aspects of decision trees

Introduction

Loans! A liability for the borrower and an asset for the bank! Banks would certainly like to give only loans and not any of the savings schemes, such as savings accounts, fixed deposits, recurring deposits, and so on. The simple reason is that banks must pay the customer after some period and if they don't earn enough, they can't give away the interest. Though the banks would like to give away as many loans possibly can, there are plenty of reason that loans would never be given on a first-come-first-serve basis. The apparently simple reason being that if the customer defaults, the bank stands out as well as an opportunity to serve a better customer. The obvious question is how does one define a better customer and will analytical methods help here. A practical data set is the German data set, which consists of the final status of whether or not the customer fully paid back their loan and a host of other important variables.

A lot of analyses has been performed and it has now become an important benchmark data set for the classification problem. It has been made available at https://archive.ics.uci.edu/ml/datasets/Statlog+(German+Credit+Data). It has been used across many research works and it has a total hit visit of 228982 at the time of writing. Its analyses from various perspectives using R software can be found at https://cran.r-project.org/doc/contrib/Sharma-CreditScoring.pdf. Additional details can be sought at https://onlinecourses.science.psu.edu/stat857/node/216. For an in-depth analysis of the German credit data, refer to **Tattar (2013)**. We will draw this dataset from the RSADBE package and will do simple transformations in the next section. A detailed description of the dataset is given here.

The GC dataset has 1,000 observations in 21 variables. The variable of interest in this credit data is whether the loan has been a good loan, customer paid back the loan amount completely, or a bad loan, and the information of this status is put in the variable good_bad. Here, 700 out of the 1,000 observations are good loans while the rest are bad loans. A host of important variable data is also collected, which gives information on the type of the customer. The additional variables consist of both quantitative (numerical) as well as qualitative (categorical) variables. The numerical variables are duration in month (duration), credit amount (credit), installment as a fraction of disposable income (installp), duration of stay at present residence (resident), age in years (age), number of existing credits at the bank (existcr), and number of the applicant's dependents (depends). The rest of the other 21 variables are categorical variables.

The GC dataset has simplified numerical representation for the factor levels of the categorical variables and as such most of them are identified as integer variables, which is not appropriate. For instance, status of the current checking account (checking) is simply numbered from 1-4 while they should represent factor levels < 0 DM, 0 <= ... < 200 DM, >= 200 DM, and No Acc. The next section fixes the required levels of the factor variables.

Simple data transformations

The German credit data available from the **RSADBE** 1.0 version has certain limitations. The data file in the package is named GC. Many of the categorical variables are stored as integer classes, which affects the overall analysis. Also, some variables are not important here and after conversion from the integer class to the factor class, re-labeling is needed. For instance, detailed information about the variables can be obtained at https://archive.ics.uci.edu /ml/datasets/Statlog+(German+Credit+Data). In this section, we'll use the data set and carry out the necessary transformation.

Getting ready

The reader will need to install the RSADBE package, which consists of the GC dataset. As earlier, we first load all the pre-requisite libraries:

```
library (data.table)
library (dplyr)
library (RSADBE)
library (rpart)
library (randomForestSRC)
library (ROCR)
library (plyr)
```

How to do it...

The GC dataset is available in the RSADBE R package. As mentioned earlier, datasets consist of many variables that are integer when those integers are indicators of the factor level. For instance, as seen earlier, we need to have the factor levels as < 0 DM, 0 <= ... < 200 DM, >= 200 DM, and No Acc, instead of 1-4. This re-labeling needs to be done for the 1,000 observations, which is achieved by using the functions as.factor and revalue:

1. Convert the checking variable to factor from its current integer class and then apply the revalue (from the plyr package) function to get the desired result:

```
data (GC)
GC2 <- GC
GC2$checking <- as.factor (GC2$checking)
GC2$checking <- revalue (GC2$checking, c ( "1" = "< 0 DM" , "2" =
"0 <= ... < 200 DM" ,
  "3" = ">= 200 DM" , "4" = "No Acc" ))
```

2. The other `integer` objects are similarly converted to the desired `factor` objects:

```
GC2$history <- as.factor (GC2$history)
 GC2$history <- revalue (GC2$history, c ( "0" = "All Paid" , "1" =
"Bank paid", "2" = "Existing paid" , "3" = "Delayed", "4" = "Dues
Remain" ))
 GC2$purpose <- as.factor (GC2$purpose)
 GC2$purpose <- revalue (GC2$purpose,
 c ( "0" = "New Car" , "1" = "Old Car" , "2" = "Furniture" ,
 "3" = "Television" , "4" = "Appliance" , "5" = "Repairs" ,
 "6" = "Education" , "8" = "Retraining" , "9" = "Business" ,
 "X" = "Others" ))
 GC2$savings <- as.factor (GC2$savings)
 GC2$savings <- revalue (GC2$savings,
 c ( "1" = "< 100 DM " , "2" = "100-500 DM" ,
 "3" = "500-1000 DM" , "4" = ">1000 DM" ,
 "5" = "Unknown" ))
 GC2$employed <- as.factor (GC2$employed)
 GC2$employed <- revalue (GC2$employed,
 c ( "1" = "Unemployed" , "2" = "1 Year" , "3" = "1-4 Years" ,
 "4" = "4-7 Years" , "5" = ">7 Years" ))
 GC2$marital <- as.factor (GC2$marital)
 GC2$marital <- revalue (GC2$marital,
 c ( "1" = "Female S" , "2" = "Female M/D" , "3" = "Male M/D" ,
 "4" = "Male S" ))
 GC2$coapp <- as.factor (GC2$coapp)
 GC2$coapp <- revalue (GC2$coapp,
 c ( "1" = "None" , "2" = "Co-app" , "3" = "Guarantor" ))
 GC2$property <- as.factor (GC2$property)
 GC2$property <- revalue (GC2$property,
 c ( "1" = "Real Estate" , "2" = "Building society" ,
 "3" = "Others" , "4" = "Unknown" ))
 GC2$other <- NULL # because "none" is dominating frequency
 GC2$housing <- as.factor (GC2$housing)
 GC2$housing <- revalue (GC2$housing, c ( "1" = "Rent" , "2" =
"Own",
 "3" = "Free" ))
 GC2$job <- as.factor (GC2$job)
 GC2$job <- revalue (GC2$job, c ( "1" = "Unemployed" , "2" =
"Unskilled", "3" = "Skilled",
 "4" = "Highly Qualified" ))
 GC2$telephon <- as.factor (GC2$telephon)
 GC2$telephon <- revalue (GC2$telephon, c ( "1" = "None" , "2" =
"Registered" ))
 GC2$foreign <- as.factor (GC2$foreign)
 GC2$foreign <- revalue (GC2$foreign, c ( "1" = "No" , "2" = "Yes"
))
```

Note here that the other object is now removed from GC2.

How it works...

Data is not always in a ready-to-analyze format and may require fine tuning in many cases. In this recipe, we used the technique of converting integer object to a factor first and then re-labeled it as appropriate. A lot of data re-structuring is easily possible and we'll use them as required.

There's more...

The `data.table` R package is also very useful. Data re-structuring can be performed on the same object and as such there is no need to create another object as we created GC2 here.

Visualizing categorical data

Visualization is an important aspect of any kind of exploratory analysis. Suppose that we had no additional information on the customer's history and we merely know that there were 700 good loans out of thousand sanctioned. In this case, the prediction for the next customer to have a good loan payment would have a probability 0.7. When the variable of interest is a numeric variable, we can plot histograms, boxplots, and so on, to get a good understanding of the problem. Here, the output `good_bad` is a factor variable and such a plot won't make any sense. A simple understanding of the distribution of the factor variable can be obtained using the bar plot where we would have two bars with the length reflecting the proportionate frequency. However, a bar plot is a one-dimensional plot in the sense that the x-axis labels as good and bad won't add any value.

Scatter plots reveal relationships between two variables when both are numeric variables. In our case, the main variable of interest `good_bad` is a categorical/factor variable and plotting other variables against it won't bring out the nature of the relationship, and hence we require different kinds of visualizing techniques. Categorical variable visualization requires specialized techniques and we use here the mosaic plot. For more details, please refer to *Friendly and Meyer (2015)*.

Getting ready

The R data frame **GC2** as created in the previous recipe will be required here.

How to do it...

1. Bar plot and mosaic plots are obtained here and we begin with the former first.
2. The `barplot` function gives the desired graph:

```
barplot ( table (GC2$good_bad))
```

3. The visual output is given next:

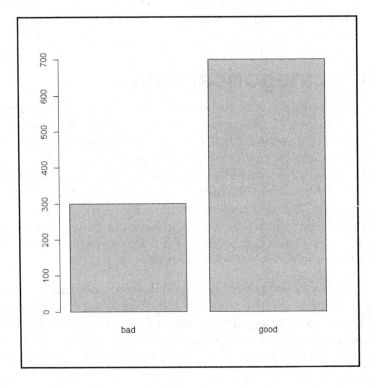

The `barplot` is a simple depiction of the number of bad and good loans. Additional information about the variables is always useful. Mosaic plots are a stacked arrangement of barplots for multiple variables and it gives an indication of the type of relationship between two categorical variables. Now, we will first look at the proportion of the good/bad loans across different categories of the variables `housing`, `employed`, and `checking` and follow it up with the useful mosaic plot.

4. Using the functions `table` and `prop.table`, we obtain the percentage of good/bad loans at each category variable:

```
table (GC2$good_bad, GC2$housing)

## Rent Own Free
## bad 70 186 44
## good 109 527 64

prop.table ( table (GC2$good_bad, GC2$housing), margin= 2 )

## Rent Own Free
## bad 0.3911 0.2609 0.4074
## good 0.6089 0.7391 0.5926
```

The good/bad loans ratio is 700/300 and we now see that if the population is divided into three parts according to whether the housing is Rent, Own, and Free, the proportion of good in these parts is respectively *0.6089, 0.7391*, and *0.5926*. Thus, in the Own part, we see a higher proportion of good loans than in the population. Of course, the other two parts see an increase in the proportion of bad loans though improvisations can be made further in these parts.

5. Similarly, the proportion table of `employed` and `checking` against the loan variable are given next:

```
prop.table ( table (GC2$good_bad, GC2$employed), margin= 2 )
  ## Unemployed 1 Year 1-4 Years 4-7 Years >7 Years
  ## bad 0.3710 0.4070 0.3068 0.2241 0.2530
  ## good 0.6290 0.5930 0.6932 0.7759 0.7470

prop.table ( table (GC2$good_bad, GC2$checking), margin= 2 )
  ## < 0 DM 0 <= ... < 200 DM >= 200 DM No Acc
  ## bad 0.4927 0.3903 0.2222 0.1168
  ## good 0.5073 0.6097 0.7778 0.8832
```

It is clear from the preceding proportion tables that if an applicant has employment of 4+ years, the possibility of loan repayment is higher than other parts as identified by the employed variable. Similarly, if the `checking` loan amount is either `>= 200 DM` or `No Acc`, the good payment proportion is higher. If the reader wishes to visualize the numbers, mosaic plots help here.

6. The mosaic plot for two categorical variables can be obtained easily as follows:

```
windows ( height= 15 , width= 10 )
par ( mfrow= c ( 3 , 1 ))
mosaicplot (~good_bad+housing,GC2)
mosaicplot (~good_bad+employed,GC2)
mosaicplot (~good_bad+checking,GC2)
```

7. The resulting mosaic plots is given as follows:

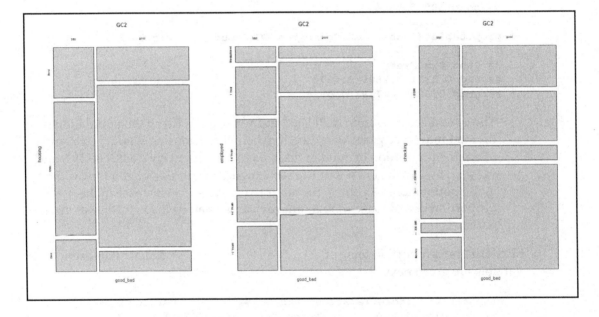

The proportions are well reflected on the mosaic plots and as such we have an effective visualization method here.

How it works...

The R function `table` is very important for understanding categorical variables and it does the frequency count by the factor levels. When the `prop.table` is applied on an array/table, we get the column proportions with the option margin=2.

Mosaic plots and bar plots provide visual insights in the analysis of categorical data. With the initial impressions, we can now build statistical techniques for statistical methods for identifying whether the customer will turn out to be a good payer or a defaulter.

Discriminant analysis

Discriminant analysis is one of the earliest statistical methods that is used to classify observations into distinct populations. As with many of the earlier pioneering works in statistics, this technique too had been invented by the great *Sir R. A. Fisher*. The theory of discriminant analysis is beyond the scope of this book. We would simply be content with the use of the `lda` function from the MASS package. Before applying the `lda` R technique to the German credit data, we will first apply it on the `iris` dataset, which is also popular thanks to Fisher. Following the application of the method to the `iris` dataset, we will then apply it to the German credit data problem.

Getting ready

The requirement of the `iris` dataset and the MASS package is met by default R software. The reader needs to have prepared the GC2 data frame as in the first section.

How to do it...

We get an initial understanding of the `iris` data set with simple functions. In this dataset, we have five variables `Sepal.Length`, `Sepal.Width`, `Petal.Length`, `Petal.Width`, and `Species`. We have three types of iris species `setosa`, `versicolor`, and `virginica` that need to be identified by length and width of sepals and petals:

1. Load the `iris` object from the `datasets` package and get initial insight using the `str`, `summary`, and `pairs` functions:

```
data (iris)
 str (iris)

## 'data.frame': 150 obs. of 5 variables:
## $ Sepal.Length: num 5.1 4.9 4.7 4.6 5 5.4 4.6 5 4.4 4.9 ...
## $ Sepal.Width : num 3.5 3 3.2 3.1 3.6 3.9 3.4 3.4 2.9 3.1 ...
## $ Petal.Length: num 1.4 1.4 1.3 1.5 1.4 1.7 1.4 1.5 1.4 1.5 ...
## $ Petal.Width : num 0.2 0.2 0.2 0.2 0.2 0.4 0.3 0.2 0.2 0.1 ...
## $ Species : Factor w/ 3 levels "setosa","versicolor",..: 1 1 1
1 1 1 1 1 1 1 ...

summary (iris)

## Sepal.Length Sepal.Width Petal.Length Petal.Width
## Min.  :4.30 Min.  :2.00 Min.  :1.00 Min.  :0.1
## 1st Qu.:5.10 1st Qu.:2.80 1st Qu.:1.60 1st Qu.:0.3
## Median :5.80 Median :3.00 Median :4.35 Median :1.3
## Mean  :5.84 Mean  :3.06 Mean  :3.76 Mean  :1.2
## 3rd Qu.:6.40 3rd Qu.:3.30 3rd Qu.:5.10 3rd Qu.:1.8
## Max.  :7.90 Max.  :4.40 Max.  :6.90 Max.  :2.5
## Species
## setosa  :50
## versicolor:50
## virginica :50
##pairs (iris[,- 5 ]) # Output suppressed
```

2. The preliminary summary gives an idea about the range of variables and other essential summaries. It is desirable to have the summaries by each type of species, the matrix of a scatterplot as identified by the pairs function indicates the presence of at least two distinct species.

3. Now, apply the `lda` function from the `MASS` package on the `iris` dataset:

```
iris_lda <- lda (Species~.,iris)
iris_lda

## Call:
## lda(Species ~ ., data = iris)
##
## Prior probabilities of groups:
## setosa versicolor virginica
## 0.3333 0.3333 0.3333
##
## Group means:
## Sepal.Length Sepal.Width Petal.Length Petal.Width
## setosa 5.006 3.428 1.462 0.246
## versicolor 5.936 2.770 4.260 1.326
## virginica 6.588 2.974 5.552 2.026
##
## Coefficients of linear discriminants:
## LD1 LD2
## Sepal.Length 0.8294 0.0241
## Sepal.Width 1.5345 2.1645
## Petal.Length -2.2012 -0.9319
## Petal.Width -2.8105 2.8392
##
## Proportion of trace:
## LD1 LD2
## 0.9912 0.0088
```

4. By running the line `lda(Species~.,...)`, we are asking R to create an `lda` object by the formula `.~.`, where species is the group indicator that needs to be identified by using all other variables from the dataset. Here, we have two linear discriminant functions, which is a linear combination of the four variables length and width of the sepal and petals. The first linear discriminant function is

$$Z_1 = 0.8294 \times \text{Sepal.Length} + 1.5345 \times \text{Sepal.Width}$$
$$-2.2012 \times \text{Petal.Length} - 2.8105 \times \text{Petal.Width}$$

5. while the second one is

$$Z_2 = 0.0241 \times \text{Sepal.Length} + 2.1645 \times \text{Sepal.Width}$$
$$-0.9319 \times \text{Petal.Length} + 2.8392 \times \text{Petal.Width}$$

6. Importantly, the first discriminant itself explains 99% of the trace here and seems good enough to identify the three groups. Now, we look at how the scores of the discriminant look across the three species.

7. Predict the discriminant scores and use the histogram for the scores across the three species:

```
iris_lda_values <- predict (iris_lda)
windows ( height= 20 , width= 10 )
ldahist (iris_lda_values$x[, 1 ], g= iris$Species)
```

8. The resulting diagram is as follows:

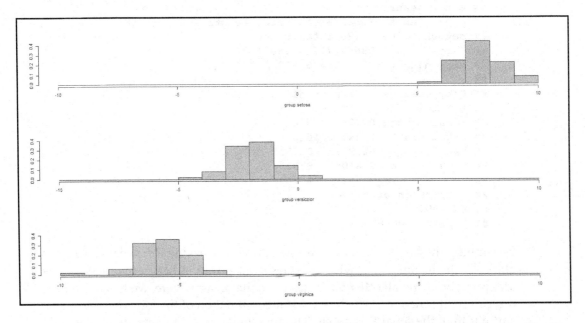

9. We can clearly see three distinct groups based on the discriminant scores. Finally, we check for misclassification.

10. Using the table function, evaluate the performance of the technique:

```
table ( predict (iris_lda) $class)

## setosa versicolor virginica
## 50 49 51

table (iris$Species, predict (iris_lda) $class)

## setosa versicolor virginica
## setosa 50 0 0
```

```
## versicolor 0 48 2
## virginica 0 1 49
```

11. Note that using the function table on the predictions gives us the frequency of each of the Species. However, it does not tell us which of the original iris plants species is correctly predicted. Using the table with the original and predicted class gives us the misclassification count. Overall, a *3/150 = 0.02%* error looks very impressive. Next, we apply this technique to the German credit data.

12. The `lda` function is now applied on **GC2**:

```
GB_lda <- lda (good_bad~.,GC2)
GB_lda

## Call:
## lda(good_bad ~ ., data = GC2)
##
## Prior probabilities of groups:
## bad good
## 0.3 0.7
##

## Coefficients of linear discriminants:
## LD1
## checking0 <= ... < 200 DM 3.808e-01
## checking>= 200 DM 9.029e-01
## checkingNo Acc 1.317e+00

## telephonRegistered 2.159e-01
## foreignYes 7.212e-01

table ( predict (GB_lda)$class)

##
## bad good
## 244 756

table (GC2$good_bad, predict (GB_lda)$class)

##
## bad good
## bad 158 142
## good 86 614
```

We can see that nearly 50% of the bad loans are not identified here by the `lda` technique. Hence, we need to improve on it and use different methods in the rest of this chapter.

How it works...

The `lda` function from the `MASS` package is useful in carrying out linear discriminant analysis.

See also

For details of the discriminant analysis technique, read *McLachlan (1992)*.

Dividing the data and the ROC

If one uses the entire dataset to build a model, it is possible that we might have over trained the model. A consequence is that the true performance of the model goes unnoticed for the unknown cases. Essentially, we need to build a good model for the credit problem and if the performance is unknown for the new or unforeseen cases, skepticism is bound to creep into our minds. A good practice then is to divide the available in three regions: (i) data for building the model, (ii) data to validate the model, and (iii) data to test the model. Thus, a set of models is built for a problem and then they are evaluated over the validated part of the data, and the model that does best at this stage is chosen for the test portion of the data. Data partitioning in three regions can be easily performed and we can quickly show how it is done on the German credit data.

Receiving operating curves, or ROC, is a very effective tool for accessing the performance of a classification model. We borrow heavily from *Chapter 7 of Tattar (2013)*. In many classification models, if the predicted probability of success is greater than 0.5, the observation is predicted as a successful observation, and a failure otherwise. At least with the training and validate data we know the true labels of the observations and hence a comparison of the true labels with the predicted label makes sense. In an ideal case we expect the predicted labels to match perfectly with the actual labels. However, in reality, it is rarely the case, which means that there are some observations that are predicted as success/failure when the true labels are actually failure/success.

In other words, we make mistakes! It is possible to put these notes in the form of a table widely known as the **confusion matrix**.

		Observed	
		Success	Failure
Predicted	Success	True Positive (TP)	False Positive (FP)
	Failure	False Negative (FN)	True Negative (TN)

We consider the following metrics for comparison across models:

$$\textbf{Accuracy:}\ \frac{TP+TN}{TP+TN+FP+FN}$$

$$\textbf{Precision:}\ \frac{TP}{TP+FP}$$

$$\textbf{Recall:}\ \frac{TP}{TP+FN}$$

Now, when we have class imbalanced problems, it is easier to have very high accuracy and precision, but that would be useless. For example, if there are 100 fraudulent transactions out of 1,00,000 observations, a classifier that identifies all as good transactions will have more than 99.99% accuracy and very high precision. However, such models won't identify even a single fraudulent transaction. In such scenarios, the ROC method is very useful. The ROC construction requires two metrics: **true positive rate (tpr)** and **false positive rate (fpr)**:

$$tpr = \frac{TP}{TP+FN}, \quad fpr = \frac{FP}{TN+FP}$$

The ROC graphs are constructed by plotting the **tpr** against the **fpr.** The diagonal line is about the performance of a random classifier in that it simply says Yes or No without looking at any characteristic of an observation. Any good classifier must sit, rather be displayed, above this line. The classifier, albeit an unknown one, seems to be a much better classifier than the random classifier. The ROC curve is useful in comparison to the competitive classifiers in the sense that if one classifier is always above another, we select the former. Another important metric associated with ROC is **Area Under Curve (AUC)**. The higher the AUC, the better the model is and it is a number between 0 and 1.

Getting ready

We need the GC2 object in the current session as prepared in the earlier part of the chapter.

How to do it...

Reproducibility is an important aspect at the initial stages of learning. We set a seed for the random splitting of the data so that the results in the reading and the results obtained from running them in an R environment are the same.

1. Use `set.seed` for reproducibility:

   ```
   set.seed ( 1234567 )
   ```

2. Create three labels `Train`, `Validate`, and `Test`:

   ```
   data_part_label <- c ( "Train" , "Validate" , "Test" )
   ```

3. Now, sample from the vector `data_part_label` 1,000 times (with replacement) with a probability 0.6, 0.2, and 0.2, and subset `GC2` accordingly:

   ```
   indv_label = sample (data_part_label, size= 1000 , replace= TRUE
   ,prob
   = c ( 0.6 , 0.2 , 0.2 ))
   GC_Train <- GC2[indv_label== "Train" ,]
   GC_Validate <- GC2[indv_label== "Validate" ,]
   GC_Test <- GC2[indv_label== "Test" ,]
   ```

   We would now roughly have 600 observations in `GC_Train` and 200 each in `GC_Validate` and `GC_Test`.

4. Run the example for performance from the `ROCR` package:

   ```
   example(performance)
   ```

In the plots seen on the screen, you would find the `tpr` plotted against `tfr`. A perfect classifier would begin at 1 on the y-axis. For cross-model comparison, we prefer a model whose ROC curve is uniformly higher than others. As an example, we would like to generate the ROC curves for the `Train` and `Validate` portions of the data set. Typically, the ROC curve for the `Train` part would be better than the corresponding one for the `Validate` part.

Fitting the logistic regression model

The discriminant analysis technique works well only when the set of independent variables/covariates follows multivariate normal distribution. At the starting point, it does not show flexibility by ruling out categorical variables. Many economic variables, such as salary, savings, and so on, are known not to follow normal distribution and are also skewed in general. Thus, the assumption of multivariate normal distribution is rather restrictive and we need a general framework for the classification problem. A very important class of model is provided by the *logistic regression model*. In fact, it is known to have very nice theoretical properties. For example, it is theoretically known that the logistic regression model provides as much accuracy as the discriminant analysis in the case of the independent variable following the multivariate normal distribution. The logistic regression model is a member of the important exponential family, and it belongs to the class of generalized linear models. Given the vector of independent observations:

$$\pi(y|\mathbf{x}) = P(Y = 1|\mathbf{x}) = \frac{e^{\beta'\mathbf{x}}}{1 + e^{\beta'\mathbf{x}}}$$

$$= \frac{e^{\beta_0 + \beta_1 x_1 + \cdots + \beta_k x_k}}{1 + e^{\beta_0 + \beta_1 x_1 + \cdots + \beta_k x_k}}$$

Here, we have k independent variables while the random variable Y is a binary random variable and the dependent variable for the logistic regression model, refer to *Chapter 7 of Tattar (2013)* or *Chapter 17 of Tattar, et al. (2016)* for more details and depth. For our purpose, we will simply use functions from R, `glm` for the moment. The ROC packages ROCR and pROC are useful for carrying out the tasks related to it. First, we'll fit the logistic regression model and obtain the summary to find which variables are significant.

Getting ready

Apart from the GC2 object in the working session, we would need the ROC packages ROCR and pROC to complete the session.

How to do it...

We will now build a logistic regression model here:

1. Using the `glm` function, we build a logistic regression model for the `training` dataset `GC_Train` and then apply the `summary` function to get the details of the fitted model:

```
GC_Logistic <- glm (good_bad~., data= GC_Train, family= 'binomial'
)
 summary (GC_Logistic)

 ##
 ## Call:
 ## glm(formula = good_bad ~ ., family = "binomial", data =
GC_Train)
 ##
 ## Deviance Residuals:
 ## Min 1Q Median 3Q Max
 ## -2.428 -0.725 0.374 0.715 2.222
 ##
 ## Coefficients:
 ## Estimate Std. Error z value Pr(>|z|)
 ## (Intercept) 1.42e+00 1.35e+00 1.05 0.2927
 ## checking0 <= ... < 200 DM 1.24e-01 2.86e-01 0.44 0.6634
 ## checking>= 200 DM 5.08e-01 4.81e-01 1.06 0.2913
 ## checkingNo Acc 1.65e+00 3.06e-01 5.40 6.7e-08 ***
 ## duration -2.95e-02 1.22e-02 -2.43 0.0153 *
 ## historyBank paid -2.20e-01 6.78e-01 -0.33 0.7451
 ## historyExisting paid 3.67e-01 5.29e-01 0.69 0.4880
 ## historyDelayed 3.93e-01 5.83e-01 0.67 0.4999
 ## historyDues Remain 1.47e+00 5.46e-01 2.69 0.0071 **
 ## purposeOld Car 1.58e+00 5.07e-01 3.12 0.0018 **
 ## purposeFurniture 8.66e-01 3.58e-01 2.42 0.0156 *
 ## purposeTelevision 6.42e-01 3.20e-01 2.01 0.0448 *
 ## purposeAppliance 6.17e-01 1.06e+00 0.58 0.5594
 ## purposeRepairs -3.12e-01 7.32e-01 -0.43 0.6699
 ## purposeEducation -5.74e-01 5.42e-01 -1.06 0.2896
 ## purposeRetraining 1.50e+01 8.96e+02 0.02 0.9867
 ## purposeBusiness 7.10e-01 4.36e-01 1.63 0.1032
 ## purposeOthers 1.50e+01 8.37e+02 0.02 0.9857
 ## amount -1.09e-04 5.74e-05 -1.90 0.0569 .
 ## savings100-500 DM 3.22e-01 3.77e-01 0.85 0.3931
 ## savings500-1000 DM 2.13e-01 4.69e-01 0.46 0.6491
 ## savings>1000 DM 7.19e-01 6.49e-01 1.11 0.2685
 ## savingsUnknown 1.24e+00 3.65e-01 3.39 0.0007 ***
 ## employed1 Year 1.69e-01 5.69e-01 0.30 0.7662
```

```
## employed1-4 Years 2.50e-01 5.53e-01 0.45 0.6518
## employed4-7 Years 7.69e-01 6.01e-01 1.28 0.2005
## employed>7 Years 2.62e-01 5.50e-01 0.48 0.6345
## installp -3.34e-01 1.17e-01 -2.84 0.0045 **
## maritalFemale M/D -2.30e-01 5.33e-01 -0.43 0.6661
## maritalMale M/D 5.49e-01 5.29e-01 1.04 0.2987
## maritalMale S 1.57e-01 6.18e-01 0.25 0.7992
## coappCo-app 4.02e-01 6.05e-01 0.66 0.5069
## coappGuarantor 1.34e+00 5.78e-01 2.33 0.0201 *
## resident 4.00e-02 1.10e-01 0.36 0.7162
## propertyBuilding society -4.23e-01 3.31e-01 -1.28 0.2019
## propertyOthers -2.47e-01 3.10e-01 -0.80 0.4250
## propertyUnknown -8.60e-01 5.66e-01 -1.52 0.1284
## age 1.32e-02 1.14e-02 1.16 0.2472
## housingOwn 1.28e-01 3.27e-01 0.39 0.6946
## housingFree 4.41e-01 6.27e-01 0.70 0.4824
## existcr -3.32e-01 2.57e-01 -1.29 0.1970
## jobUnskilled -5.35e-01 8.72e-01 -0.61 0.5395
## jobSkilled -4.76e-01 8.47e-01 -0.56 0.5739
## jobHighly Qualified -6.57e-01 8.65e-01 -0.76 0.4476
## depends -5.90e-01 3.25e-01 -1.81 0.0696 .
## telephonRegistered 2.99e-01 2.61e-01 1.14 0.2526
## foreignYes 1.47e+00 1.08e+00 1.36 0.1739
## ---
## Signif. codes: 0 '***' 0.001 '**' 0.01 '*' 0.05 '.' 0.1 ' ' 1
##
## (Dispersion parameter for binomial family taken to be 1)
##
## Null deviance: 734.00 on 598 degrees of freedom
## Residual deviance: 535.08 on 552 degrees of freedom
## AIC: 629.1
##
## Number of Fisher Scoring iterations: 14
```

2. As in the regular regression model, a factor variable with *k* factors is converted into *k-1* new variables. Here, the statistically insignificant variables are employed, marital, resident, property, age, housing, exist, job, telephone, and foreign. That is, 10 out of the 20 variables specified are insignificant, while the others are significant. In the case of factor variables, if any one of the levels is significant, the overall variable is significant too. The underlying algorithm has converged after 14 iterations. We will next look at the accuracy of the model for the training part.

3. Using the `table` function, we compute the accuracy of the model as follows:

```
table (GC_Train$good_bad)

##
## bad good
## 181  418

table (GC_Train$good_bad, ifelse ( predict (GC_Logistic, type=
"response" )> 0.5 , "good" , "bad" ))

##
## bad good
## bad 96  85
## good 46 372
```

4. In the training dataset, we have 181 bad loans, and the logistic regression model correctly identifies 96 out of them, which is slightly above 50% accuracy. Improvements in the accuracy is of course desirable. However, we will instead check first how the model performs on the data points that were not used to build the model and carry out the ROC analysis.

5. For the training and validate partition, **predict** the class identification by the fitted logistic regression model. Also, use the `prediction` and `performance` function from the ROCR package to set up the ROC curves:

```
GC_Logistic_Train_Prob <- predict(GC_Logistic,newdata=GC_Train[,-21],
                          type="response")
GC_Logistic_Validate_Prob <- predict(GC_Logistic,newdata=GC_Validate[,-21],
                          type="response")
Train_Pred_Logistic <- prediction(GC_Logistic_Train_Prob,
                          GC_Train$good_bad)
Perf_Train_Logistic <- performance(Train_Pred_Logistic,"tpr","fpr")
Validate_Pred_Logistic <- prediction(GC_Logistic_Validate_Prob,
                          GC_Validate$good_bad)
Perf_Validate_Logistic <- performance(Validate_Pred_Logistic,"tpr","fpr")
plot(Perf_Train_Logistic,col="red",lty=2)
plot(Perf_Validate_Logistic,add=TRUE,col="green",lty=2)
legend(0.6,0.5,c("ROC Train Curve","ROC Validate
Curve"),col=c("red","green"),pch="-")
```

6. The resulting diagram is as follows:

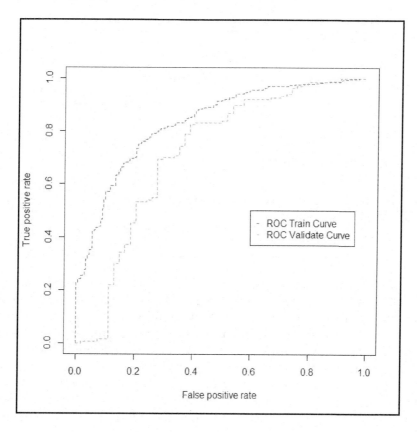

7. It can be seen from the ROC curves that the performance of the logistic regression declines in unseen cases or the validation part, as expected. Next, we calculate the area under the curve metric for the model in both the regions.

8. Calculate the area under curve using the `roc` function from the pROC package:

```
GB_Logistic_Train_roc <- roc(GC_Train$good_bad,GC_Logistic_Train_Prob)
GB_Logistic_Train_roc

##
## Call:
## roc.default(response = GC_Train$good_bad, predictor =
GC_Logistic_Train_Prob)
##
## Data: GC_Logistic_Train_Prob in 181 controls (GC_Train$good_bad bad) < 418
cases (GC_Train$good_bad good).
## Area under the curve: 0.836

GB_Logistic_Validate_roc <-
roc(GC_Validate$good_bad,GC_Logistic_Validate_Prob)
GB_Logistic_Validate_roc

##
## Call:
## roc.default(response = GC_Validate$good_bad, predictor =
GC_Logistic_Validate_Prob)
##
## Data: GC_Logistic_Validate_Prob in 54 controls (GC_Validate$good_bad bad)
< 137 cases (GC_Validate$good_bad good).
## Area under the curve: 0.72
```

9. Thus, the logistic regression model has higher AUC in the training part than the validate part. Many ways of improving the logistic regression model exists, for example, one might look in to model selection issues, multi-collinearity problems, and so on. A detailed digression in logistic regression model is not necessary here though. Here, the AUC difference is *0.836 - 0.72 = 0.116* and it seems very high. The ideal is to find those models where this difference is as small as possible, which would then imply that the model has learnt the features/patterns and it is able to generalize quite well too. In the next section, we will quickly see what the decision rules and in the following section we will see how the rules are generated.

How it works...

The `glm` function is very versatile and it can be used to fit models in the class of generalized linear models. Here, we used it fit the logistic regression model with the option `family='binomial'`. The `summary` function gives the details of the fitted model. The `table` function is used to access the accuracy of the fitted model over the training and validate portions of the data. The `predict` function returns the probability P(Y=1) given the values of the independent variables. The `prediction` and `performance` functions from the ROCR package help in setting up the ROC curves, while the `roc` function from the pROC package is used to calculate the AUC.

See also

For more details try `?glm,` `library(help=ROCR)` and `library(help=pROC).`

Decision trees and rules

The logistic regression model is a powerful technique. For a practitioner, it possesses some difficulties in terms of the p-values, the threshold values of prediction, and so on. The decision rules provide a simple framework wherein the practitioner should simply look up at certain variables and the values to arrive at a decision. For instance, if a customer calls up a bank help desk and tries to find out whether they are eligible for a loan, the call center employee asks for some details such as age, income, gender, existing loans, and so on, and tells them whether they are eligible for the loan. Generally, such a decision is arrived at using sets of decision rules. Similarly, if an emergency patient is on the way to hospital with suspicion of heart related problems, a simple set of rules might help in deciding whether it is a gastric problem or an attack and in the latter case, the hospital can begin the necessary preparations as every single minute would prove crucial in the diagnostics. The important question is how does one arrive at such a set of decision rules.

Decision rules are easily derived from decision trees and we'll look at `rpart` example. We will first build a classification tree and then visualize the decision tree. The decision rules from the tree are extracted and we will then look at the percentile splits at each of the terminal nodes using the table function.

Getting ready

We will need the `kyphosis` dataset from the `rpart` package.

How to do it...

1. Using the `kyphosis` data, we will learn about decision tress and rules:
2. Load the `kyphosis` dataset from the `rpart` package:

```
library (rpart)
  data (kyphosis)
```

3. Build the classification tree using the `rpart` function and visualize the decision tree:

```
kyphosis_rpart <- rpart (Kyphosis~.,kyphosis)
plot (kyphosis_rpart, uniform= TRUE )
text (kyphosis_rpart)
```

4. The resulting decision tree is as follows:

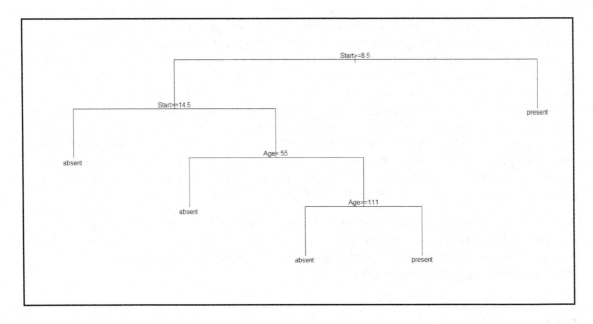

5. The rules of the tree can be extracted by using the **asRules** function from the **rattle** package:

```
asRules (kyphosis_rpart)

##
## Rule number: 3 [Kyphosis=present cover=19 (23%) prob=0.58]
## Start< 8.5
##
## Rule number: 23 [Kyphosis=present cover=7 (9%) prob=0.57]
## Start>=8.5
## Start< 14.5
## Age>=55
## Age< 111
##
## Rule number: 22 [Kyphosis=absent cover=14 (17%) prob=0.14]
## Start>=8.5
```

```
## Start< 14.5
## Age>=55
## Age>=111
##
## Rule number: 10 [Kyphosis=absent cover=12 (15%) prob=0.00]
## Start>=8.5
## Start< 14.5
## Age< 55
##
## Rule number: 4 [Kyphosis=absent cover=29 (36%) prob=0.00]
## Start>=8.5
## Start>=14.5
```

6. We can easily get a count of the number of cases per terminal node as shown next.

7. Use the `where` variable of the `rpart` function to find which terminal node a case is assigned:

```
kyphosis$where <- kyphosis_rpart$where
table (kyphosis$Kyphosis, kyphosis$where)

##
##          3  5  7  8  9
## absent  29 12 12  3  8
## present  0  0  2  4 11
```

8. Now, these numbers can also be obtained through the simple **table** function. First, we convert the `data.frame` object to a `data.table` object.

9. Convert the `data.frame` kyphosis into a `data.table` object:

```
K2 <- data.table (kyphosis)
```

10. Since the preceding tree diagram suggests that if the start value is greater than 12.5, Kyphosis would be absent in the individual, we check it.

11. Using the `data.table` structure, find the proportional count by the **Start** variable:

```
K2[, prop.table ( table (Kyphosis))]

## Kyphosis
## absent present
## 0.7901 0.2099
```

12. Similarly, verify the proportional count at each terminal node:

```
K2[Start>= 12.5 , prop.table ( table (Kyphosis))]

## Kyphosis
## absent present
## 0.95652 0.04348

K2[Start < 12.5 & Age <= 35 , prop.table ( table (Kyphosis))]

## Kyphosis
## absent present
## 0.9 0.1

K2[Start < 12.5 & Age > 35 & Number < 4.5 , prop.table ( table
(Kyphosis))]

## Kyphosis
## absent present
## 0.5833 0.4167

K2[Start < 12.5 & Age > 35 & Number >= 4.5 , prop.table ( table
(Kyphosis))]

## Kyphosis
## absent present
## 0.3077 0.6923
```

Thus, a decision tree creates partitions of the data set where each terminal node has as high cases of a factor variable as possible. In general, a decision tree looks at distinct values of each of the variables and accordingly partitions the data into distinct region. Then, it accesses how good each of the partitions is and selects that split which leads to maximum gain in accuracy at each of the terminal nodes. Thus, the data is recursively split in multiple regions and the process is concluded until each of the terminal node consists of as many pure nodes as possible.

Next, we will build decision trees for the German credit data.

How it works...

The `rpart` package helps in constructing classification, regression, and survival trees. The decision trees can be easily visualized using the `plot` function. We have extracted the rules of the decision tree using the `asRules` function from the `rattle` package.

See also

Decision trees can be built in R using multiple packages, for example `partykit`, `tree`, and so on.

Decision tree for german data

We have fit a logistic regression model for the German data. Now, we will create a decision tree for it.

Getting ready

The `GC2` object along with the partitioned data will be required here. Also, the fitted logistic regression model is needed.

How to do it ...

We will create the decision tree using the `rpart` package and its functionalities:

1. Create the decision tree and plot it as follows:

```
GC_CT <- rpart (good_bad~., data= GC_Train)
windows ( height= 20 , width= 20 )
plot (GC_CT, uniform = TRUE ); text (GC_CT)
```

2. The decision tree plot is given as follows:

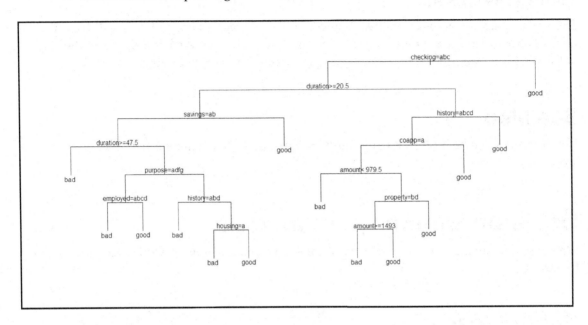

3. The properties of the fitted tree need to be evaluated.
4. Check the complexity parameter and important variables of the fitted tree:

```
table (GC_Train$good_bad, predict (GC_CT, type= "class" ))
```

```
##
## bad good
## bad 107 74
## good 32 386
```

```
GC_CT$cptable
```

```
## CP nsplit rel error xerror xstd
## 1 0.06262 0 1.0000 1.0000 0.06209
## 2 0.02486 3 0.8122 0.9503 0.06118
## 3 0.02210 6 0.7348 1.0055 0.06219
## 4 0.01842 8 0.6906 0.9724 0.06159
## 5 0.01657 12 0.6022 0.9779 0.06170
## 6 0.01000 13 0.5856 0.9724 0.06159
```

```
GC_CT$variable.importance
```

```
## checking duration amount history savings purpose coapp property
## 29.4516 15.0985 12.8465 11.2774 10.8025 9.7595 7.2114 6.7423
```

```
## employed housing age installp existcr job marital resident
## 6.7003 6.1063 3.6083 2.8071 1.6281 1.4417 1.3372 0.9983
```

5. Thus, we see that the variables in order of importance are checking, duration, amount, history, and so forth. Out of the 181 bad loans in the training dataset, we have identified 107 of them as compared with only 96 using the logistic regression model. Whether this is indeed an improvement will be evaluated later. We will now complete the ROC analysis.

6. As with the logistic regression model, we first fit the ROC curves and then compare it with the earlier logistic regression solutions:

```
  GC_CT_Train_Prob <- predict (GC_CT, newdata= GC_Train[,- 21 ],
type= "prob" )[, 2 ]
  GC_CT_Validate_Prob <- predict (GC_CT, newdata= GC_Validate[,- 21
], type= "prob" )[, 2 ]
  GB_CT_Train_roc <- roc (GC_Train$good_bad, GC_CT_Train_Prob)
  GB_CT_Validate_roc <- roc
(GC_Validate$good_bad, GC_CT_Validate_Prob) roc.test
(GB_Logistic_Train_roc, GB_CT_Train_roc)

  ##
  ## DeLong's test for two correlated ROC curves
  ##
  ## data: GB_Logistic_Train_roc and GB_CT_Train_roc
  ## Z = 0.92, p-value = 0.4
  ## alternative hypothesis: true difference in AUC is not equal to
0
  ## sample estimates:
  ## AUC of roc1 AUC of roc2
  ## 0.8358 0.8206

roc.test (GB_Logistic_Validate_roc, GB_CT_Validate_roc)

  ##
  ## DeLong's test for two correlated ROC curves
  ##
  ## data: GB_Logistic_Validate_roc and GB_CT_Validate_roc
  ## Z = -0.2, p-value = 0.8
  ## alternative hypothesis: true difference in AUC is not equal to
0
  ## sample estimates:
  ## AUC of roc1 AUC of roc2
  ## 0.7198 0.7301
```

The higher gain in the accuracy for the decision tree is not statistically significant. Thus, the ROC curves are not much different for the logistic regression model and the decision tree. However, if we were to ignore the results from the ROC tests, we might as well say that the decision tree gives higher accuracy.

How it works...

The `rpart` function continues to be useful. Also, we applied `roc.test` for the first time in the book.

A lot of advancement has taken in the context of decision trees and we restrict ourselves with the simple decision tree only.

Index

CPSIA information can be obtained
at www.ICGtesting.com
Printed in the USA
FSOW03n1845050717
35897FS